Pursuing th

Also by Dan Cohn-Sherbok

AN ENCYCLOPEDIA OF JUDAISM AND CHRISTIANITY
(with Lavinia Cohn-Sherbok)

—◦⊚◦—

Also by Mary Grey

THE OUTRAGEOUS PURSUIT OF HOPE

Pursuing the Dream

A Jewish—Christian Conversation

—◦◦◦—

DAN COHN-SHERBOK
AND MARY GREY

DARTON · LONGMAN + TODD

FOR LAVINIA AND NICHOLAS

First published in 2005 by
Darton, Longman and Todd Ltd
1 Spencer Court
140–142 Wandsworth High Street
London
SW18 4JJ

ISBN 0 232 52540 4

A catalogue record for this book is available from the British Library.

Designed by Sandie Boccacci
Phototypeset in 11/13.5pt Bembo by IntypeLibra Ltd
Printed and bound in Great Britain by
CPI, Bath

Contents

Foreword

Professors Mary Grey and Dan Cohn-Sherbok are both thinkers 'outside the box' in terms of their respective religious traditions. But both continue to draw deeply from the resources of those traditions despite their significant disagreements with aspects of their religious heritages.

In this volume they share their lives of faith with us in an exchange of letters that covers well over a year. We see how each responds to some of the core issues facing all people of religious faith in our time in the light of current social and political challenges. We also see how difficult interreligious understanding can be, despite good intentions and a profound commitment to the project. As they themselves admit at the end of the book, after more than one year many barriers to understanding remain between them, though they have become stronger in their shared commitment to social responsibility in the name of their individual faith traditions.

While I have some important differences with their views on a number of points — as they do with each other — I found myself profoundly engaged in their ongoing conversation. Their discussions forced me to reflect more deeply on my own faith perspectives in several key areas. I remain confident that other readers will have a similar experience.

Grey and Cohn-Sherbok take up issues central to the theological understanding of Judaism and Christianity such as God, Jesus and Judaism, Trinity, and the interpretation of Scripture. But they focus as well on contemporary social concerns — ecology, feminism, non-violence, the role of animals, the struggle for justice in the Middle East, understandings of the family, forgiveness, and anti-Semitism.

Both authors raise some critical questions that demand comment. Cohn-Sherbok strongly argues that Christian faith is inherently anti-Jewish. Here I agree with Mary Grey that while we must clearly acknowledge how endemic anti-Judaism has been to expressions of Christian faith (and still remains so in many quarters), possibilities do exist for reshaping the fundamental theological self-identity of Christianity in a way that abrogates its anti-Judaic core. Several individual Christian theologians, myself included, have proposed such new models, as have recent institutional documents from various church bodies. And in December 2004 in London there was launched a multi-year project in which a group of leading theologians from various countries and from a variety of Christian denominations addressed this issue under the auspices of the World Council of Churches, the International Council of Christians & Jews, the Cardinal Bernardin Center at Catholic Theological Union in Chicago and the Centre for the Study of Jewish—Christian Relations in Cambridge.

I appreciate the emphasis by both Grey and Cohn-Sherbok on the notion of 'divine vulnerability'. This perspective on God has been a central feature of reflections about God against the background of the Holocaust experience in my own writings on the Shoah and Christian theology. The reflections on feminism, ecology and non-violence are also quite rich in their perspectives. I do side with Cohn-Sherbok on the question of Jesus and the state of women in his day. Cohn-Sherbok is correct in criticising Grey in her claim that Jesus represented a new day for women, a common motif in feminist theology which has been critiqued as lacking documentary evidence by several Jewish and Christian feminist scholars. Regarding ecology, and particularly the role of animals, Grey has gone somewhat too far. Here I stand with Cohn-Sherbok, while understanding that both of us agree with Grey on the urgent need for new ecological awareness as a basic spiritual concern in both Judaism and Christianity.

As with anti-Judaism, Cohn-Sherbok's strong emphasis on anti-Semitism within the core of Christianity needs some tempering. But in saying this I do not minimise its continuing strength. I fully agree with him on the deep-seated anti-Semitism in Mel Gibson's film *The Passion of the Christ*, to which Christian leadership has given a feeble response.

All in all, *Pursuing the Dream* achieves a depth of dialogue that mere theological documents cannot. Neither format is the only way to go in terms of enhanced interreligious understanding. But Grey and Cohn-Sherbok have done a masterful job with the format they have chosen.

John T. Pawlikowski, OSM, Ph.D
Professor and Director of Catholic–Jewish Studies
Catholic Theological Union, Chicago

Visiting Fellow, St Edmund's College and the Centre for the Study of Jewish–Christian Relations, Wesley House, University of Cambridge

Introduction

The idea for this conversation emerged from the time when, a few years ago, we were both involved in a colloquium dealing with the topic of reconciliation in the world's religions. We both wrote essays about the ways in which our two faiths might contribute to the project of creating a better world, but unfortunately the intended volume was never published. Later, both of us were appointed to chairs of theology at the University of Wales, Lampeter. Finding ourselves in the same place, we discussed the possibility of renewing the project by focusing on the ways in which our two faiths provide spiritual resources for achieving reconciliation in the contemporary world.

The difficulty, however, was that for part of the year both of us live in different places: Mary has a home near Winchester, and Dan has a holiday flat in London. How, we wondered, could we communicate with each other at such a distance? The solution, we concluded, was to write letters to each other: in this way we would have the opportunity to ponder each other's views and respond critically. There would also, we hoped, be an element of surprise and spontaneity. What we did not foresee, however, was that — paradoxically in an age of advanced technology! — it would be so very difficult to share our views.

How were we to communicate? Initially we pondered whether we should simply write letters to each other by post. But we thought this would slow up the process. Possibly we should send faxes. Mary's fax machine, however, was not working properly. In the end we decided to send each other email attachments. Yet this too turned out to be problematic. Mary's computer was protected by anti-virus software and refused to receive Dan's attachments. As a result, we decided to include our letters in the email itself. The difficulty, however, was that Dan did not know how to transfer his letters from a disk on to an email. Yet eventually, with the help of a computer expert, Dan learned how to do this. Another issue was that we both travel. Mary found herself writing from the desert of Rajasthan and Dan from Colorado, USA.

So, for the last year, we have been writing to one another. The theme of our book is reconciliation, but it became obvious after the first few weeks that we disagreed about nearly everything except the general principle that our two traditions contain invaluable spiritual resources for creating a better world. The problem was that both of us have very different visions of what such a world should be. In addition, it became clear that in fundamental ways we also took a radical attitude and sometimes critical distance from the two religions we represented.

As readers will see, the letter-writing style is a personal one. Our family histories and backgrounds are included from time to time. Our concern for world events, specifically the climate of insecurity and violence following the events of September 11th 2001, forms a kind of backcloth to our discussions. It will become very obvious that our conversation is as much a dialogue of conflict as of reconciliation. Yet this is not surprising, given the history of Jewish—Christian relations through the centuries. In a post-Holocaust world, it is exceedingly difficult to transcend the horrors of the past in attempting to attain reconciliation and harmony. But we do believe that this extensive correspondence — covering central areas of theological conflict as well as pressing social problems — illustrates the possibility for mutual sympathy and understanding. In all likelihood readers will not agree with either of us, but it is our hope that they too will join in this dialogue and encounter. In a world beset with misunderstanding and conflict, it is vital that our faith traditions contribute to the quest for the age-old Jewish hope of *tikkun olam*.

Throughout this process we have been encouraged and supported by the comments of our reader, Helen Fry, who is herself a recognised scholar in the field of Jewish— Christian relations. We are grateful for her guidance and insights.

Dan Cohn-Sherbok and Mary Grey

Part One

1. God

———❧❦❧———

21 June 2003

A JEWISH UPBRINGING

Mary,

Perhaps I should start with something about my religious upbringing.

Growing up in the leafy suburbs of Denver, Colorado, I had a typical Jewish education at the local Reform Temple. At the age of eight I was sent to the Temple summer camp located in the Rocky Mountains about fifty miles from Denver. I remember sleeping in a wood cabin by a mountain stream with a group of other boys. One day the rabbi travelled from Denver to visit the camp. After lunch, he came to inspect our cabin. Accompanied by the camp director, he stopped by my bed and asked my name. 'Dan Cohn-Sherbok,' I replied. He looked me over. 'That bed is a mess,' he said. 'And you look a mess. You're a messy little kid.'

This unpromising beginning was followed by years of religious education at the Temple Sunday school. Jewish boys and girls from throughout the city were taken by their parents on Sunday to the Temple, located in an affluent part of the city. For two hours, our teachers attempted to impart knowledge of Judaism to unwilling students. Most had no interest in the tradition. Instead of listening, they made paper airplanes, threw spit balls, and giggled throughout lessons. After class each Sunday, we flooded into the sanctuary for a worship service. The rabbi, robed in black, recited the prayers, read from the Torah and preached a sermon to an inattentive congregation.

These dispiriting experiences in religion school, however, did not dampen my interest in the Jewish faith. Unlike most of my high school friends, I found Judaism fascinating. I liked Temple services. I enjoyed the classes in Sunday school despite the raucous behaviour of the other students. Following my *bar mitzvah*, I had decided that I wanted to become a congregational rabbi. When I went east to study at Williams College, I majored in philosophy; after graduation, I enrolled at the Hebrew Union College — Jewish Institute of Religion in Cincinnati, Ohio — the largest seminary for Reform rabbis in the United States. Most of the students were from Reform homes, but a few had a traditional Jewish background.

Among religious Jews, the great divide is between the Orthodox and the non-Orthodox. Orthodox Judaism is based on the belief that God revealed the Torah (Five Books of Moses) to Moses on Mount Sinai. As a consequence, every word of the Pentateuch is of divine origin and all the legal precepts in the Torah are binding on the Jewish people. Reform Judaism, on the other hand, views the Jewish heritage as evolutionary. In the view of these modernisers, the tradition has undergone continual change over nearly four thousand years. Both Scripture and rabbinic sources are understood as historically conditioned. As early as 1885, the movement declared in the Pittsburgh Platform (a distillation of Reform theology): 'We accept as binding only [Judaism's] moral laws and such ceremonies as elevate and sanctify our lives and reject all such as are not adapted to the views and habits of modern civilization.'[1]

All of us at the Hebrew Union College subscribed to such modernising convictions. Yet, theologically, Reform Judaism has not distanced itself from the tradition. Like the Orthodox, Reform Jews believe in a personal God who created the universe and providentially rules over his creation. As a child, I remember reading such prayers in the Reform prayer book as the following:

> Praised be Thou, O Lord our God, ruler of the world, by whose law the shadows of evening fall and the gates of morn are opened. In wisdom Thou hast established the changes of times and seasons and ordered the ways of the stars in their heavenly courses.[2]

In the Sabbath worship services at the College, we acknowledged God's power and involvement in Jewish life in such responsive readings from the prayer book as the following:

> And through thy power alone has Israel been redeemed.
> Great deeds hast Thou wrought on our behalf and
>   wonders without number.
> Thou hast kept us in life; Thou hast not let our footsteps
>   falter.
> Thy love has watched over us in the night of oppression;
> Thy mercy has sustained us in the hour of trial.[3]

I hope this gives you some idea of my orientation to the faith. But as you will discover, over the years I have changed some of my ideas about the nature of divine reality.

Dan

1.2   *24 June 2003*

A CATHOLIC CHILDHOOD

Dan,

That was fascinating — I see both connections and differences with my own Roman Catholic upbringing. I grew up in the north-east of England as the eldest of seven children, in a close-knit Roman Catholic community. (Close-knit in the sense we were taught to relate only to fellow Roman Catholics and simply didn't notice anyone else. I first entered an Anglican church to watch the Coronation on TV — at that time not many families possessed one!) My parents, deeply committed religious people, teachers, both of Irish ancestry — indeed my father was born in Cork — gave us the strong impression that Ireland was the true source of faith (and we wore the shamrock with pride on St Patrick's Day). Alongside we were nourished by the Anglo-Saxon saints of Northumberland and Durham — Cuthbert, Hilda, Aidan and Oswald — whose abbeys and churches were popular places of pilgrimage. Despite the narrowness and strictness of the tightly woven Catholic web that surrounded us, the tight observations that were imposed on us (the Communion fast, weekly confessions, Friday abstinence from meat,

Sunday obligation under pain of mortal sin), there was a richness of religious experience for which I'm now grateful. The celebration of the feasts, especially Christmas and Easter, gave a sense of mystery and wonder. The symbolism of light shining in the darkness, of goodness triumphing over evil, of Resurrection joy that touched all creation — these affected us children at a non-verbal level.

But at a verbal level, where *you* had the Bible, *we* had the Catechism. (Remember this is before the second Vatican council where things radically changed.) We had to learn by heart chunks of text that we barely understood. 'What must I do before going to bed?' we were asked. 'We occupy ourselves with thoughts of death and give our last thoughts to our crucified Saviour.' Terrifying language for nine- or ten-year-olds!

God was very distant in those days. We were told 'He' was a God of love: yet the language of sin and guilt, the need to strive to 'get to heaven', 'save our souls', coupled with the cloying sweet-ness of some of our devotional practices (the Rosary, the Nine Fridays, the Nine Tuesdays to St Anthony), sentimentality around the Child Jesus and the narrowness regarding sexuality, were huge barriers. We could — thanks to St Thomas Aquinas — prove He existed (or thought we could — more about that later!) but expe-riences of divine presence were beyond our grasp.

If this sounds negative, and you are wondering why on earth I would want to study theology, there were other things going on at the same time. The official sacramental experience of the Church was routinised and boring, but there was a wider sacra-mental reality that opened our eyes to beauty around us: despite it being mining country, we were entranced by the countryside, seasons, hills, forest and the cold north-east sea. God the Creator was showering all these gifts on us — even if I could appreciate it then more in poetry and music than in official Church language. The second thing was that I knew God wanted justice and hated suffering and poverty. I discovered my mother crying one Christmas. She had received a letter from the late Archbishop of Durban — the famous Denis Hurley — in which he told her about apartheid. From early on she instilled in all of us children a love and commitment to social justice, as being what God wanted.

So it was completely natural to me to want to study theology

— and to be a priest or nun. The day I discovered that as a girl, priesthood was barred to me, was a complete shock. As was the discovery that even to study theology — at that time — was almost impossible. So I went to Oxford and studied Classics and Philosophy (called Greats), spending my free time studying every form of theology I could. I joined a lay Jesuit group, a Third Order Franciscan group, and a Russian Orthodox Fellowship! But I didn't actually study theology until after I was married with four small children, the youngest only a baby. This was in Belgium at the University of Louvain. By then my understanding of God had changed dramatically and clashed with the theology I was being taught.

But that's another story,
Mary

I.3   *25 June 2003*

GOD IN NATURE

Mary,
I think we couldn't have had a more different background. The close-knit Irish Catholicism of North-East England is an utterly different world from Jewish Denver. Yet, despite these differences, it appears that both of us were drawn to religion through nature. You write about the countryside, seasons, hills and forests that seemed infused with God's presence. For me, the mountains of Colorado had the same impact — at summer camp where I was a camper and counsellor, we were surrounded by green forests, rolling streams, and snow-capped peaks. Every Sabbath all of us assembled at our outdoor sanctuary where the visiting rabbi from the Temple led us in prayer.

As a little boy, I remember how the Psalms captured this sense of wonder at God's creation. In this respect my early awareness of divine reality was related to God's manifestation in the natural world. Over the years such an apprehension has not faded in intensity; this, no doubt, is why I love living in Wales. It is certainly not the land of my fathers, nor do I feel any affinity with Celtic Christianity. But the green valleys, deep gorges, and wooded countryside remind me of the Colorado landscape, and evoke the same feeling of divine presence.

In rabbinical seminary we studied the traditional proofs for God's existence including the ontological, cosmological and teleological arguments. You may be surprised that, along with medieval Jewish philosophers, we were exposed to the works of the great scholastic thinkers, such as Aquinas. Although I am convinced that the majority of these proofs are mistaken, I am nonetheless persuaded by the argument by design. My wife Lavinia, who studied philosophical theology at Cambridge, thinks I am profoundly wrong. She keeps telling me to reread David Hume's critique. But I am unmoved.

As you know, some philosophers of religion are adamant that modern physics points to the existence of a divine creator. In their view, the fact is that if the most significant physical features of the universe had been infinitesimally different, galaxies would not have formed, planetary systems would not have developed, and human beings would never have evolved. Hence, they contend, the universe appears to have been designed — how else can one account for the astonishing fine-tuning of the universe?

Such conclusions support what our two traditions claim about the nature of God. He is the transcendent creator of all things. For Jews, this is a cardinal belief. According to Moses Maimonides — the greatest Jewish philosopher of the Middle Ages — such a conviction is one of the thirteen tenets of the faith. Here, I think we can agree. But there are crucial and contentious issues that divide us. You mention the sacramental elements of your faith. The celebration of the feasts, you write, convey a sense of mystery and wonder. Light shining in the darkness is symbolic of goodness triumphing as illustrated by the Resurrection.

The centrality of Christ is, for me, incomprehensible. The notion of an immanent Deity whose purposes unfold in the life and death of His only Son is not a mystery, but rather a muddle. For nearly four thousand years, the doctrines of the Incarnation and the Trinity have divided Jew from Christian and led to suspicion and hostility on both sides. In speaking about God, I think we need to face up to this central dilemma. Can the two of us attain some sort of religious reconciliation, given the theological chasm that separates us?

Dan

1.4 *27 June 2003*

GOD IN PROCESS AND DYNAMIC MOVEMENT

Dan,

That was quite a challenge ... Can we cross this chasm? At least we have to try. If we cannot achieve a common understanding on the Creator we haven't created a language to talk meaningfully about peace and reconciliation. It's interesting that it is the experience of the majesty and beauty of nature that inclines you to consider Aquinas's Design Argument sympathetically. Lavinia is quite right that Hume's critique logically refutes it. But Aquinas (influenced of course by Maimonides, among others!), who probably had no conception of what we today mean by 'atheist', wasn't trying to prove God's existence anyway. He was probably more like Anselm, 'faith seeking understanding'.[4] The 'thinking man' — I won't mention his views on women at this point — can use his brain to make sense of his faith in God.

But I would want to question that argument more from a contemporary scientific point of view. Neither of us are scientists — my daughter Clare, who is, is constantly telling me to leave science to the scientists! — yet we are very aware that the world-view in which the medievalists operated has changed. Newton's laws have given way to a different world through the new understanding of quantum physics. All those arguments about 'Unmoved Mover', 'Uncaused Cause', based on a notion of some great power external to the world and controlling what goes on within it — intervening at certain key moments — gives way to something far more exciting. God as intimately involved in all processes of reality. God, not as Unchanging, in whom there is no potential, but God *in becoming, in process* ... A God of movement, dynamic ... (Before you start citing 'I am God, I change not' as part of biblical faith, seeing what I have said as conflicting, I want to argue that 'I change not' highlights God's fidelity, not the lack of movement and change in God. Love and fidelity never change but they reach out to us, evoke our response and allow us to contribute to the rich profundity of God.)[5]

Do you see where I am going? I see two important directions. God's involvement with the entire web of creation, not only at its beginnings, but now, in the processes of its becoming, cuts through the dominance and superiority of humanity vis-à-vis creation. In a way, it makes theological and ecological sense of the Psalmist saying 'The heavens are telling the glory of God', involving all creation in praise of the Creator — we often forget that creation is more faithful than we are! Secondly, we are given the sense of a God-in-movement and I believe that this is the truth behind the doctrine of Trinity. I agree with you that to imagine God as three persons (three men, or two men and a bird!) is hard to justify. I am reminded of the French jingle:

> Il y avait un jeune homme de Dijon,
> Qui n'aimait pas le religion!
> Il dit, 'Par ma foi!
> Comme c'est drôle, les Trois!
> Le Père, Le Fils et Le Pigeon!'[6]

It just seems nonsense! But if we re-vision *both* transcendence *and* immanence within the worldview of the web of connections between all things, immanence becomes a many-levelled interiority, God as present in the depth of all living beings and organisms. Transcendence means the power that connects us, inspires us to act, to love, to relate, to connect meaningfully with other beings, to co-create with God according to the capacities God gives us.

You'll see that I think of God as the power that drives to relate, to connect, to be aflame for the kind of world God wants. And divine power in this relational world is exercised through compassion, mercy, empathy, faithfulness — all the biblical qualities you believe in. Why the Trinity then? Because Jesus is the earthly embodiment of relational power, the power for relational justice — in my belief not the only embodiment, and I know that's controversial. And the Spirit is God the energiser, the inspirer, the power that draws the I to the Thou, to use Martin Buber's term.[7]

But in the end I come back to the idea of a God in dynamic

movement, and the Trinity as one way of conceptualising this. But let me throw the gauntlet back to you: the Hebrew God of the Bible is a patriarchal God. The God of both our traditions is most frequently worshipped as a Father God. And I see this as a stumbling block for the egalitarian society we long for, and a stumbling block to the reconciliation between men and women. Another chasm to bridge?

Mary

1.5   *30 June 2003*

DIVINE IMMANENCE

Mary,

I appreciate your daughter's observation — scientific cosmological speculations are certainly beyond my competence. But what scientists who are also philosophers of religion say about creation is relevant. As I mentioned, there is an increasing awareness among a number of these thinkers that the findings of astronomers and other scientists support the hypothesis that the universe was created. This is certainly of significance for theology! You're right that Aquinas did not conceive of the teleological argument as a rigorous proof of the existence of God; it was meant rather as a means of rational support of what he believed on the basis of faith: it was faith seeking understanding, rather than understanding demonstrating the validity of belief. Yet it seems to me that the argument by design is powerful and, if not a proof, then at least a strong foundation for religious conviction.

Here possibly there is a meeting point for both Christian and Jew. But there is no doubt that we have very different views about God's action. It is of course true that biblical writers and rabbinic sages subscribed to the conviction that God is active in the world He created. Such sentiments are widely shared by many Orthodox, Conservative and Reform Jews. However, for other Jews it has become increasingly difficult if not impossible to believe in a benevolent and all-powerful Deity who is present in human affairs. In a post-Holocaust world, many Jews fail to see how there could be an omniscient God who is anxious to rescue his chosen people from disaster and destruction.

A typical response to God's seeming inaction during the Holocaust is found in the notorious tract *After Auschwitz* by the Conservative rabbi Richard Rubenstein. In this radical work, he contends that it no longer makes sense to believe that God chose the Jewish nation as his own, freed the ancient Israelites from bondage, revealed Himself on Mount Sinai, and providentially guides their destiny.

You indicate that you think that God is dynamically involved in human affairs. You write that God is immanent in the sense that He is involved in the interconnected web of all creation. Previously you implied that He is benevolent and loving. I wonder what evidence you would give in support of such claims. Why do you believe that He is involved in the created order, and that He calls us to engage with Him in creating a better world?

Dan

1.6   *1 July 2003*

GOD, NOT OF INTERVENTION, BUT OF VULNERABILITY

Dan,

It's the beginning of a new month, and my Celtic lectionary tells me that July is a month for reconciliation! Would it were so easy — my response to you is one of both agreement and disagreement. I want to agree with you about the design of creation pointing to the transcendent Creator, but *not* from the old deterministic model of an external cause, mover, designer — as I tried to argue in my last letter. Maybe not persuasively enough! As you yourself indicate, appealing to modern science (forget my daughter for the moment!), the worldview emerging from quantum physics, from Einstein's relativity, from Heisenberg's Uncertainty Principle, gives us more exciting possibility of the interrelatedness of organic life, not only on this planet but in the entire universe. It cuts through the God/world dichotomy and restores a cosmology, a cosmic consciousness of ourselves within a wider whole — and I would call the wider cosmos God. A God in whom all life forms find their origin and fulfilment. A God whose energies permeate the entirety of creation. Very much something we can share and celebrate in worship!

But not only does this eliminate anthropocentrism — the superiority of humanity over the rest of life forms — it reveals the falsity of all dualisms including that of men over women, and humanity over animals. Don't you agree that both our faiths exhibit extraordinary reluctance to let go of the patriarchal Father God in His omnipotence, who intervenes when 'He' makes things good? It's not that the Christian feminist argument would dispute the biblical supremacy of the 'Father' naming of God: it's more common in the Christian than in the Jewish scriptures anyway and is the usual way that Jesus addressed God. It's the link between Fatherhood and power that is the concern, because of the way this has allowed violence and abuse in the family, both past and present, and the way the *authority* of fatherhood has even served to conceal this abuse. This is what we try to balance with a richer, inclusive nexus of images of God. God as Creator, Sustainer, Mother and Father, Lover and Friend, God as Love and Compassion, God as Flowing Water, Fire and Rock.

I can hear you say that these are positive images and reinforce the conviction that God acts benevolently, and that, as I said earlier, 'God strives for justice and makes it!' In the present state of the world, amidst the immense failure of peace and justice movements, what evidence do I bring?

Can I invite you to take a step back and look at the old model, of God as omnipotent Father? Now, on this model, God is both external and internal to the world and can choose to 'intervene' from time to time, to rescue the Chosen People from disaster. I can understand how terrible the loss of faith could be, that (it would appear) God did not choose to intervene to save the Jews from the Holocaust, and why Rubenstein might make the remark you quoted. But within the model of the web of interconnected life forms, God does not arbitrarily decide to intervene on one occasion and not on another. That makes nonsense of a God of love, and I refuse to go down the track of 'God permitted this suffering to make you a better person!' I wonder if that is one thing we could agree on?

Within the connected worldview God is present all the time and does not have to leap in from outer space. But God is vulnerable to the very autonomy and freedom of the processes of reality — for which God is ultimately responsible. This vulnerability is witnessed to in a very poignant way by the diaries of Etty Hillesum, who went voluntarily to Westerbork in 1943, wanting to be the 'thinking, praying heart of the Concentration Camp'. And her prayer to God was that 'Alas, there is not very much you can do for us now — it's what we can do for you!' She took so seriously the suffering vulnerability of God, that she felt it was the responsibility of people like herself to make a home for God in the hearts of the people of the camp, her responsibility to keep the presence of God alive.[8] The same experience comes from Christian women in diverse situations of oppression.

But can you accept this idea of a vulnerable God, despite the way this seems to render God powerless in the face of injustice? Could there be a different concept of divine agency?

In case this ending seems too bleak, let me tell you there is a beautiful evening light outside, the wind is blowing in the willows, the river is flowing. These are the kinds of natural elements that gave joy to Etty Hillesum even in a situation that offered no hope.

Mary

1.7   *2 July 2003*

THEOLOGY AND GENDER

Mary,

Your comments about contemporary physics are intriguing. I am not a physicist so I cannot provide any detailed response. But I am aware that a number of leading scientists, such as John Polkinghorne, are convinced that the order of the universe would be incredible without a divine cause. Given the existence of the Creator (as well as the process of evolution), all life must be interrelated. But such interconnectedness does not necessarily imply that there is a cosmic consciousness which is continually cognisant of all things. Arguably, it is possible — as Deists maintain —

that God created the cosmos, but does not concern himself with His creation.

You are right that both Judaism and Christianity are patriarchal in character, and that God is conceived in both traditions in masculine terms. In Scripture, He is depicted as a benevolent Father who watches over his children. He is the 'Lord of Hosts', the Almighty Redeemer of Israel. Judaism is a religion created by men, for men. The biblical writers as well as the rabbis formulated a wide range of laws, curtailing women's rights: husbands, not wives, are empowered to initiate divorce; women are not entitled to act as judges; women are excluded from the quorum necessary for a full religious service; women must be separated from men during prayer; women are exempt from a wide range of religious laws; women are not entitled to serve as rabbis. Typical of such misogynistic attitudes is the traditional prayer men are obligated to recite every morning: 'Blessed art Thou, O Lord our God, King of the Universe, who has not made me a woman.'

As a consequence of such a bias, theological discussions about divine theodicy have focused on the seeming incompatibility of beliefs about God's nature, in particular omnipotence, and the existence of human suffering. I agree that both of our faiths have been reluctant to let go of the patriarchal Father God and his omnipotence. There is no doubt that the notion of the Fatherhood of God has had disastrous consequences, leading to violence, militarism, and the persecution of the vulnerable. Yet I am not persuaded that such a patriarchal bias must be corrected by counterbalancing the traditional image of God as Father with attributes such as Mother, Lover, or Friend. If God does have such qualities, there must be independent evidence for believing that He has such a nature. Ascribing such positive attributes to God must be justified on other grounds than the fact that our traditions have been prejudiced against women.

You urge me to step back and look at the traditional image of God as Father. On this model, you point out, God is both external and internal to the world and can intervene when He wishes. However, it is not a question of masculinity or femininity, but of ontology. Either God is external to the world, or He isn't. Either God intervenes in the world, or He doesn't. Gender is irrelevant.

You assert that God is vulnerable, and cite the work of Etty Hillesum who was convinced of the suffering vulnerability of God. If God is vulnerable, as you suggest, then again I want to ask you what grounds you have for believing this.

Recently I reviewed a pioneering work on Holocaust theology — *The Female Face of God in Auschwitz* by Melissa Raphael.[9] Like you, she insists that we must now abandon masculine conceptions of God's nature. Drawing on the testimonies of women who were imprisoned in Auschwitz, she argues that women's experiences should be seen as an act of sacralisation in the death camps. This, she believes, is an invitation of God's presence in the most horrific place on earth. According to Raphael, God's face as the exiled *Shekhinah* (divine presence) was not hidden at Auschwitz. Instead, it was revealed in the female face as a refracting image of God. Specifically, women's attempts to wash themselves and others, and to deal with the bodies of the suffering, have deep spiritual significance.

What I cannot understand, however, is why she believes that these experiences are pointers to God's nature as a compassionate and loving mother. The fact that women were kind to one another in the most terrible circumstances does not necessarily reflect anything about God's character. All that one can say with certainty is that these individuals were caring and compassionate. Similarly, I want to ask you what your grounds are for assuming that God has the nature that you describe. This is a metaphysical question, rather than a moral one. What basis is there for believing, as you say, that God wants justice and hates suffering and poverty, that God's love and fidelity reach out to us, and that God is vulnerable and suffers?

Dan

1.8   *4 July 2003*

EXPERIENCING THE SUFFERING COMPASSION OF GOD

Dan,
It's clear we agree on the misogyny of both traditions, but not on the response to it! Yet if we long for reconciliation it cannot be

ignored. There is a way to answer your challenge from abstract principles. For example, you say, 'What's the evidence?' and I answer, think of the most important transcendental principles around — like Truth, Justice, Beauty, Love, Goodness — and say 'that's what I mean by God' and wherever I find these, I experience divine presence. But I prefer to answer from our faith traditions.

I think that if there were not alternative strands to both of these, there would not be much hope! Surely, when feminist theology draws on *Shekhinah* traditions, on Wisdom traditions (*Hokhmah, Sophia*), it is legitimate to regard these as in some way revealing a female dimension to the Divinity. (Although I regard God as above and beyond gender.) It is also true that there is an ancient goddess tradition that took longer than is supposed to give way to the rise of Jahwism: the worship of Asherah lingered on in the hearts of the people and was one of the features that angered the prophets. Why does Jeremiah (7:17—18) rail against the people who are baking cakes for the Queen of Heaven?

But the real faith argument is that the writer of Genesis 1:27 states that God created both 'male and female' in his image: thus both genders are called to image the Divine. Somehow female personhood too finds a home and inspiration in the Godhead, even if the dominant tradition — and power structures — privilege the masculine. I fully admit it is a minor tradition, often forgotten, but there are traces of what could be called a female dimension of God both in the Hebrew Bible, and in Christian tradition. For example, the word used for the compassion of God is *rehem/rahamim*, womb (as Phyllis Trible so beautifully shows us),[10] and is continually used for God's love for Ephraim (Israel) his darling child, for whom he yearns (Jer. 31:20b). The Bible seems happy to use imagery of giving birth in terms of giving birth to the new Israel. Isaiah speaks of the same compassionate motherly love of God, when God cries that even if a mother abandoned her sucking child, God will not abandon Israel (Hos. 11:11). The compassionate, tender love of God is immensely more powerful than human compassion and means that God will not give way to anger against human wickedness. In the Bible it is also an expression of God's Fatherhood — which is an indication that

Divine Fatherhood is not to be thought of in terms of power and punishment.

But a more powerful argument than a minor textual tradition (I can also give examples of Jesus as mother) is that of religious experience. We do — women and men — experience the love of God as compassionate, tender and forgiving. We do — and the stories flood in from many parts of the world — experience that God suffers with us. 'God weeps with our pain,' cries Kwok Pui Lan, a Chinese theologian.[11] God accompanies us in suffering, offers strength and consolation, fuels anger at injustice and courage for resistance. I can well understand how Melissa Raphael can argue that women consoling each other is an expression of Divine Presence in the death camps.

I think the vulnerability of God follows from the participation of God in human — and non-human — suffering. It is a consequence of the radical immanence of God. An immanence which is not bound by human limitations. But it also follows from rethinking omnipotence and power. (Remember the old argument fell apart because it seemed that God could be either omnipotent or all-loving but not both?) If we lose the Aristotelian basis on which that argument was built, you then think about love and God's actions more in terms of how people relate to each other. If we are open and vulnerable to each other (fears, hopes, dreams), we are more able to act for the good of each other. God, by definition, longs for the ultimate good of each of us: but given the cruel, oppressive structures in which we engage daily, we persist in blocking the actions and possibilities of redeeming grace. Is it not an act of ultimate love for God to remain open and vulnerable to the atrocities that humanity commits? Surely the act of keeping hope and love alive in the death camps in whatever humble way is justifiably experienced as Divine Presence?

Mary

─◦⊙─ ⊙◦─

1.9   *6 July 2003*

GOD AND THE HOLOCAUST

Mary,

You are right that within both of our traditions, there is ample
support for the doctrine of divine goodness. According to
Scripture, God is the all-good ruler of the universe. In the Psalms
He is described as good and upright (Ps. 25:8); his name is good
(Ps. 52:11); He is good and ready to forgive (Ps. 86:5); He is good
and does good (Ps. 118:68); He is good to all (Ps. 145:9). In rabbinic literature the same view prevails: God is the supremely
beneficent Creator who guides all things to their ultimate destiny.
In the unfolding of his plan, He has chosen Israel as his messen-
ger to all peoples — as Creator and Redeemer, He is the Father
to all.

Yet, as I noted, in the modern world serious questions have
been raised about such a conception of God's intervention in the
life of the Jewish nation. The horrors of the Holocaust have
caused a wide range of thinkers to question the traditional understanding of God's nature. Typical of such writers is the Reform
rabbi Steven Jacobs, who in *Rethinking Jewish Faith* argues that
Jewish theology must be reformulated in a radically new fashion:

> Both the Bible and post-biblical or rabbinic Judaism pres-
> ent their understanding of Deity as the God-who-acts-in-
> history, whose caring and concern for Jews was ultimately
> expressed at Sinai ... No amount of rationalization can
> overcome the enormity of the loss of 6 million ... What
> is now demanded in the realm of theological integrity is
> a notion of a Deity compatible with the reality of radical
> evil at work and at play in our world ... Such an under-
> standing is ... contingent upon accepting a notion of God
> as other than historically and traditionally presented by
> both Judaism and Christianity.[12]

The problem of evil is now a central issue for Jews. Is it possible
to believe in a God who saves given the enormity of the

Holocaust? In *After Auschwitz*, the Conservative rabbi Richard Rubenstein maintains that we must abandon belief in the God of the Bible and rabbinic Judaism:

> I believe that the greatest single challenge to modern Judaism arises out of the question of God and the death camps. I am amazed at the silence of contemporary Jewish theologians on this most crucial and agonizing of all Jewish issues. How can Jews believe in an omnipotent, beneficent God after Auschwitz? Traditional Jewish theology maintains that God is the ultimate, omnipotent actor in historical drama. It has interpreted every major catastrophe in Jewish history as God's punishment of a sinful Israel. I fail to see how this position can be maintained without regarding Hitler and the SS as instruments of God's will.[13]

When I ask you for independent evidence of the claims you make about God's immanence, these questions serve as the background to my challenge. You contend that whenever you find truth, justice, beauty, love and goodness, you experience God's presence. Why is this so? How can you be sure that there is a direct connection between such experiences and the Divine? It is not enough to cite what our traditions have said about God in the past. Nor is it sufficient to point to the patriarchal orientation of our two faiths, to demonstrate that there are attributes of God which have been neglected in describing the reality of God. Further, the fact that the author of Genesis viewed God in a particular way does not in itself demonstrate that God has the qualities that are attributed to him. I am asking you, in the light of the events of the twentieth century, how can you be so certain God loves human beings with compassion and tenderness? The fact that human beings have experienced God in this way does not demonstrate that what they experience is veridical. How can you be so sure that God weeps with the pain of those who died in the camps, that He accompanied those who were led to the gas chambers, and that He is filled with anger at the injustices of the Nazis?

Dan

1.10   *8 July 2003*

IS GOD RESPONSIBLE FOR EVIL?

Dan,

Your last challenge is almost unanswerable: I realise that for so
many Jewish theologians and communities the Holocaust eradi-
cates hope and faith in the goodness of God. I'm aware too that a
Christian history of anti-Semitism and anti-Judaism has prompted
some Christians to look for purpose and meaning where it is an
affront to find any. There are other responses too that I'll come
to later. I hope in our exchanges you'll tell me if I'm under-
estimating the horror and falling into a trap of finding easy
meaning, citing other atrocities numerically worse, or attempting
to exonerate all involved.

Christianity has particular difficulty in believing in a God
responsible for radical evil. For traditional Christians God is all-
good, the summit of all perfection. The Jewish feminist theologian
Judith Plaskow, in her book *Standing Again at Sinai*, challenges
Christian feminists on this point with Isaiah's statement, 'I am
God, I create weal and woe' (45:7), saying that Christianity is the
only religion that will not admit evil into the being of God.[11]

But it is not so straightforward for Jews either! There seems to
be innate faith in the goodness of God — despite evidence
against! Think of the legendary story told by both Jews and
Christians, where a group of rabbis put God on trial for evil, find
him guilty, and then proceed to evening prayer![12]

I wonder what kind of facts and experiences you would regard
as evidence? It just is true, that despite what seems to be evidence
against, people persist in believing in the goodness and compassion of God. Believers read scriptures as evidence — and there is
no way that we can get behind texts to an independent reality.
Even what appears to be 'pure experience' is always mediated
experience. What presents itself as 'pure revelation' — a vision
for example — springs from a particular context, culture and
expectation.

I have to go back to what I said to you earlier, that I reject this idea of an interventionist God! It fits neither with contemporary science which has moved on from Newtonian physics; nor with a God who respects the laws of God's own creation. If God chooses to be vulnerable to the complex realities of creation, there has to be a different understanding about how divine power works. And as I also wrote to you earlier, we can draw on the intuition that we are created in the image of God, and that where we practise love, mutuality and compassion, and 'blessed rage for justice', we can do this because we are in the image of the Divine. If God's power is the power of compassion, it doesn't work in an interventionist way — like sending in the troops to Iraq or Bosnia. Compassionate power is for the long haul! It works through empathy, through perseverance and fidelity — all qualities that are radiated through Jewish traditions.

There is plenty of evidence that believers do experience the compassionate presence of God, in the most desperate of circumstances. They also experience the absence of God, the impotence and vulnerability of God — what St John of the Cross calls the darkness of God, the Dark Night of the Soul. And this is one way of responding to the challenge that a tough faith in God is capable of surviving oppression.

But the one argument that Christians will use consistently in responding to your challenge is — Jesus of Nazareth, the Christ. In Jesus' death on the cross we see how God was prepared to be vulnerable, that vulnerability was a way of showing love, and that from this vulnerability came — in some mysterious way — hope and a changed quality of life.

How can our interchange possibly achieve a shared understanding on this subject given our troubled history?

Mary

I.11 *10 July 2003*

A NEW JEWISH THEOLOGY

Mary

You are right that there is an innate faith in the goodness of God amongst many contemporary Jewish theologians. Like you, they conceive of God as a source of goodness, even though they do not think He actively intervenes in history. Rabbi Edward Feld in *The Spirit of Renewal: Finding Faith after the Holocaust,* for example, rejects various traditional responses to the problem of evil. In his view, it is now necessary to formulate a new theology in which God is understood as manifest in human life:

> We can no longer believe in divine intervention that will come from the outside, but we must learn that we can let holiness enter, that we can make space for the divine, that which is most deeply nourishing, that which sparks the soul of each of us ... We believe not in an omnipotent God who will transform the reality closing in around us ... but in a God who in a delicate voice calls us from within that reality to break through its hardness and create a resting place for the Divine Presence.[13]

But this is not my view. Arguably in our post-Holocaust world we can no longer accept that traditional doctrines about God's goodness are valid. I believe that what is required today is a complete reorientation in theological reflection. Such a revised theology should be based on the distinction between the Divine-as-it-is-in-itself and the Divine-as-perceived. As you know, this contrast is a central feature of many of the world's faiths.

In Judaism God the transcendental Infinite is conceived as *En Sof,* as distinct from the *Shekhinah* (God's Presence) which is manifest in the terrestrial plane. In Hindu thought the *nirguna Brahman,* the Ultimate in itself, beyond all human categories, is distinguished from the *saguna Brahman,* the Ultimate as known to finite consciousness as a personal deity, in *Isvara.* In Taoist thought, the Tao that can be expressed is not the eternal Tao. In Mahayana Buddhism there is a contrast between the eternal cosmic Buddha-nature, which is also the infinite void, and on the other hand the realm of the heavenly Buddha figures in their incarnations in the earthly Buddhas.

In attempting to represent Ultimate Reality, the different religions have conceptualised the Divine in two distinct modes: the Divine personalised and the Divine as absolute. In Judaism, God is understood as Lord; in the Christian faith as Father; in Islam as

Allah; in the Indian traditions as Shiva or Vishnu, or Parameter. In each case these personal deities are conceived as acting within the history of the various communities. The concept of the Divine is alternatively schematised to form a range of divine conceptualisations in the world's religions such as Brahman, the Dharma, the Tao, Nirvana and Sunyata in Eastern traditions.

Given these varied images of the Divine among the various religious systems that emerged throughout history, it is not surprising that there are innumerable conflicts between the teachings of the world's faiths — in all cases believers have maintained that the doctrines of their respective traditions are true and superior to competing claims. Thus Jews contend that they are God's chosen people and partners in a special covenant — their mission is to be a light to the nations. Christians, on the other hand, have traditionally believed that only those who belong to the true faith can be saved, and the Christian community has continually sought to convert all human beings to the Gospel.

Each religious tradition then affirms its own superiority — all rival claims are regarded as misapprehensions of Divine Reality. From a pluralistic perspective, however, there is no way to ascertain which, if any, of these spiritual paths accurately reflects the nature of the Divine-as-it-is-in-itself. Hence, I believe it is impossible to make judgements about the veracity of the various conceptions of the Divine within the world's religions. Instead, the adherents of all the world's religions must recognise the inevitable human subjectivity of religious conceptualisation.

This recognition calls for a complete reorientation of religious apprehension. What is now required is for both Jews and Christians to acknowledge that their conceptual systems, forms of worship, lifestyle and scriptures are in the end nothing more than lenses through which Divine Reality is perceived. Yet the Divine-as-it-is-in-itself is beyond human understanding, regardless of the religious experiences of the faithful. Within this theological framework, claims about God's goodness, justice and mercy (like those you have made in previous letters) should be understood as human conceptions stemming from the religious experience of Jews and Christians through the centuries. In all cases pious believers and thinkers have expressed their understanding of

God's nature on the basis of their own personal as well as communal encounter with the Divine. But given that the Divine-as-it-is-in-itself is beyond human understanding, such claims cannot be viewed as definitive and final. In this respect it makes no sense for either Jews or Christians to believe that they possess unique truth about God.

Dan

2. Jesus

━◦◦◦◦━

2.1   11 July 2003

JESUS — A NEW BEGINNING?

Dan,

Your letter ends with the declaration that no views about God are definitive and final — and now, I'm beginning to see what you yourself think! At least in part. That they are human constructions, I agree. I would argue that all contribute something important to our understanding of Sacred Mystery.

But, if we are having difficulties in reaching a common understanding of God, it is obvious that we will have a much harder task when it comes to Jesus! As I said to you in my last letter a few days ago (1.10): 'In Jesus' death on the cross we see how God was prepared to be vulnerable, that vulnerability was a way of showing love, and that from this vulnerability came — in some mysterious way — hope and a changed quality of life.' But even before we come to discuss this, the fact of two thousand years of Christian anti-Semitism and anti-Judaism blocks the way.

Even though the last two decades have seen Christian theologians embarking on a journey of *metanoia* or repentance of the terrible treatment of the Jewish people through history, and there are many efforts at understanding through interfaith dialogues and shared pilgrimages to places of violence, we both know that this only nibbles at the damage. In my own church, since the important document of the second Vatican council, *Nostra Aetate*,[1] and the efforts of the present Pope, John Paul II, attitudes have certainly changed. The New Catholic Catechism states clearly that 'The Jews are not collectively responsible for the death of Jesus.'[2]

But it still remains a deep-seated prejudice in the psyches of many Christians that the Jews were responsible — ignoring the complex involvement of the Roman authorities. When Christians read on Good Friday in the Scriptures a line such as 'his blood be on us and on our children' (Matt. 27:26), when they read Jesus' anger with regard to the Pharisees, calling them blind hypocrites, 'snakes, vipers' brood' (Matt. 23:27, 33), prejudices are reinforced.

Of course theology has moved on: we now see the 'Jesus movement' as a reform movement within Judaism and there seem to have been many at that time — like the Essene community and the call to repentance of John the Baptist. We now know that Jesus had no plan to split from Judaism — that he did not even plan to found a church! Paul had to deal with these difficult issues. Jesus observed Jewish feasts and was angry with what he saw as a ritualistic, superficial observance of the Law, not the Law itself. So he followed in a clear line of prophets like Isaiah and Hosea calling for 'mercy, not sacrifice'.

If it is the Gospel of John that seems to keeps alive this presumption of Jewish guilt, with constant references to 'the Jews' in a hostile tone, even this — according to Johannine specialists — needs to be understood not in an anti-Judaistic way, but as emerging from John's own community which was experiencing dissension and internal splits as well as persecution. Witnesses were now becoming martyrs.

I'm not trying to pretend that everything can be harmonised: I am the first to agree that there are huge obstacles to be overcome. Feminist theology itself is not innocent of anti-Judaism. Although I don't think we fall into the trap of regarding the Hebrew scriptures as 'background' for the coming of Jesus, yet, frequently blaming Judaism for patriarchy, we have also been guilty of defining the uniqueness of Jesus over against contemporary Judaism. On the other hand, I don't think the solution is to be discovered by downplaying Jesus: more that we should be looking to different fulfilments and developments of the Jewish scriptures — is that something you would go along with? Or is there no way you can make sense of the claims that Christians make for Jesus?

Mary

2.2   *13 July 2003*

CHRISTIAN ANTI-SEMITISM

Mary,

From your previous letters I think I have a clearer picture of what you mean by God's goodness and compassion. Traditionally this has been understood in both of our faiths as divine, beneficent action. In Scripture as well as in rabbinic and Christian literature, God is portrayed as intervening in human affairs. But you state that you reject the idea of an interventionist God because it does not fit with contemporary science; further, you state that such a Deity would not respect the laws of nature if He were to interfere directly in our lives. You may be aware that a number of contemporary Jewish theologians have adopted a similar view. In the best-selling book, *Why Do Bad Things Happen to Good People?*, Rabbi Harold Kushner contends that even though God is not an actor in history, He is nonetheless present in our lives as a source of goodness. It is a mistake, therefore, to blame God for human suffering. God is present in everyday life, not as a causal agent, but as a source of mercy, goodness and comfort.[3]

But even though Jews and Christians might be able to find common ground in such a reformulation of the notion of God, you are right that Jesus is a stumbling-block in Jewish—Christian encounter. For Christians, Jesus on the cross symbolises God's vulnerability; in his death the world is redeemed, and all of creation is reconciled. But for Jews, the crucified Christ symbolises the Church triumphant. You refer briefly to the background of Christian anti-Semitism. But I would argue that the Christian faith is inherently anti-Jewish, regardless of Jesus' own attitudes. I know this is a strong claim, but I think it can be illustrated by surveying the history of Jewish—Christian relations:

In the years after Jesus' death, the followers of Christ believed themselves to be the true heirs of the covenant. For these Christians Jesus' Messiahship was understood as bringing about a new age in which the true Israel would become a light to the nations. Given this vision, the Jewish people were regarded with animosity. The writers of the gospels depicted Jesus attacking the leaders of the nation, and the Church taught that circumcision of the heart, rather than obedience to the Law, was what God required.

In proclaiming this message, Paul stressed that the Jewish nation had been rejected by God and the old covenant had been superseded. The Epistle to the Hebrews emphasises the antithesis between the Jewish people and the Christian community, and this contrast is highlighted in the fourth gospel which differentiates between the spiritual universe of Christianity and the realm of darkness represented by the Jews. In the light of this teaching, the Fathers of the Church developed an *Adversos Judaeos* tradition which vilified the Jews. According to the Fathers, Jews were guilty in the past of indecent actions, and they have continued to be a contemptible people.

The tradition of Christian anti-Semitism as created by the Church Fathers continued through the centuries. In the fifth and sixth centuries the *Codex Theodosianus* and the Justinian Code denied Jews various rights. Later, during the Crusades, Jewish communities were devastated throughout western Europe. In the Middle Ages Jews were frequently accused of killing Christian children to use their blood in preparations for the Passover; they were also charged with blaspheming the Christian faith in the Talmud. Further, Jews were blamed for causing the Black Death by poisoning wells, were continually portrayed as dark, demonic figures; as the personification of evil, they were regarded as sub-human.

Such images continued into the early modern period: centuries-old Christian prejudice combined with commercial interest provoked antipathy towards the Jewish population in western lands. Even though the Enlightenment brought about the improvement of Jewish existence, Christian writers continued to attack Jewry on rationalist grounds, and in the nineteenth century the Jewish community suffered frequent outbreaks of hostility. In Germany various racist publications attacked Jews, and the researches of Christian biblical scholars undermined the traditional belief that the Torah was given by God to Moses. At the end of the century the Dreyfus affair raised fundamental questions about the viability of Jewish life in the Diaspora.

As you know, such anti-Jewish attitudes served as the background to the emergence of Nazism and the horrors of the Holocaust. You are right that steps have been taken since the end of the Second World War to confront this legacy of two millennia of Christian anti-Judaism.

Yet, such attitudes are deeply rooted in your tradition. The injustices and pogroms inflicted on the Jewish community have been the result of Christian contempt for the Jew. We must acknowledge that both of us are heirs of a fearful tradition — for the Jewish community Jesus and his Church continue to be regarded as the enemy.

Dan

2.3   *18 July 2003*

CHURCH HISTORY AS THE PROBLEM

Dan,

I am glad you acknowledge that we agree about something — namely, that we cannot blame God for suffering, but share an awareness of God's presence as comfort, consolation. Actually, I think there's more to it than that, as I hope to show. I think we have to rethink causality. But I remain perplexed even when using the word 'we'. I still do not know if it includes your own perspective. You cite Rabbi Kushner, but what does Rabbi Cohn-Sherbok think? As well as being loyal to our traditions, we each represent a distinct context with distinctive reactions — don't we?

So, moving to Jesus, when you say, 'I would argue that Christian faith is inherently anti-Jewish regardless of Jesus' attitudes', does this actually represent what you yourself believe? Do you really think that anti-Judaism and anti-Semitism are like viruses that cannot be detached, cannot be eradicated from the system? There is no way that I will argue against you about the horrendous history of anti-Judaism or that this was the seed bed for the anti-Semitism that would erupt into the tragic evil of the Holocaust. I will always argue that the commitment of Christians to *metanoia*, repentance, requires ongoing expression of deeds as well as words, and even if this is sincere and whole-hearted, can never make up for the lost communities, bereft families, and memories of such total violation.

Agreed, that the history of Jewish—Christian relations means that the guilt of Christians can never be denied or excused. The conversion required is ongoing, and it is a conversion on many levels. But, surely, the fact that Christians are now so anxious to explore the fact of Jesus' Jewishness and to understand Christian origins as part of Judaism does give hope for new relations and shared explorations. You say that the gospel writers depicted Jesus as criticising the nation's leaders: but if Jesus was a prophet within the Jewish tradition, isn't this exactly what prophets did? Compared with Amos Jesus can even seem rather mild! The earliest tradition seems to have understood the meaning of the life and death of Jesus through the expectations of the Hebrew scriptures. It is not even clear any more that Paul envisaged the break with Judaism as clearly as was supposed. His early writings were written well before the destruction of the Temple — and the earliest Christian communities continued to pray in the synagogues. The tensions around circumcision and the eating of certain foods reflect more the question as to whether all traditional practices and marks of identity were to be imposed on non-Jewish converts to Christianity.

I don't pretend that there are not problems: but what sets the pattern for the terrible persecution of the next two thousand years, that we have just begun to redress, was not the 'Jesus movement' as such — all kinds of groups experienced this as a liberating, healing moment — but was, first, the encounter with the dualism of Greek philosophy, and second, the triumphalistic attitude of the Church, especially when Constantine made Christianity the established religion of the Roman empire. 'Jesus came preaching the Kingdom but what happened was the Church' expresses this sad fact, as the messianic future in Christ is melted into the Church's reign as Christ on earth. Rosemary Ruether calls this false consciousness the 'false reifying of the experience of the eschatological in history'.[4]

Liberation Theology has been trying for the last thirty years to redress the balance by re-envisioning the theology of the Church from the underside of history. Conscious of the legacies of geno-cide, ecological devastation, and wiping out of indigenous peoples that the hegemony of the Christian empires has produced, there are many attempts in different continents to become the church of the poor, in solidarity with the poor. New understandings of the crucifixion of Christ emerge: Jesus is reclaimed as a suffering brother with the rejected and vulnerable people of the world. They are the crucified peoples, crucified not by an act in the past, but by the oppressive and brutalising regimes today, political and economic.

So, not for a minute trying to soften or escape the legacy of anti-Judaism in history, would *you yourself* be willing to admit that these new developments offer a hope for a shared Jewish and Christian spiritual search?

Mary

2.4   *19 July 2003*

BEYOND CHRISTIAN HOSTILITY

Mary,

I agree that the developments that have taken place since the Second World War in Jewish—Christian relations provide a new framework for Jewish—Christian encounter and understanding. Yet I do believe that the anti-Jewish bias of Christianity cannot be eradicated. It is a virus that contaminates the entire body of Christian life and thought. Even if Jesus' denunciation of the Jewish religious establishment was in line with the prophets' con-demnation of the leaders of the nation, his words have served as a basis for vilifying the Jewish people. Similarly, in the epistles Paul appears highly critical of Pharisaic Judaism. In his view, obedience is not possible under the Mosaic covenant; rather, a new covenant including baptism is now required. Through such an act it is pos-sible to put off the body of flesh and be raised with Christ (Col. 2:11—12). Only this covenant can provide the power to become a living law when God's commands are written on the tablets of the human heart (2 Cor. 3:3).

You are right to point out that there is currently an attempt to exonerate Paul from the charge that he showed contempt for the Jewish faith. Some scholars contend that, in making a case against Judaism, he misunderstood or possibly distorted the Judaism of his own time. Others stress that Paul was concerned exclusively with the relationship of gentiles to the Torah; hence he does not deal with the question of Jewish observance of the Law because it is irrelevant to his concerns. Alternatively, it has been proposed that Paul's opposition to Judaism was a stand against Jewish nationalism rather than Jewish legalism.

Yet, no matter what one makes of this scholarly debate, there is no question that the synoptic gospels, the fourth gospel, and Paul's epistles have been used by the Church to foster anti-Semitism through the ages. According to early Christian theologians such as John Chrysostom, Ephrem and Hippolytus, the Jews were guilty of indecency: the Jewish nation, they argued, is a lawless and dissolute people. Hence all future promises apply solely to the Church. On the basis of Scripture, early Christian theologians sought to demonstrate that the conflict between the Church and Synagogue was prefigured in the Bible: because of their rejection of Christ, Jews have continually been subject to God's wrath. Hence it is Christians, rather than Jews, who constitute the elect. This is the fulfilment of the messianic vision of the ingathering of all people to Zion. Later, as the religion of the Roman empire, Christianity served as the vehicle for bringing God's redemption to all human beings. The Jews, on the other hand, suffer rejection and misery because of their unwillingness to accept Jesus as Christ. The Jewish nation is destined to wander in exile, and Jewish law has been superseded through Christ's death and resurrection.

This terrible legacy of Christian contempt for the Jew should not be forgotten — it must not be softened or denied. In the minds of many Jews, the Church's attitude to the Jews paved the way to the gas chambers. Nonetheless, as you suggest, it is now possible to build bridges between our two faiths. In recent decades the Roman Catholic Church and the World Council of Churches have issued numerous decrees denouncing anti-Semitism and have encouraged Jewish—Christian dialogue.

Pioneering Christian scholars have attempted to understand the Jewishness of Jesus — modern Christology, they believe, must be purged of any anti-Jewish bias. God's enduring covenant with the Jewish nation has also repeatedly been emphasised, and various theories have been propounded to illustrate that Jesus' death and resurrection do not supersede God's revelation on Mount Sinai. In this context the traditional idea of mission has been replaced by the notion of Christian witness. No longer do most Christians feel compelled to convert the Jewish people to the one, true, faith; rather Judaism is affirmed as a valid religious tradition with its own spiritual integrity. These are all positive steps towards reconciliation between Christian and Jew despite two millennia of Jewish persecution, suffering and death.

Dan

2.5   *24 July 2003*

CAN CHRISTIANITY BE FORGIVEN?

Dan,

I'm confused! Your letter states that 'the anti-Jewish bias of Christianity cannot be eradicated' and you proceed to outline horrific examples of this, which you already stated in your previous letter — 13 July — yet you end on a positive note, citing examples of recent scholars who have changed the compulsion for conversion to one of common witness, for example. *What do you really think?* Is it actually possible to start all over again?

On the one hand, I agree with you that in no way must we soften or deny Christian contempt for the Jew. I've already said that the many-levelled journey for repentance for the Christian must be ongoing. The memory of two millennia of persecution cannot be blotted out — indeed it is an intrinsic part of Jewish identity.

But this leads me to the heart of what our conversation turns on — namely, on reconciliation. Many Christians take forgiveness as the centre of the teaching of Jesus. They often quote Jesus saying, in response to Peter, that one must forgive seventy times over (Matt. 18). This answer is then transposed to the context

of Jewish—Christian relations and Jews are asked to forgive
Christians for the atrocities of the Holocaust-Shoah. There are so
many post-war stories of encounters with SS guards in this
context — and the Jewish answer is that only God can forgive.

I remember a shocked undergraduate of mine, when Rabbi
Friedlander made that response to him after a lecture on
forgiveness.

If I approach the issue from feminist theology I see equal resistance to the centrality of forgiveness. Women have frequently been
told to forgive in order to keep peace in the family, regardless of
the justice issues around the disputes. Is this what is behind the
reluctance to forgive — that there is scant regard to the injustices
inflicted on Jews through the centuries?

I think there is a clue given from Jesus' own life and teaching
— when isolated from any anti-Judaistic bias. Jesus set his face to
Jerusalem in a freely chosen path of suffering love, emerging from
a being totally reconciled with God, the power and source of life
and justice; a path also chosen by the community that formed and
nurtured him. The struggle that appeared to end for Jesus with
crucifixion was a protest against all crucifixions, against the necessity of the violent putting to death of the innocent, poor and vulnerable. The feminist ethicist Beverley Harrison wrote that Jesus'
death on the cross, his sacrifice, was no abstract exercise in moral
virtue but the price he paid for refusing to abandon the radical
activity of love:[5] His sacrifice was *for* the cause of radical love, to
make and sustain relationship and above all, to right wrong
relationship. And all this, within a prophetic Jewish understanding.

A similar refusal to separate forgiveness and reconciliation was
glimpsed recently in the all-too-brief presidency of President
Aristide of Haiti. Would reconciliation mean amnesty, a sweeping
under the carpet, or what degree of justice could be striven for?
Leslie Griffiths wrote: 'The fiery priest was very clear that there
could be no question of accepting "reconciliation" understood as
"papering over the cracks of the past" without a clear recognition
of the demands of justice.'[6]

I argue that forgiveness can find meaning within such a vision
of structural justice. That Jesus was very aware of unjust power
structures can be seen by the fact that the forgiveness parables and

injunctions are always from the powerful to the less powerful and not the other way round. There is no urging that the battered woman must forgive her abuser, that land-hungry peasants must forgive rapacious landlords. The woman from the town (Luke 7) is forgiven because she has loved much. Even Peter's famous question — mentioned above — as to how often we have to forgive, is answered in terms of the parable of the unjust servant, where the forgiveness/debt cancellation went from the powerful king to the powerless servant, not vice versa. What Christians have not seen is that the initiative for reconciliation must come from the wronged person or community, and to utter words on someone's behalf is to sow seeds for more injustice.

So, if we put forgiveness within the context of justice and reparation, can Christianity be forgiven? And if not, how can there be a new beginning for Jews and Christians?

Mary

2.6   26 July 2003

RECONCILIATION AND THE THEOLOGICAL CHASM

Mary,

You are right that there is a problem. Christianity, I believe, is intractably anti-Jewish. The New Testament contains venomous sayings about Jews, and the history of the Church is scarred by persecution and murder of the Jewish people. Modern Jews and Christians are the inheritors of nineteen centuries of suspicion, hatred and contempt. My point in rehearsing the history of Christian anti-Semitism is to emphasise that a dark shadow of past atrocities is cast over all attempts at positive Jewish—Christian dialogue.

This does not mean, however, that Christian repentance for two millennia of Jewish suffering is impossible. On the contrary, Jews are obliged to forgive those who are truly penitent. But I should stress that the Jewish concept of forgiveness is different from the Christian. According to the New Testament view, God does not demand a prior restitution from the offender; instead, God takes upon himself the act of reparation. In this way, the sinner can be restored to a true relationship with God. God's love is thus wholly unconditional, free, and unmerited, and as such it naturally calls out repentance from human beings. When Christians see God's reconciling love in Christ, their hearts are moved to repentance towards God and forgiveness towards others. Forgiveness is thus from God, and by God through Jesus' teaching and ministry.

In the Hebrew Bible, God's forgiving nature is repeatedly asserted. A central theme of the prophetic books is the need for repentance — an act made possible by God's capacity for forgiveness. Yet, in the Jewish tradition, divine forgiveness is dependent on confession, repentance and the determination not to repeat the offence. In the tradition, these stages are highlighted and reflected in the liturgy, particularly on the Day of Atonement. Each individual is to seek forgiveness from God and from his neighbour. God is conceived as ready to forgive at the first sign of repentance, and human beings are urged to follow his example. However, it is understood that when one has committed an offence against another person, restitution is necessary and the offender must seek the injured party's forgiveness.

In short, in Judaism forgiveness is not unconditional: it is dependent on the attitude of the offender. In this light, Jews are compelled to forgive the Christian community if Christians are truly repentant about past terrors unleashed by the Church against the Jewish community. The reason that Rabbi Friedlander was not prepared to forgive the Nazis was because they did not repent of the atrocities committed against the Jewish nation, nor did they seek forgiveness. But this does not apply to those Christians who genuinely feel remorse about the history of Christian anti-Semitism. Jewish—Christian encounter and dialogue is possible today because of such a change of heart.

You refer to Jesus' life and teaching as a possible bridge between the two faiths — his radical love, symbolised by the Cross, points the way to reconciliation between Christian and Jew. I myself am drawn to the image of Jesus as a prophet of Israel, protesting against unjust power structures. Some time ago, I wrote a book about Jewish liberation theology, *On Earth as it is in Heaven: Jews,*

Christians and Liberation Theology, in which I argued that Jesus can be understood as a prophet of Israel. I wrote:

> This prophetic understanding of Jesus should make it possible for the Jew to gain a sympathetic insight into Jesus' ministry. His attack on the scribes and Pharisees can be seen, not as a rejection of the Torah, but as a prophetic renunciation of a corrupt religious establishment. Such a conception of Jesus should enable both Jews and Christians to set aside previous barriers to interfaith dialogue and concentrate on a shared prophetic vision.[7]

I still believe this to be so. But I am aware that there are major theological barriers between our two faiths. The doctrines of the Trinity and the Incarnation constitute a deep chasm separating the Christian and the Jew, and these fundamental religious differences will make it difficult for us to find common ground even if we can now achieve a measure of reconciliation in a post-Holocaust world.

     Dan

2.7   *26 July 2003*

SON OF GOD

Dan,

For the first time I sensed a measure of agreement in this correspondence, and that brings with it a sense of hope on this rainy summer morning! Jewish understanding of forgiveness is remarkably similar to my Catholic upbringing: whatever the shortcomings in the practice, we were taught that forgiveness has three elements — contrition, confession and satisfaction (or restitution). Even if nothing can undo the crime that has been committed. But even more significant in this measure of agreement is your understanding of Jesus as prophet — which I had tried to develop on 18 July.

    But there is always a sting in the tail — and this has now emerged in the chasm created by the doctrines of Incarnation and Trinity. Jesus himself never claimed to be the Son of God, but

rather called himself 'Son of Man' — just as God addressed
Ezekiel as 'Son of Man'. The problem develops first over the intimate relationship that Jesus has with the 'Father' whom he
addresses as 'Abba', 'Daddy'. This in turn has been used in an anti-
Judaist way to assert that Jesus' relationship with the Divine was
far more intense than any Jewish precedent. Even in feminist
circles there has been a tendency to set up Jesus as the antithesis
of Judaism — part of the dreadful antithesis between 'God of
wrath, God of love'.[8]

But even if there are few other examples of the use of 'Abba'
in relation to God, I am convinced that Jesus' language of inti-
macy with God is part of his Jewish heritage. Being a 'Son of God'
is also inherited from Judaism. When we sing at Midnight Mass
on Christmas Eve, 'Thou art my Son, this day have I begotten
thee' (Ps. 2:7), even if the primary context is the Davidic kingship,
Christian devotion understands the *sensus plenior*, deeper understanding, to refer to Jesus. And this is the real obstacle for Jewish—
Christian relations, that titles springing from early Christian
devotional circles formed the basis of a theology that came to be
defined over against and in competition with Judaism. So
'Lord/*kurios*', '*Christos*', even the baptismal formula, 'In the name
of the Father, Son and Holy Spirit' sprang from devotional
contexts.

But isn't there a way forward in trying to redefine Christology
within Jewish monotheism? God is One, but *Hokhmah/Sophia* is
also a divine figure associated with God. *Elohim* is a plural name
for God. The *Logos*, Word, is spoken of by Philo of Alexandria as
a second god, 'First-born'.[9] God speaks through angelic messengers. The New Testament scholar Larry Hurtado even suggests
that the kind of agency ascribed to principal angels gave the early
followers of Jesus a 'basic scheme for accommodating the resur-
rected Christ next to God without having to depart from their
monotheistic tradition'.[10]

So I'm arguing that in the earliest stages of the formation of
Christology, there was still an effort to situate Jesus within Jewish
monotheism. He is Son of God — but so are many others. He is
Son of Man — and so is Ezekiel. He sits at God's right hand —
but along with angelic presences. He ascends to heaven — and so

did Elijah. He has a miraculous birth, as did Isaac, Ishmael and Samuel. He speaks in the spirit, as do the prophets; he gives his spirit to his followers, as did Elijah to Elisha.

Don't get me wrong: I'm not pretending that all problems can be eliminated. I think there did come a decisive break with the Synagogue. By that time anti-Judaism had set in, so that the doctrines that developed around Christology assumed a confrontational and polemical nature. But I'm eternally optimistic that there can be a new start!

Mary

2.8   *28 July 2003*

JESUS AS MESSIAH AND SAVIOUR

Mary,

I am aware of the scholarly debate concerning Jesus' claims about himself. In all likelihood, Jesus did not think of himself as the Second Person of the Trinity — the doctrine of the Incarnation only developed at a later stage in the history of the Church. I think you are right that if Jesus is understood as the 'Son of God' in the same way that such biblical figures as Ezekiel are 'sons of God', Christology would not be a barrier to Jewish—Christian dialogue. But are you really proposing such a fundamental shift in the Christian understanding of Jesus?

For nearly two thousand years the Church has asserted that Jesus is the long-awaited Messiah. He is literally the unique Son of God, and as God's anointed, he ushers in the Kingdom of God in which the Old Torah is superseded. Forgiveness, atonement and salvation are offered through God's redemptive intervention in human history. Jesus summons all to enter into a new covenant with God based on divine love and grace. In your opinion, are such notions to be jettisoned?

This is a fundamentally important issue for our conversation. I had assumed that as a Catholic theologian, you subscribe to the essential Christian teachings about Jesus. It is clear from our correspondence so far, that you do not believe in an interventionist God, even though you think his goodness and justice are manifest in human experience. Are you now saying that you think the traditional Christian notion of Jesus as Lord and Saviour must be set aside? If so, this will have vitally important consequences for our future discussion.

As you know, in the past Christians viewed Jesus as the Alpha and Omega of all creation. Jews have always rejected this doctrine. According to rabbinic sources, the belief that God was in Christ is heretical; the doctrine that God is both Father and Son was seen as a dualistic theology. In the Middle Ages the concept of the Trinity was bitterly denounced. The twelfth-century philosopher Moses Maimonides, for example, maintained that Christians are polytheists rather than monotheists. Modern Jewish thought is equally critical of any attempt to harmonise the belief in God's unity with the doctrine of a triune God. Contemporary Jewish theologians of all degrees of observance affirm that Judaism is fundamentally incompatible with what they perceive as the polytheistic character of Trinitarian belief.

Now if you are saying that you go along with the Jewish community in rejecting these fundamental doctrines of the Christian faith, we can certainly bridge the theological divide that previously separated the Christian and the Jew. But is this really your position? Distancing yourself from the notion of an interventionist God is a radical step, but discarding the traditional belief in the divinity of Christ would arguably remove you altogether from the circle of Christian believers. Have I misunderstood you?

Dan

2.9   *28 July 2003*

JESUS AND REDEMPTION VIA HIS CROSS

Dan,

The optimism of my last letter has been quickly replaced by the consequences of the challenge of your response. Do not be so quick to cast me out of the Christian Church! We are in a new phase — that's the *kairos* of this moment. But it is beyond credibility to assume that the efforts at understanding we are now making can undo two thousand years of persecution and deliberate misunderstandings.

When I rejected an interventionist God I argued (1 July) that this deepens rather than rejects faith in the God of creation of both our traditions. It is an *agential* view rather than an interventionist one. In my last letter I was not denying the Jesus of salvation and Trinity, but rooting Christology in Jewish monotheism as a matter of historical fact. But I also recognised that the philosophical doctrines expressed in credal formulae were defined in a context of anti-Judaism, and at times when the Christian Church had long lost touch with its ethnic roots in Judaism. The question for us now is whether they can be recovered to our mutual benefit.

For example, the Trinity doctrine has always been placed on the horns of the dilemma of tri-theism on the one hand and modalism on the other, and the Church has always denied both extremes. But if the fundamental insight of the doctrine is that in Jesus, people experienced an encounter with God, Divine Mystery, and that this continues through his spirit, how is this to be expressed? Surely, it does not have to be quintessentially anti-Judaistic?

It all hinges on the qualitative meaning of Jesus as encounter with God. I argue that the messianic quality of Jesus' life and the community he gathered around him is expressed in the degree of compassion and identification with the poorest and most vulnerable groups of people he engaged with (lepers, women, ethnic minorities, mentally deranged). It is his *life* in this commitment lived through to a violent death, and the post-Easter conviction of his followers that he was still with them, that was the basis of *ecclesia*, where his presence was experienced in 'the breaking of the bread' (Luke 24:30). Tragically, this became diverted into the Jews being blamed for his death, and the cross being used as an instrument of violence in the Crusades and the conquest of the 'New World'. Meditation on the sufferings of Jesus and identification with them intensified the blame and anti-Jewish sentiment. I cannot deny that the mystique of the cross, and 'being washed in the blood of the lamb', is still a popular evangelical expression of what is saving about Jesus. I cannot deny the strength of the hatred of the cross because of what the Jewish people have suffered through it. This is made very clear in the poignant novel *My Name is Asher Lev*, where the young artist Asher Lev is flung out of his Brooklyn Hasidic community because of his painting of his mother on the cross-panes of a large window in a gallery, which seems to be depicting her as a symbol of suffering on a cross.[11] But we are making huge efforts to move away from all damaging interpretations. Some would see the Cross as a symbol of protest, a protest against the oppression of the innocent. Jesus died to end this suffering and to end the need for all innocents to be put to death. Sandra Schneiders invites Christians to examine how the symbol functions, to repent of its abuse and to look carefully at what it inspires.[12] I think the symbol is so integral to Christianity that to remove it is to lose its essence: following 'The Way of the Cross' has become integral to Christian life. But if this way is a way of repentance, of protest against injustice, imperialism and corruption in the name of a crucified Jew, this offers a way forward.

It also gives a clue to what the reality of Trinity is for Jesus' followers today: if those who follow the Way of the Cross experience meeting Jesus again in the poor Indian woman of the desert, the Nicaraguan peasant, the prisoner on Death Row — then Jesus' spirit is bringing close the suffering love of God in a healing way. That is what I believe salvation is about now — and it's the substance of the Kingdom that Jesus proclaimed.

Mary

2.10 *30 July 2003*

JEWISH OBJECTIONS TO JESUS

Mary,
I do not wish to diminish your optimism. But I do think there are difficulties about the possibility of reconciliation between Jew and Christian given Christian claims about Jesus. I was very glad to receive your fascinating new book *Sacred Longings*, which I have read. I appreciate that when you say you do not believe in an interventionist God, you are referring to the notion of God as

causal agent in the world. But, as you explain in your new book, you nonetheless regard God as actively renewing the human spirit. Further, you state that in your understanding of the Trinity what is crucial is relatedness. You write: 'Many of us see related-ness as the defining metaphor, both intra-Trinitarian and as an outpouring of liberating and compassionate love to the world.'[13]

Given such emphasis on liberating and compassionate love, I can understand your conviction that those who follow the Way of the Cross experience Jesus in his confrontation with the margin-alised — in these meetings his spirit brings close the suffering of God in a healing fashion.

Your desire to redefine Christology within Jewish monotheism is admirable. After so many centuries of misunderstanding and dis-trust, we do need to find common ground. I see that the way in which you have interpreted the doctrines of the Messiahship, Incarnation and the Trinity could provide a basis for common cause. I am certainly sympathetic to this quest. Yet these central Christian doctrines, even as you explain them, are still barriers to Jewish—Christian encounter and dialogue.

I cannot overlook the ways in which Jews have traditionally recoiled from these doctrines. Regarding Jesus' Messiahship, for example, Jews have refused to accept Jesus as their Messiah and Saviour for several reasons. First, according to Judaism, it is obvi-ous that he did not fulfil the Jewish messianic expectations — he did not restore the kingdom of David to its former glory; nor did he gather in the dispersed ones of Israel and restore all the laws of the Torah that were in abeyance. He did not compel all Israel to walk in the way of the Torah nor did he rebuild the Temple and usher in a new order in the world and nature.

In other words, Jesus did not inaugurate a cataclysmic change in history. Universal peace, in which there is neither war nor com-petition, did not come about on earth. Thus for Jews, and I include myself in this, Jesus did not fulfil the prophetic messianic hope in a redeemer who would bring political and spiritual redemption as well as earthly blessings and moral perfection to the human race.

A second objection to Jesus concerns the Christian claim that he possesses a special relationship with God. In the Gospel of

Matthew, for example, we read: 'No one knows the Son except the Father; and no one knows the Father, except the Son' (Matt. 11:27). In John's gospel, Jesus declares: 'I am the way, and the truth, and the life; no one comes to the Father but by me. If you had known me, you would have known my Father also; henceforth you have known him and have seen him' (John 14:6—7). I simply cannot believe that Jesus, unique among all human beings, occupies such an elevated position.

But most important, the Christian claim that Jesus is not simply the Messiah, but God himself is, I believe, totally incompatible with the Jewish belief in God's unity. Among medieval Jewish thinkers this doctrine embraced the idea that there is no plurality in God's being: God is absolute simplicity. As Maimonides wrote: 'This God is One, not two or more than two, but One whose unity is different from all other unities that there are ... Nor is He one as a body, containing parts and dimensions ... But His is a unity than that which there is no other anywhere.'[14]

A classic formulation of this view is contained in *The Kingly Crown* by the medieval poet Solomon Ibn Gabirol:

> Thou art One, the beginning of all computation, the
>   base of all construction.
> Thou art One, and in the mystery of Thy Oneness the
>   wise of heart are astonished, for they know not what it
>   is.
> Thou art One, but not as the one that is counted or
>   owned,
> for number and chance cannot reach thee, nor attribute,
>   nor form.[15]

No matter how you redefine the belief in Jesus' Messiahship and his divinity, the theological chasm between Christian and Jew remains. As I said previously, both Jews and Christians can read Jesus' words as prophetic utterances similar to the message of the prophets of the Northern and Southern Kingdoms. Throughout their history the Jewish people have suffered at the hands of their enemies; they have been exploited and marginalised. As such, they should ideally be sympathetic to the plight of those who are downtrodden today. In this Jews and Christians can draw together, and find in Jesus' life and death a source of inspiration. But the central theological beliefs of the Christian faith, even as you interpret them, will inevitably pull us apart.

Dan

2.11   *30 July*

WILL THE CHASMS EVER BE BRIDGED?

Dan,

The force of your argument in one sense is unanswerable and there seem to be more chasms than bridges between us. And certain chasms may never be bridged.

We can agree that sharing a belief in the prophetic sayings and wisdom of Jesus is a small step. Redefining Christology within Jewish monotheism is another. But our discussions have made it clear that Christianity claims more than this, and makes such enormous claims that an unbridgeable gulf has appeared.

To your challenge that Jesus did not fulfil messianic expectations, did not restore David's kingdom to its former glory, rebuild the Temple and so on, I can argue that this was not the kind of Messiah that Jesus was. Indeed he went out of his way to show that — and disciples left him because he disappointed them in his own lifetime. He was a failed Messiah in that sense. When John the Baptist's disciples came to him and said: 'Are you he who is to come or should we look for another?' (Matt. 11:3), Jesus replied, 'Go and tell John what you hear and see: the blind receive their sight and the lame walk, lepers are cleansed and the deaf hear, and the dead are raised up, and the poor have the good news preached to them' (4—5).

At the level of his own self-understanding, or the understanding of Matthew and his community, Jesus was comparing himself with Isaiah (35:5—6), where the healing of land and people was to be a sign of messianic times. You might be interested to know that when I am in the desert of Rajasthan, at the Gandhian ashram of Wells for India's partners,[16] at early morning prayer, the leader will ask for the teachings of Jesus. (The group is mostly Hindu, with some Muslims.) It is extraordinary how poignant it is to speak of faith in how the desert will blossom — as both Jewish and Christian belief — to dedicated field workers facing, as a matter of daily routine, drought and sandstorms among poor, hungry and thirsty villagers. It seems to bring us close in imagination and experience to the expectation of the biblical communities both before and at the time of Jesus. (It is a reminder that we who read these texts are eons away from the historical biblical expectation — is that not where we should now be searching for common ground?)

I could attempt to argue that the Trinity does not interfere with the Oneness, the Unity and Simplicity of God and that classical theologians like St Thomas — whom we touched on in 1.4, 27 June — fell over themselves trying to prove that the threeness did not destroy the oneness! But a more important argument is that the heart of Christian faith *as experienced* is belief in *One* God: 'Credo in Unum Deum' is the community prayer at every solemn gathering. All attempts to explain God as 'Being itself' (like Paul Tillich's), or St John's 'God is love' or my own as 'passion for relational justice' — all depend on this unity, that is capable of different expressions.

So we cannot agree on Christian claims as to the nature of Jesus. But there is a way forward in understanding more than one fulfilment to the Hebrew scriptures, in seeing that messianic expectations could develop as blessing in more than one way. But to follow that trail we need to encounter the role that the scriptures play in our two traditions. No doubt more chasms will appear! This is beginning to sound more like adventures of hobbits — *Lord of the Rings* — than a 'safe' conversation!

Mary

3. The Bible

—◦◦◦◦—

3.1 4 August 2003

SCRIPTURE: A PARTING OF THE WAYS?

Mary,

In discussing the concept of God and Jesus' life and death, we have referred on numerous occasions to Scripture. Through the centuries, the Bible has served as the foundation of both our faiths. Yet, despite this common understanding, there are fundamental differences between the Jewish and the Christian perception of the biblical text. For the Jewish people, the Bible consists of three types of books: the Torah (Five Books of Moses), the *Neviim* (prophets), and the *Ketuvim* (writings). According to tradition, all these books are sacred and inspired, but the Torah is of pre-eminence since it is viewed as having been revealed directly by God to Moses on Mount Sinai. This means that all the words of Genesis, Exodus, Leviticus, Numbers and Deuteronomy are true, even though their meaning is interpreted in a variety of ways.

In rabbinic literature a distinction is drawn between the revelation of the Torah and the prophetic writings. This is frequently expressed by saying that the Torah (Five Books of Moses) was given directly by God, whereas the prophetic books were given by means of prophecy. The remaining books of the Bible are viewed as conveyed by means of the holy spirit rather than through prophecy. Nonetheless, all these writings constitute the canon of Scripture. According to the rabbis, the expositions and elaborations of the Written Law were also revealed by God to Moses on Mount Sinai, and subsequently passed from generation to generation. By this means additional legislation was incorporated into the corpus of Jewish law. This process is referred to as the Oral, as opposed to the Written, Torah. Thus traditional Judaism affirms that God's revelation is twofold (the Written and the Oral Torah) and binding for all time.

You will not be surprised to hear that, as a Reform Jew, I cannot accept this traditional understanding of the Oral and the Written Torah. In the Reform liturgy, we express our dedication to the Torah in the Sabbath service: 'It is a tree of life to those who hold fast to it,' we declare. But, unlike the Orthodox, we have embraced the findings of biblical scholarship. Today there is a general recognition among non-Orthodox Jews that the Written Torah was not composed by Moses. Rather, it is seen as a collection of traditions originating at different times in the history of ancient Israel. I know you are not a Christian fundamentalist! I imagine we would both generally agree about the status and authority of the Hebrew Bible.

But what about the New Testament? Jesus was perceived by his followers as the fulfilment of the Jewish tradition. Consequently, the Christian community has accepted the Hebrew scriptures as canonical — but in addition to these scriptural books, the Church added 27 writings which they also viewed as inspired by God. These works emerged from living communities that bore witness to Jesus. Like the Hebrew scriptures, the New Testament grew out of the life of a people who believed themselves to have been chosen by God. For Christianity, the Hebrew scriptures constitute the Old Testament — a prelude to the New. Jesus is perceived as the Word made flesh, and in his life and death he was thought to have presented the Jewish community with a new perception of God's demands. According to the Christian Church, it is in the New Testament that the Old Testament promise of salvation for all people is fulfilled. If we have had difficulty finding common ground so far, has the chasm between us opened even further?

Dan

3.2   *4 August 2003*

SCRIPTURE — FULFILLED, OR STILL WAITING IN HOPE?

Dan,

What a relief to learn that we can agree on a critical, scholarly approach to the Bible! I refuse to fall down the chasm yet ... But I have to be honest that many Christians don't have a good track record with regard to actually knowing the Bible, and the Catholic tradition, to which I belong, is about the worst in this respect. It was not until after the Encyclical of Pope Pius XII, *Divino Afflante Spiritu*, in 1943 that Scripture — both Hebrew and Christian — was opened up for ordinary believing Catholics and we were actively encouraged to study it! I'll never forget my surprise when, as an undergraduate, I was invited by a friend to visit her home in the Welsh valleys: she and her family were keen Methodists, and we went with her parents to a Bible-study evening in someone's home. I felt very much in awe, and very humbled, when I saw how well these people knew and loved the Bible.

Even now the Catholic Catechism issues strict guidelines as to how the Bible must be read — 'attentive to the content and unity of the whole', with Christ as its centre, 'within the living tradition of the whole Church', and 'attentive to the analogy of faith' — which means the coherence of the truths of faith among themselves and within the whole plan of revelation.[1] It seems that doctrine dictates the way Scripture should be read. And the basic Christian hermeneutic, or method of reading the Bible, has been to see in Christ the fulfilment of so much that has gone before. As I said to you already, we have been taught to look for the *sensus plenior* or deeper meaning as being that which points towards Christ. A good example of this would be the passage in Acts 8 (27—40) where the Ethiopian eunuch is reading Isaiah, the passage where the Servant of the Lord is led like a lamb to the slaughter. Philip then interprets the passage in terms of the death of Jesus, the Ethiopian believes this and is led to baptism.

It becomes a paradigm of the conversion process. Other typologies would be the sacrifice of Isaac and David as God's anointed son.

Now, Christians sensitive to the way that Scripture has been read with anti-Jewish eyes, and who were even taught to be critical of Jews because they have not recognised Jesus as Messiah, are trying to approach the text with new eyes. (Or some of us are.) But I would have to agree with you that the attitude is still widespread that the Hebrew scriptures are 'Old Testament' and the Christian scriptures are 'New'. The 'Old' is the background — the 'New' is what matters. Even enlightened people who are part of the new approaches still 'colonise' Jewish scriptures for Christianity. Isaiah is treated like a fifth Gospel.[2] Feminist Christology can also define the Christian Jesus over against Judaism.

Supersessionism is deep in the psyches of ordinary people. However, I think there is a clear way forward. (Don't forget that women have special problems with the whole of Scripture, since both Christian and Jewish texts are patriarchal and at some times misogynistic — but that's another story.) The Church consistently affirms the sacredness of Scripture, and that the Hebrew Scriptures are part of divine revelation. Inevitably, Christians will keep reading texts as pointing to Christ — but that could only be one level of meaning of a text that has many meanings. Reading Scripture with new eyes involves discerning the many layers, and becoming sensitive to liturgical, apologetic and ecclesial purposes for which texts have been used. If we are adopting the approach I have argued for already, Jesus as Jewish, Jesus and within Jewish monotheism, then we have to reject supersessionism and find a more complex way of understanding how God reaches out to all God's people. If 'election of chosen people' is problematic, the whole schema of 'Salvation History' is equally problematic. The way forward must come in devising ways for reading and interpreting that move us out of the narrow traditional device of 'promise—fulfilment'.

Mary

3.3   *6 August 2003*

UNDERSTANDING THE BIBLE

Mary,

There are clearly important areas of disagreement between us
about the status of the New Testament, but I am glad that we can
agree that the findings of biblical scholarship are of vital importance in understanding the meaning of Scripture. As you may
know, this is not the traditional Jewish view: biblical scholarship is
regarded as irrelevant. According to traditional Judaism, Moses is
the author of the Torah, and that is the end of the matter. There is
no doubt that Jesus and his followers would have believed this too.

As I mentioned, this doctrine is referred to as *Torah MiSinai*
(Torah from Sinai). The idea is that while Moses was on the top
of Mount Sinai for forty days and forty nights, he received a
divine revelation from God and recorded every word of Genesis,
Exodus, Leviticus, Numbers and Deuteronomy from the mouth
of the Almighty. This is how the twelfth-century Jewish
philosopher Moses Maimonides explained this process:

> The Torah was revealed from heaven. This implies our
> belief that the whole of the Torah found in our hands this
> day is the Torah that was handed down by Moses, and that
> it is all of divine origin. By this I mean that the whole of
> the Torah came unto him from before God in a manner
> which is metaphorically called 'speaking'; but the real
> nature of that communication is unknown to everybody
> except to Moses.[3]

Another philosopher of the medieval period, Nahmanides, argued
that although the Torah was revealed on Mount Sinai, Moses
wrote Genesis and part of Exodus when he descended from
Mount Sinai. And at the end of forty years in the wilderness he
completed the rest of the Pentateuch.

The belief in *Torah MiSinai* is one of Maimonides' 13 principles
of the Jewish faith, and it is of fundamental importance. Because
the entire Torah is of divine origin, it is inerrant — the account

of creation, the flood, the stories about the patriarchs, the exodus from Egypt are accurate in every detail. Further, the 613 laws in the Five Books of Moses are binding on Jews for all time. You may not know that today all strictly Orthodox Jews subscribe to this view.

Some time ago the Chief Rabbi, Jonathan Sacks, and the distinguished Jewish scholar Rabbi Louis Jacobs had a ferocious debate in the *Jewish Chronicle* concerning this issue. The Chief Rabbi insisted that the Written Torah was revealed to Moses on Mount Sinai; Louis Jacobs disagreed, and cited the findings of a century of biblical scholarship in support of his position. Jonathan Sacks refused to listen: for him, as for all Orthodox Jews, the doctrine of *Torah MiSinai* is a matter of faith.

But, for Reform Jews, this is not the case: it is taken for granted that the Written Law was not recorded by Moses, but instead was the work of many hands. It is not Mosaic, but rather a mosaic of different traditions which have been incorporated into a unified whole. For this reason Reform Jews do not accept that the account of God presented in the Torah is necessarily a true account, nor do they regard the legal code in the Pentateuch as authoritative. That is why, for example, Reform Jews do not follow the dietary laws or observe the multifarious regulations concerning Sabbath observance. At the end of the nineteenth century, Reform leaders gathered in Pittsburgh, Pennsylvania and formally declared their position regarding the Bible (in what is known as the Pittsburgh Platform):

> We hold that the modern discoveries of scientific researches in the domain of nature and history are not antagonistic to the doctrines of Judaism, the Bible reflecting the primitive ideas of its own age and at times clothing its conception of divine providence and justice dealing with men in miraculous narratives.[4]

Further, these reformers emphasised that only the moral law should be regarded as obligatory:

> We recognize in the Mosaic legislation a system of training the Jewish people for its mission during its national

life in Palestine, and today we accept as binding only the
moral laws and maintain only such ceremonies as elevate
and sanctify our lives, but reject all such as are not adapted
to the views and habits of modern civilization.[5]

This is a radical departure from Orthodoxy, and it is not surprising that Orthodox Judaism has castigated Reform Jews for their
lack of adherence to the tradition. As a Reform rabbi, I agree with
the stance of these reformers. But the rejection of the traditional
teaching about the Torah has important implications for our dialogue about reconciliation. If the Bible can no longer be regarded
as authoritative in the way it once was, what are the grounds for
our religious opinions? We have already referred to the Bible as
support for our views, but if it is the product of the religious
experience of the ancient Israelites, can it speak to us today? If it
contains revelation or divine inspiration, where is it to be found?

    Dan

3.4   6 August 2003

IN WHAT SENSE CAN THE BIBLE BE AN INSPIRED TEXT?

Dan,

Your struggle — or the struggle of Reform Judaism — to maintain a critical perspective on the Bible in Jewish circles is mirrored
by a very similar tension in Christian biblical scholarship. The
Orthodox Jewish case is similar to the fundamentalist — usually
evangelical — Christian wing, which resists any effort to place a
text in its historical circumstances or literary genre. Take the
anguish around the case of homosexuality, for example. The tradi-
tionalists (fundamentalists) claim that the 'Bible' condemns homosexuality. The principal text cited is Genesis 19, the destruction of
Sodom and Gomorrah, where the sin in question is presumed to
be homosexual acts. But when textual analysis is brought to bear
on the text, it becomes clear that the real sin is the violation of
hospitality through threatened homosexual rape of God's messengers (v. 5). A clear sign that this analysis is correct (and a further

argument that both Jews and Christians can benefit from reading
First and Second Testaments together) is Jesus' command when
sending his disciples on their first mission (Luke 10:1—16). On
being refused hospitality by a town, they are to 'Go into the streets
and say, "Even the dust of your town that clings to our feet, we
wipe off against you ... I tell you it shall be more tolerable on that
day for Sodom than for that town"' (v. 12). Again, the offence is
one against hospitality, so important for ancient Near East cultures. (I'm not trying to argue that the Bible gives a clear brief for
homosexual acts: rather, the current issue of lifelong fidelity in a
gay, committed relationship is not one that the Bible considers at
all.)

I think the problem both our traditions wrestle with is the issue
of the Bible being wrong. And if so, how can it be inspired? If not
inspired, how can it be a sacred text? I think we gave up the old
idea that inspiration literally meant that the Holy Spirit took over
the pen (quill) of whatever writer, Moses or his deputy, and dic-
tated every word. Mostly we hear a watered-down version of this.
The Catholic Catechism again — apologies if this is too often
quoted!

> To compose the sacred books God chose certain men
> [sic!] who, all the while he employed them in this task,
> made full use of their faculties and powers so that,
> although he acted in them and by them, it was as true
> authors that they consigned to writing whatever he
> wanted written and no more.[6]

Feminist biblical scholars find this inadequate to explain how, in
the text cited, the fact that Lot offered the violent men in the city
his virgin daughters to 'do to them what you please' (v. 8) goes
unremarked on and uncriticised as violence against women by
biblical interpreters both Christian and Jewish, both then and
now. Phyllis Trible calls this a 'text of terror'[7] — and there are
many others. We can bring in factors like historical context,
literary genre, hermeneutic and extenuating circumstances, but
the fact is that the Bible is frequently *horribly wrong*.

Rosemary Ruether tries to solve the problem by invoking the
prophetic principle as a principle whereby the Bible critiques

itself, and invites other prophetic communities to do the same, as moral sensitivity is sharpened through the centuries. I am drawn to this argument. But it also means ignoring many texts that are arguably part of the biblical canon. Elizabeth Schüssler Fiorenza takes a different tack, arguing that the Bible must be taken as a whole as an ambiguous document(s), both oppressive and liberating. What gives it inspirational potential is not the written word as such, nor even the selection of certain inspiring texts and the elimination of others, but the recognition of the patriarchal and *kyriarchal* nature and politics of the texts. (*Kyriarchal* means the discourse of domination.) But it doesn't mean a focus on a few courageous biblical women. Rather, the attempt is to retrieve — via a multi-strategic approach — the liberating potential of a given text, hearing this via the silences and the gaps between the written words. Then the liberating message is taken up by feminist communities in contemporary and historical struggles for the transformation of injustices.

In this way, I think we can speak of the Bible as inspired text.
Mary

3.5   *12 August 2003*

THE HUMAN FACE OF SCRIPTURE

Mary,

You mention the old idea of revelation as divine dictation. But you must remember that the Jewish fundamentalist notion of direct communication from God pertains only to the Torah; the prophetic books and the Writings by contrast are viewed as inspired by God. Here the Catholic understanding (which you refer to) is very similar to the Jewish view of the origin of the *Neviim* (prophetic books) and the *Ketuvim* (Writings): God is viewed as choosing certain individuals as his messengers. The books of the Bible they composed are ultimately of divine origin even though these persons made use of their own powers and faculties when writing them.

I am afraid, however, that I do not accept either notion of divine disclosure. If the Bible is wrong historically, morally and theologically, then what sense does it make to say that the text is in some sense divinely inspired? Wouldn't it be much simpler to view the biblical text as a flawed document, written thousands of years ago by ancient Israelites who in many ways were mistaken about the origin of the universe as well as the history of the world, and whose moral sensitivities and theological insights were unrefined? You are looking for a reflection of the Divine in the Bible, whereas I think it would be much more useful to search for its human origins.

You mention Rosemary Ruether's view that the Bible critiques itself and invites other prophetic communities to do the same. In this way, she implies, it is possible to isolate God's message embedded within the text. But I don't think the Bible does this at all. In no sense does Scripture encourage the questioning of God's word in the Torah and his message in the other books through heightened moral sensitivity. Nor am I persuaded by Schüssler Fiorenza's argument that the Bible as an ambiguous document is susceptible of revision so that its divinely liberating message can be extracted. Rather, I view the Bible as a religious text composed by ancient Israelites over two thousand years ago. It contains a spiritual interpretation of the history of the Jewish people, written from a Judeo-centred perspective.

As such, it is not surprising that many of its historical details are wrong, and its moral assumptions questionable. In addition, numerous stories about God's actions are, to my mind, theologically unacceptable (such as the account of the flood, and Abraham's sacrifice of Isaac). In a word, the Bible — like all religious texts (including the Qur'an, the Vedas, etc.) — originates from specific historical and sociological contexts and reflects the religious opinions of its authors.

If the Bible is inspired as you state, where is such inspiration to be found? In the narrative concerning God's creation of the cosmos? Or the story about Noah and the flood? Is God's word to be discovered in the Decalogue or the other commandments recorded in the Five Books of Moses? Or, perhaps, in the account of the ancient Israelites' liberation from Egyptian oppression (as South American liberationists have argued)? Alternatively, is it in the depiction of the conquest of the land? Or, as Reform Jews have traditionally maintained, is God's message to be uncovered in the prophetic books where the classical prophets inveighed against moral transgression? Or, again, in the prophetic books, such as Isaiah, which describe the messianic kingdom?

At the beginning of your last letter, you state that Jews and Christians can benefit from reading both Testaments together. But if we are to do this profitably, I think we must both accept that the Hebrew Bible and the New Testament reflect the social, political, economic and cultural worldview of their authors. We must not confuse our own spiritual, moral and theological assumptions with those of the writers of these texts, nor should we identify those parts of Scripture of which we approve with what we believe to be God's inspired message.

Dan

3.6   *13 August 2003*

SCRIPTURE AS TEXT THAT LIBERATES

Dan,

Let's agree to jettison any crude notion of inspiration, the Spirit guiding the pen and so on. Even the 'God writes straight with crooked lines' argument. Let us also agree that Scripture reflects the worldview of its writers in all their misguidedness and prejudices. (And their flashes of insight too!) And that we as readers can reinscribe our own limitations and prejudices in the way we read the text, as Christians still continually do in reading the New Testament with anti-Judaistic eyes.

Now I want to take you back to what I said about divine agency on 27 June. There I saw God as involved with all the processes of reality — 'God as the power that drives to relate, to connect, to be aflame for the kind of world God wants. And divine power in this relational world is exercised through compassion, mercy, empathy, faithfulness.'

But this relational world is shaped partly by sacred texts. Both our communities are 'People of the Book', in a way that is true of Islam, but not of the Greek and Roman religions. And if God is involved with sacred texts, how could this work? I don't rule out inspiration, for example the prophetic texts. But it would work more like imagination, a poetic and sensitive imagination, based on commitment to God's Spirit and discernment of God's will for the well-being of community, in this case the Jewish people.

But the extraordinary fact about this sacred text (or collection of texts), that you say has a human face, is that it *can* work in a liberating way. But it involves, first of all, a hermeneutic of suspicion, to use Elizabeth Schüssler Fiorenza's phrase.[8] This is what Judith Plaskow did in her ground-breaking study, *Standing Again at Sinai*, when she discovered that women were not included in the revelation given to Moses. She retorts: 'Of course we were at Sinai: how then is it that the text could imply we were not there?'[9] She sees the presumed exclusion as the product of an unjust social order — *but this does not have to be.* How to use the text to achieve a transformed, just order is then her quest for Jewish theology.

But this hermeneutic and raised awareness is operating also in Christian feminist circles. It is never a question of rescuing biblical texts *for their own sake*, but of how they are used in the search for justice and in liberating communities from oppression. So even using historical-critical methods is inadequate: these may fail to challenge the androcentric prejudices and positions of privilege of both writer and reader! The Dutch liberation theologian Lieve Troch writes that feminist hermeneutics grounds its analysis and reflection in the experience of women's oppression, suffering and resistance.[10] Reflections on texts are undertaken from within a commitment to the *discipleship of equals* and this requires ongoing analysis of economic and political realities, both local and global. Texts are chosen by the community for their *destabilising function*, the destabilising of oppressive power structures. So when the Book of Ruth is read from the perspective of poor African women, it is Ruth's status as widow with which they empathise, whereas from a European perspective it is the empowering nature of the sisterhood of Ruth and Naomi that receives attention.[11] Reading *against* the grain of the patriarchal text is encouraged in order to achieve justice for the poorest and most vulnerable sections in the community. It is in this sense that I believe that the Bible can be read by both our faith communities for the achievement of the peace and justice of the Kingdom of God. But God is in the process too, as what does God long for other than the well-being of all creatures?

Mary

⌐◯──◯⌐

3.7   *15 August 2003*

SUBJECTIVELY INTERPRETING SCRIPTURE

Mary,

Some time ago I argued along similar lines about the liberationist dimensions of Scripture in the book I wrote about liberation theology: *On Earth as it is in Heaven: Jews, Christians, and Liberation Theology*. Following the path of South American Christian liberationists, I stressed the importance of the theme of the Exodus. Like those feminist theologians you mention, I sought to ground my reflections on the experience of suffering and oppression in this biblical narrative. The texts I selected were chosen for their destabilising characteristics. It was my aim to achieve justice for the poorest and most vulnerable sections of the community. Referring to the Passover ceremony which commemorates the departure of the ancient Hebrews from Egypt, I said:

> Reflecting on the significance of Passover, it becomes clear that Jews, like liberation theologians, have found renewed strength and hope in the message of the Exodus. The Passover ceremony unites the Jewish people with their ancestors who endured slavery and oppression in Egyptian bondage. Despite the persecution of centuries, the Jewish nation is confident of eventual deliverance and the ultimate redemption of humankind ... Thus Jews and Christians share a common biblical heritage and vision of the transformation of society, and the Exodus unites them in a common hope and aspiration for the triumph of justice.[12]

I think you would approve of such sentiments. But I now see that there are some serious difficulties with the position I espoused in this study. The first is that scholars have raised serious doubts about the historicity of the Exodus account. Some scholars, for example, have suggested that the crossing of the Red Sea took place, not at the head of the Gulf of Suez which is a long way from the Israelites' point of departure, but at one of the lakes now joined by the Suez Canal. Other suggestions include the head of the Gulf of Aqaba or alternatively Lake Sirbonis. It is now widely accepted that the Jewish people did not escape en masse, but that there were a series of migrations of the Hebrew clan into Canaan. If the ancient Israelites did not actually flee from their oppressors under Moses' leadership as Scripture relates, then there is little point in citing this text as evidence of God's liberating actions.

But, most importantly, if God is not a causal agent in human affairs, then it makes no sense to believe that He is on the side of those who are exploited and oppressed, and that He seeks to liberate them. In your last letter, you say that we should jettison crude notions of divine intervention. Yet you imply that this does not rule out the concept of divine agency in a much weaker form: on this account, God is viewed as active in human life as a force impelling human beings to seek goodness and justice. In this respect, those elements of Scripture which embody this quest can be understood as inspired.

My response, however, is to question such a hermeneutic. If the Hebrew Bible contains pernicious features — including an espousal of patriarchy, an acceptance of slavery, fierce punishments for crimes such as homosexuality, vivid depictions of divine wrath — how can one determine which, if any, features of the biblical narrative are divinely inspired? Aren't such exegetes as Rosemary Radford Ruether, Elizabeth Schüssler Fiorenza, Judith Plaskow, Lieve Troch — and perhaps even Mary Grey — isolating those elements of Scripture of which they approve and using them as a framework for criticising those aspects of Scripture which they regard as flawed? In so doing, these critics are simply imposing their own values on the biblical narrative. It is not the Bible then which determines their outlook; instead, they are appealing to non-biblical standards (such as the principle of justice) to evaluate the biblical text. Scripture thus ceases to be authoritative for these writers — instead moral principles which are derived from other sources have become all-important.

Dan

3.8 *17 August 2003*

THE POWER DYNAMICS OF THE 'HOLY TEXT'

Dan,

This gets complicated: let's take stock. Initially what appeared to be a consensus has given way to struggling in murky waters. (If that is an appropriate metaphor!) I argued that divine agency is involved in the *process* of interaction between text and community action for justice. I told you that I had sympathy with Ruether's argument that the Bible critiques itself through the prophetic texts but ultimately must agree with Schüssler Fiorenza's insistence on taking the Bible as a whole — I realise that canons differ — in both its liberating and oppressive elements. This will involve a 'hermeneutics of proclamation', where violent texts are declared to be 'not the Word of God'. For example, however you explain Judges 19, the story of the violated concubine, as having some logic in the text, it cannot be reckoned as sacred scripture because of its misogyny.

From a historical point of view, discoveries of archaeologists and historians do not invalidate the liberating meaning of the Exodus story. It is the fact that the mythic memory of liberation functioned to shape the identity of the Jewish people and subsequent liberation movements in history that is crucial. Remember that even as recently as the anti-apartheid struggle in South Africa, the people were calling for a 'new Moses' to deliver them? Christians base their claims for social justice partly on the fact that Jesus chose a Passover setting as the clue to the meaning of his ministry and death. 'Exodus' continues to be reworked even outside Christian and Jewish settings: Toni Morrison, the black American novelist, in her novel *Beloved* used it as a frame for the deliverance of the slave Sethe from 'Sweet Home' (the slave-owner's house) to a kind of freedom, with some tragic consequences.[13]

The question now becomes: how does all this work for Jewish—Christian relations? The hermeneutic I work with takes account of androcentrism/racism/logic of domination *both* in the community relations of text production *and* in the reading community. What is central in both cases is the power dynamics. If we take no account of the power motif operating in the world of the text, we risk reinscribing the inequalities of the text in our own communities. Both of us have examples of congregations, or sections of them, reduced to silence, passive listeners, by careless or even deliberate misuse of an ancient text, composed in answer to a long-gone historical situation. (For example, Paul's injunction for women to keep silent in church and not to uncover their heads.)

Let's take a difficult example for Jewish—Christian relations, namely Jesus' harsh critiques against the Pharisees. How can these be 'holy texts' when such criticisms form a major part of the anti-Jewish power dynamics, and Christians still read them with 'anti-Jewish eyes'? What difference would it make if we entered the 'world of the text', respected the scholarship of the Pharisees, and tried to understand that their method of reform was to emphasise fulfilling ritual obligations as the way to holiness? In other words, if the power dynamics changed from being 'innocent, radical Jesus clashes with corrupt power establishment' to 'two opposing Jewish reform groups move, tragically, to irreconcilable positions that will end in the suppression of the group that holds no institutional power' — would it move us to a more irenic understanding?

In brief, no breakthrough without coming clean about power dynamics!

Mary

3.9 *20 August 2003*

MORALITY AND SCRIPTURE

Mary,
You are right: these are murky waters. But I think it is possible to clarify the assumptions of our hermeneutical approach to the Bible. If I understand correctly, you wish to distinguish between those elements of Scripture which you believe are morally objectionable, and those which you wish to commend. The Bible thus contains:

(1) Morally commendable features (such as the prophetic denun-
    ciation of moral corruption; the liberation of the ancient
    Hebrews from Egyptian bondage)

and

(2) Morally objectionable features (patriarchy; misogyny; andro-
    centrism)

Further, you contend that the moral features you approve of are
the product of divine intervention, whereas those features you
regard as morally reprehensible are human in origin, having
nothing to do with God's will. Am I right?

If so, then I think you will admit that you are appealing to
moral values independent of Scripture which you are using to distinguish between what you regard as morally acceptable in the
Bible, and what is morally undesirable. Further, you are using
moral criteria to determine what is divinely inspired and what
is not. Assuming I have correctly interpreted your approach, I
must ask you to explain from where you have derived these moral
values.

Presumably you think such moral principles are objective, having ontological status — but from your argument it is clear that
such absolutes are not divinely revealed in Scripture (as Orthodox
Jews contend) since you are using them to isolate the features of
Scripture which you believe are of divine origin. So where do
these values come from, and how do you know them? Possibly,
you believe that they are ultimately derived from God because
He is benevolent. But, again, I want to ask you — as I have in
previous letters — how can you know that?

If you reply that you know this on the basis of personal
religious experience, how can you be sure that your religious
experience, or anyone else's, provides that person with access to
knowledge of God's true nature?

As I explained in the letter I wrote to you on 10 July, I do not
believe that we can have definitive knowledge about the nature of
Ultimate Reality: the Divine as-it-is-in-itself is beyond human
comprehension. Therefore, I think it is misguided to derive an
ethical system from an assumed knowledge of God's nature or

from alleged revelations (such as the revelation of the Torah on
Mount Sinai). Traditionally, Jews have based their lives on the conviction that they know God's will for them, and that they are
bound to observe God's commandments as partners in the
covenant. But, as a modern Jew, I do not think we can any longer
embrace such a doctrine.

This does not mean, however, that ethics should now be
regarded as irrelevant since they cannot be grounded in God's will
as recorded in Scripture or as enshrined in rabbinic sources (or for
that matter as disclosed in the New Testament or in classical
Christian texts). On the contrary, I think it is possible to establish
a moral system on other grounds: I believe that human beings are
able to intuit general moral principles, and for me such moral
intuitions are fundamental. Possibly here we can find common
ground. If we agree that there are overriding general ethical
concepts which can serve as the basis for establishing a moral
framework for modern living, then arguably such principles could
be employed in formulating a Judeo-Christian ethic based on our
religious traditions. Such values would thereby become filters
which we can use to select those features of the Jewish and
Christian heritage which continue to have spiritual meaning for
our time.

     Dan

3.10 *22 August 2003*

THE BIBLE AS OUR STORY

Dan,

If you don't mind my saying so, you are a curious mixture of a
modern and post-modern thinker at the same time! You use language like 'divine intervention' — which I have told you several
times I don't agree with(!) In fact 'intervention' is my hate word
in theology! And at the same time, in a post-modern way you
jettison divine revelation in the Bible in favour of 'intuited moral
principles and values' which can be the basis of, or criteria for,
acceptance or rejection of Scriptural texts. The argument here will
become circular because, like it or not, the Bible is one of the

sources of these values. (I realise there are others.) It seems here
that this has become not a Jewish—Christian conversation, but
more a philosophical argument about the basis of ethics. And I
now wonder whether you want God at all, since you continually
challenge my assumption of God's benevolence, compassion, and
so on. What's the point of faith in a malevolent deity? As I said in
my last two letters, I believe that biblical truth is manifest in the
interaction between text and a community's struggle for justice.

The need for sacred texts, I would argue, is rooted in the
human search for meaning, which throughout history has been
best expressed in narrative form. *It's a story-shaped world*, many
writers have recently said in the hugely popular narrative theology. '*Once upon a time there was* ...' seems instinctively the way the
growing child discovers a place in family, community and culture.
So sacred text has meaning and authority for the individual's personal search, for the community's shared spiritual journey and is
where the institution wields authority to guard its own identity.
And here of course lies the core of the problem for our communities — the abuse of authority in dominating the consciences
and lives of believers, as I have been saying.

I was struck by the similarity between your position and that of
the Christian theologian Don Cupitt, who dismisses the claims of
religion to metaphysical truth, and appeals, as you do, to moral
values. When asked at a conference how he would hand these on
to children, he replied, 'Through the Biblical story ... *A decree
went out from Caesar Augustus* ... and so on.' Where I do agree
with you is in discovering God's actions and presence in a wider
way than through texts. (Maybe these are your moral intuitions.)
Or I interpret text in a wider sense. By God's actions I mean all
that is good and leads to goodness, truth, beauty and justice. These
are the transcendental principles I respect and work for. As I wrote
earlier, I believe the activity of believing is to discern the presence
of God in an ever-deepening way — through the patterns of
living, through relationships and in creation. The richness of these
encounters is then picked up and deepened in sacred texts. But if
we are to encounter each other's traditions and identities in the
texts then we have to be prepared to read with 'new eyes' and
allow a plurality of interpretations.

As a feminist theologian, seeking a place within the sacred story, because of the misogyny of the texts, I also recognise other texts as sacred. I believe that, with the Jewish feminist poet Adrienne Rich (whose work for me counts as 'sacred text'),

> Miriam, Aaron, Moses
> are somewhere else, marching
> You learn to live without prophets
> without legends
> to live just where you are
> your burning bush, your seven-branched candlestick ...[14]

She ends this poem saying,

> What's sacred tries ...
> *One more time.*

And I believe this is the unique quality of sacred text: its ability, because of the way its themes speak to the depths of the human struggle, to be reshaped and readdressed in a plurality of contexts throughout history. Or again, rejected as destructive to human civilisation. What we have to do is to be honest about who we are, as interpreting community, and what is the power dynamic within which we operate. Only then can what is sacred about the story be encountered as meaning-giving for persons and communities.

Mary

3.11 *26 August 2003*

PROGRESSING BEYOND SCRIPTURE

Mary,

You are right that in certain respects I am old-fashioned — I do use theological language in its traditional sense. I regard terms such as 'God', 'revelation', 'providence', 'eschatology' as having the meaning ascribed to them by theologians through the centuries. Of course, each of these terms has a history of interpretation. Yet they none the less have a specific range of meanings: they do not mean whatever writers might wish them to mean. Unfortunately today a number of Jewish and Christian theologians seek to appear traditional in orientation and deliberately employ religious language as a badge of orthodoxy. But in fact they have emptied such terminology of its original significance.

Let me take an example from the Jewish world. You may have heard of Mordecai Kaplan — he was ordained as an Orthodox rabbi at the beginning of the twentieth century and served as a professor at the Jewish Theological Seminary in New York. In the 1930s he wrote a very influential book entitled *Judaism as a Civilization* in which he argued that the concept of a supernatural God must be discarded in the modern age. Nevertheless, he continued to refer to God as 'the sum of all the animating forces and relationships which are forever making a cosmos out of chaos'.[15]

In the United States Kaplan subsequently founded the Reconstructionist movement, which embraced his non-supernaturalist approach. In Reconstructionist synagogues, worshippers continue to use God language, even though such a religious vocabulary has been stripped of its metaphysical moorings. I believe such an approach is misleading and dangerous. Theologians who twist religious language in this way are deceiving both themselves and others. It is a great pity that so many of our colleagues — particularly those who describe themselves as proponents of Radical Orthodoxy — have fallen into this trap. It is unclear to me whether they are deliberately disingenuous or simply are unable to face up to the fact that they have abandoned the traditional doctrines of the faith. In any event, I believe that theology is a discipline with fixed boundaries: the theological language of the past constitutes a framework for exploring religious issues today.

But it is true that I am also a progressive. I think that, as modern Jews, we must wrestle with our religious inheritance in the quest to chart a meaningful Jewish life in the contemporary world. This conviction is the basis for my willingness to jettison concepts and doctrines which, I believe, are incoherent and no longer spiritually relevant. With regard to Scripture, I believe we must accept that the worldview of the ancient Israelites is in many respects outmoded. The Bible was written thousands of years ago by Jews who had little accurate information about the origins of the universe. In many ways their understanding of human life was primitive and flawed. From our conversation, I think you would agree with me about this, even if we differ about the importance of the historicity of the text in formulating a meaningful theology for today. (You'll remember that in your letter of 17 August you said that the 'discoveries of archaeologists and historians do not invalidate the liberating meaning of the Exodus story' — but if the Exodus story is simply a myth, then in my view, it is ridiculous to use such a narrative as a basis for constructing a theology of liberation.)

Further, as is obvious from our conversation, both of us reject the traditional idea that God revealed the words of the Bible to Moses on Mount Sinai. As you said in your letter of 13 August, God did not guide the pen of the author of the Five Books of Moses, nor was He the direct cause of what is written in the other books of Scripture. The Bible is not in this sense the Word of God. In this light we do not regard everything that the Hebrew Bible says about the history of ancient Israel, the covenant, and the role of God in the life of the nation as true and sacrosanct: I think we concur that the tools of critical scholarship must be applied to the scriptural text. In addition, I think we both accept that the ancient idea that the Old Testament is fulfilled in the New and that Judaism has been superseded by a new revelation and dispensation must now be discarded. I believe we can also agree that there are moral values embedded in Scripture which can serve as a basis for constructing a Judeo-Christian framework to consider the burning issues confronting our two traditions in contemporary society. Where we disagree, however, is whether these values are divinely inspired. As you have seen, I am unable to make such a claim, and I think we need to explore more fully what, if anything, is authoritative in our two traditions.

Dan

4. Authority and Tradition

❧⦿❧

4.1   1 September 2003

THE SEARCH FOR A USABLE PAST[1]

Dan,

Your assertion on 26 August that we need to explore further what is authoritative about our respective traditions is crucial. But for me this whole area opens up a hornet's nest of problems. For us as Christians and Jews, the Bible has authority — but we have already agreed that we cannot uncritically accept this. So as a Christian I cannot just fall back on 'the words of Jesus'. Someone has to decide on the ongoing meaning and authority of certain teachings for lived faith and practice in community through history.

Christians themselves are not in agreement about this process. The Orthodox Church, for example, relies on the teaching of the Church in the first six centuries — and will recognise nothing that is added later as having the same authority. Theology is more a question of making this traditional teaching intelligible and accessible for new generations. But the process can also be creative. Elisabeth Behr-Sigel writes: 'Authentic faithfulness to Tradition is creative and requires each generation to respond to new needs and challenges according to the dynamic of Tradition.'[2]

For Protestant Christians, the authority of the Bible is supreme and incontrovertible but the method of its interpretation is disputed, although in general there is more weight given to 'individual understanding in the depth of the heart'. For the Catholic tradition, faith (= *depositum fidei*) is handed on by the apostles through both Scripture and Tradition: the guardian of both is the 'teaching *magisterium*' of the Church. In practice this resides in the Congregation for the Doctrine of the Faith, at the moment chaired by Cardinal Ratzinger. The theory is that the teaching *magisterium* should not be an absolutist, top-down, authoritative body. As the Catholic Catechism itself says, the whole body of the faithful share in:

> understanding and handing on revealed truth. They have received the anointing of the holy Spirit who instructs them and guides them into all truth. (Section 91)
>
> The whole body of the faithful ... cannot err in matters of belief. This characteristic is shown in the supernatural appreciation of faith (*sensus fidei*) on the part of the whole people, when, 'from the bishops to the last of the faithful', they manifest a universal consent in matters of faith and morals. (Section 92)[3]

I am sorry to quote at length but this idea of the '*sensus fidei*' of the whole body of the faithful is absolutely crucial to my argument. We are here talking not only about doctrines at the heart of Christianity — like incarnation, Trinity and others we have touched on — but moral issues and ethical practice. Even liturgy now comes under the umbrella of the CDF. Increasingly the authority of the '*sensus fidei*', the gathered faithful, has come to be considered of little or no value. Two examples of this would be the contraception issue and the ordination of women. Artificial contraception was clearly prohibited by Pope Paul VI in the encyclical *Humanae Vitae* in 1966. Leaving aside the issue itself, it was the question of authority that was the most disturbing. The Pope ignored the findings of a commission appointed by his predecessor, Pope John XXIII, where a majority opinion favoured a change in the law, as the reasons for forbidding birth control were no longer acceptable. Instead, he supported the minority opinion of the commission, which adhered to the traditional arguments. Many people — including priests — left the church in disillusionment. The voice of the people had not been heard. If this is considered as a 'non-received truth' then its authority is still in question. Many consider the issue of the ordination of women to be in the same category. The Vatican's two documents *Inter Insigniores* (1978) and *Mulieris Dignitatem* (The Dignity of Women) (1988), both appealed to tradition to prove that this could never take place, and even that it was a non-question. Discussion itself was prohibited. But the 'tradition' appealed to in the latter case, namely that 'Jesus ordained 12 men' and the early Church did the same, and this means we have no authority to ordain women, has been shown to be both historically false and methodologically invalid.[4] Jesus did not ordain anyone; nor did he utter anything on the question of contraception.

This raises the wider question, not only for the many groups who have been discriminated against by the way tradition has been interpreted and imposed in an authoritarian manner by the teaching magisterium, but for Christians in general — how can we discover a usable past? How can we relate to tradition in a creative way, especially in a way that helps us to live peacefully together in a troubled world?

Mary

4.2   *4 September 2003*

THE CHAIN OF TRADITION

Mary,

You are right to point out that the central authoritative basis of our two faiths is Scripture, yet we can no longer view the Bible in the way generations of Jews and Christians did in previous centuries. Within the Jewish community, all the non-Orthodox movements have rejected the central doctrine of *Torah MiSinai*. In modern times we must acknowledge that the development of biblical criticism has undermined this central principle of the Jewish faith. If the Bible continues to be regarded as authoritative for modern Jews, then it is unclear exactly what this means. As I pointed out, both law and legend cannot be viewed in the way they once were. Given this shift in orientation, how is Scripture to be used today?

The same question applies to the rabbinic tradition. Previously

I emphasised that from Hellenistic times, Jews have believed that the Oral Law as well as the Written Law were revealed to Moses on Mount Sinai. As the first collection of Jewish law, the Mishnah explains:

> The Oral Law was given to Moses, passed on to the elders, and then was transferred to the prophets and from the prophets to the 'Men of the Great Assembly'. The last of these was Simon the Just. He handed it down to the generations of rabbis until it was finally written down in the second century CE by Judah-Ha Nasi.[5]

The Mishnah, which contains these decisions, is therefore an authoritative compendium of interpretations of the law: it is a record of the ritual and ethical decisions reached through such debate. Since all the law — written and oral — was revealed by God to Moses, it, too, is binding on all Jews.

I should stress, however, that this chain of tradition continued to evolve. In the following centuries, scholars in Palestine and Babylonia engaged in debate about Mishnaic law, and their discussions and decisions are recorded in later compendia of law and lore: the Palestinian and Babylonian Talmuds. These two vast collections of earlier material are viewed as sacred texts in that they contain the word of God as interpreted by these early rabbinic sages. The Babylonian Talmud — the greater of these two Talmud collections — is, like the Mishnah, an authoritative text. For over a thousand years it has served as the focus of Jewish study.

But the development of rabbinic law did not cease at this stage. In Babylonia at the great rabbinic academies as well as in *yeshivot* (academies) established in other countries the tradition of interpretation continued, and distinguished legalists issued their opinions about the meaning of the commandments. In the Middle Ages a number of leading scholars such as Moses Maimonides produced codes of Jewish law based on this corpus of material, culminating in the work of Joseph Caro, the author of the *Shulkhan Arukh*, which is regarded as the definitive code of Jewish law.

Through the centuries, then, Jews viewed both the Written

Torah and its interpretations as the authoritative basis for Jewish living. Even though the Mishnah and the Talmud require interpretation, they have served as the framework for leading a religiously Jewish life. Today Orthodox Jews continue to regard the chain of tradition as authoritative basis for Jewish existence. However, as in the case of the Hebrew Bible, the religious assumptions of the past have been challenged by the non-Orthodox. No longer is the Written Law viewed as divinely revealed. It, too, is seen as the product of human reflection: the words of the rabbis are perceived as shaped by the social and cultural conditions in which these scholars lived.

What this means in practice is that strictly religious Orthodox Jews — who constitute a tiny minority in the Jewish world — continue to perceive both the Bible and the rabbinic tradition as sacred and sacrosanct. It is the obligation of every Jew, they believe, to keep the Law and follow in the footsteps of previous generations of faithful believers. Any transgression of the legal code is a sin. For this reason, the Orthodox establishment castigates Conservative, Reform and Reconstructionist Jews for their unfaithfulness to the Jewish heritage.

Non-Orthodox Jews, on the other hand, feel free to observe only those features of the faith which they regard as spiritually significant. The vast majority of biblical commandments and the legal obligations prescribed by the rabbis have been discarded. Hence there are no clear criteria in modern Judaism for determining which, if any, aspects of the Jewish faith have authority. Instead there is a major split between Orthodox Jews, who regard both the Oral and Written Law as of divine origin and therefore of supreme authority, and non-Orthodox Jews (as well as the unaffiliated), who no longer feel bound to carry out the letter of the Law.

Dan

4.3   5 September 2003

THE AUTHORITY OF EXPERIENCE

Dan,

How interesting it is that the tension in the Catholic Church between the top-down authority of the *magisterium* and the *sensus fidei* or consensus among the faithful is reflected by your description of the tensions between Orthodox and Reform Jews' attitude to Tradition. A better parallel of course would be a strictly fundamentalist attitude to the binding word of Scripture, contrasting with the critical attitude which we have discussed. And we see the problems that causes currently in the area of homosexuality. We — Roman Catholics — have also in the past experienced many ritualistic obligations like a Eucharistic fast and we are still obliged to attend Mass on Sundays and Holy Days under pain of committing 'mortal sin'. A difference between what you cite and my position is that the source of authority in the case of Roman Catholicism is the Church herself, claiming to be the interpreter of truths revealed by God. In the early Church, authority was interpreted far more as an authority of service to others (see I Cor. 12:4—31).[6] In fact the Pope is still called the *servus servorum* (servant of the servants). But during the Middle Ages this evolved into a far more centralised, juridical-based model, dominated by the male priesthood and culminating in the declaration of Papal Infallibility in 1870. Disobedience to this authority has meant imprisonment and for many theologians even today has meant being forced into silence, when they have expressed views conflicting with the Vatican. You probably know the eminent theologian Hans Kung, who forfeited the right to teach as a Catholic theologian in the University of Tübingen. (This has not diminished his popularity!)

This punitive attitude, as you can imagine, causes an immense dilemma for ordinary believers. But rather than discussing the ethics of disobedience, I want to raise the question of an alternative source for authority.

I wonder, what authority does religious experience have in

your tradition? By this I mean the whole area of personal experience and mystical experience. At times mystical experience has
emerged as a kind of radical protest against authoritarianism
or as a witness to the power of the intuitive, non-verbal realm
of experience. Thus the Rhine mystics of the twelfth and
thirteenth centuries, Gertrude of Helfta and Mechthild of
Magdeburg, for example, claimed eucharistic visions of Christ
when female religious authority was increasingly vulnerable. Yet
Hildegard of Bingen (who died in 1179) was unique in having
her visions recognised — even by the Pope — in her own lifetime. Since mystics make direct claims as to their experience of
'the Divine', from what I am learning of your thoughts, I guess
you will not be sympathetic to these! So it's not really to indulge
ourselves in a long discussion about mysticism that I introduce
the question.

It's more about exploring the weight of personal experience as
authority. We both — I suspect — agree that experience comes
mediated through all kinds of lenses — gender, personal family
background, our religious and national adherences, economic
position, historical context, and so on. History and theology have
both suffered where these have not been factored into an analysis. That's why the 'underside of history' has become so important,
as well as the demand for 'positionality' in theology. Given all this,
does the claim to experience the presence of God, even in a very
mild way, as 'the still, small voice' of 1 Kings 19, for example, have
any authority? Or, to put it more strongly, if a group of believers
(Jewish or Christian) argue — as has happened many times in
history — that they must resist authority under the guidance of
the Holy Spirit, do we respect that? Charismatic movements making these claims abound. Indeed they have caused the foundation
of significant Christian groups like the Quakers. Waiting in silence
for the guidance of the Spirit still forms the style and content of
worship. Pentecostalism doesn't wait in silence, but certainly
claims to act through the experience of the Spirit! If I am to come
clean about my own position, it would be to assert that I do
believe strongly in the guidance of the Spirit as authority, but
more in the Ignatian sense of 'the discernment of the spirits'.[7] By
that I mean prayer or reflection as to what is 'of God' in a certain

issue. And this discernment would not be in isolation from community thinking and established tradition. But it *would* give credibility to personal experience as one factor in ethical decision making or in questions of belief.

I wonder what you think.

Mary

4.4 *11 September 2003*
TESTING AUTHORITY

Mary,

Two years ago today the world was rocked by the terrorist attack on the World Trade Center. In the light of this event and the subsequent war against Islamic terrorism, there is a pressing need for religions to find common ground. Yet our conversation so far illustrates the difficulties of this quest. Nonetheless, I think we can agree that as far as authority is concerned there has been considerable tension between the Jewish and Christian religious establishments and their critics. But, unlike Christianity where there is a clash between the top-down authority of the *magisterium* and the consensus of the faithful, modern Judaism has been torn asunder by the battle between the Orthodox and the non-Orthodox.

As I noted, Orthodox Jews are fundamentalistic not only in their approach to Scripture but also with regard to the evolving rabbinic heritage. In their view, God revealed himself to Moses and his Word was passed down through generations of sages whose decisions are recorded in the Mishnah and the Talmud. In Judaism there is no one who has the authority of the Pope, but the notion of infallibility is a central feature of the faith. Revelation itself is infallible and serves as the touchstone of truth. The covenant is binding on all Jews, and salvation is dependent on the observance of divine commands. The infringement of the Law is punishable by rabbinic courts, and ultimately results in punishment in the Hereafter.

It is not surprising, therefore, that strictly Orthodox Jews are so critical of Conservative, Reform, Reconstructionist and

Humanistic Judaism. These movements are viewed as aberrations
of the faith, distortions of Judaism which have led the Jewish
community away from God's intention for his chosen people. Nor
is it surprising that Orthodox religious leaders, such as the Chief
Rabbi, are so critical of Jews like me who have a very different
view of the development of the tradition.

You mention the role of religious and mystical experience in
challenging the authority of the Synagogue. No doubt, early
reformers experienced God differently from their Orthodox coreligionists. But this was not the basis for their rejection of the
central tenets of traditional Judaism. Rather, they were influenced
by the spirit of the Enlightenment. At the beginning of the nineteenth century Jews were no longer insulated from non-Jewish
currents of culture and thought, and this led to a transformation
of Jewish existence. During this period a number of rabbis who
had been influenced by the Enlightenment began to re-evaluate
the Jewish tradition.

In this undertaking the achievements of Jewish scholars who
engaged in the scientific study of Judaism (*Wissenschaft des
Judentums*) had a major impact. In 1842, for example, the Society
of the Friends of Reform was founded in Germany and published
a proclamation justifying their innovative approach to tradition. In
the declaration of their principles, the society proclaimed that
they recognised the possibility of unlimited progress in the Jewish
faith, and rejected the authority of the legal code as well as the
belief in messianic redemption. At the end of the nineteenth century, Reform leaders met in Pittsburgh, Pennsylvania to formulate
the principles of Reform Judaism. They stated:

> We hold that the modern discoveries of scientific
> researches in the domains of nature and history are not
> antagonistic to the doctrines of Judaism, the Bible reflect-
> ing the primitive ideas of its own age and at times cloth-
> ing its conception of divine providence and justice dealing
> with man in miraculous narratives … Today we accept
> as binding only the moral laws and maintain only such
> ceremonies as elevate and sanctify our lives, but reject
> all such as are not adapted to the views and habits of

modern civilization ... We recognize in Judaism a progressive religion, ever striving to be in accord with the
postulates of reason.[8]

In subsequent years Reform Judaism underwent significant
change as have the other non-Orthodox movements.
Nonetheless, the non-Orthodox rejection of religious authority
was not perceived as due to the influence of the Spirit, but as the
result of critical reflection on sacred texts. Jews have not been like
the Quakers, waiting in silence for the inbreaking of the divine
Spirit, but rather they have viewed their quest as motivated by
rational reflection. It is not prayer or meditation that has brought
about the transformation of Jewish life, but instead the determination of Jewish scholars to free the faith from antiquated and
outmoded religious assumptions that have confined Jewry to an
inward-looking ghetto existence for nearly two millennia.

  Dan

4.5   *11 September 2003*

A FEMINIST PARADIGM — 'AUTHORITY IN
COMMUNITY'

Dan,
I'm replying to you immediately, also on 11 September, because
in a way that tragic event, and the subsequent violence still
unfolding, illustrates the need for reconciliation, not only between
Christians and Jews but on the widest possible scale. Escalating
hatred witnesses to an unreconciled world, as well as to the model
of authority being exercised by the powerful nations, Europe and
America. This model seeks answers with military force, from the
Balkans to Iraq. It is a model of authority that exacerbates further
conflict. So, resisting the temptation to take up your reply to me
which seemed to reject the authority of 'waiting on the Spirit' in
favour of critical reflection on tradition (personally I don't see
that one cancels out the other!), with the haunting memory of
September 11th in mind, I want to argue for a different model of
authority. I argue that both our faith traditions operate largely

with top-down models of authority, largely hierarchical: in your case, whether it is Orthodox or Reformed traditions, in mine whether Catholic, Protestant or Orthodox. (Although I admit that the Quakers try very hard to operate from a different model, as does the United Reform Church.) On 1 September, you will remember, I wrote to you of a model of authority I deeply respect — the *sensus fidei*, or agreement of all the faithful — but it is a model that is largely ignored.

The problem is that both our traditions rely on what I call a pyramid of power, where power legitimates authority, and the voices on lower levels of this pyramid are unheard or ignored.[9] Letty Russell writes:

> Things are assigned a Divine order, with God at the top, men next, and so on, down through dogs, plants, and so-called impersonal nature. This paradigm reinforces ideas of authority over community and refuses to admit the ideas and persons who do not fit into established Western white, male hierarchies of thought or social structures.

But just suppose it could be different. Suppose we take a linguistic turn and understand 'authority' in its root sense of 'to make increase' or 'grow', from the Latin verb *augeo*. (You know I'm a classicist at heart!) And then we might see authority as located in the whole community, and as being concerned with what promoted this growth, in this case meaning growth in faith.

Thus a feminist liberation paradigm of authority would give preferential weight to those at the bottom of the pyramid of power, namely the powerless and marginalised — to include many categories. Instead of pyramids I would speak about 'circles of interdependence' and a concept of power that was more about empowering and enabling than the exercise of domination. This paradigm glorifies neither poverty nor marginalisation but, as Russell writes, sees authority more as partnership in building community than in the absolutised pattern where a few in power dictate to those of lesser status.

How would I begin to justify this in tradition? I would cite prophetic texts of God's preference for the poor and rejected, laws like the Jubilee laws that act as safeguards of the rights of the poor

(Lev. 25:1—17), Jesus' teachings where justice for the poor is the mark of integrity of a community, for example, in the Beatitudes (Matt. 5, Luke 6) and the way that the ethics of the Kingdom are founded on the poor having access to basic needs (Matt. 25). It's not about idealising poverty or the poor — we both know that poverty degrades and dehumanises — but, first, it's about being honest that there is much that is diseased about our inherited models of power and authority Then it's about seeking to base authority in an alternative system, an alternative method of order-ing our communities both religious and civil. But knowing we do this on the basis of this dis-eased system. 'The master's tools will not dismantle the master's house', as one writer has said.[10] True, but people of good will can still throw their energies into creat-ing an inclusive understanding of authority that truly enables the growth of the entire community.

Mary

4.6 *16 September 2003*

PERSONAL LIBERTY

Mary,

We have just returned from the United States where we visited my mother. America is in mourning about the events of two years ago — thus it is certainly appropriate that as Christian and Jew we seek a basis for reconciliation between faiths given the apparent clash of civilizations. But I am not persuaded that what is needed is a new form of authority grounded in the experience of those at the lower level of society. I accept that in the past those who exercised authority from the top of the social pyramid often manipulated the masses for their own ends. In the Jewish world, the rabbinic establishment consisted of well-educated men who shaped the tradition in their own image. The patriarchal character of Judaism for the last two thousand years has reinforced male dominance in all spheres of Jewish life.

Like you, I disapprove of such an abuse of power. But I am deeply suspicious of authority invested in the whole community. Is there any reason to believe that authority transferred to the weaker members of society will result in an improvement of conditions? Certainly such a reorientation will involve change. But I am not persuaded that it would be for the better. Such a shift in political control occurred, for example, with the Bolshevik revolution, yet it led to the terrors of the Stalinist regime and the subsequent erosion of human rights and suppression of the masses. When the powerless become empowered — as has occurred in Israel following the creation of the Jewish state in 1948 — state domination has often led to the most terrible abuses. The victimisation of the Palestinian people is a current example of what can occur when the pyramid of authority is reversed.

You champion empowering and enabling the oppressed, but my fear is that such restructuring of society will simply result in further misuse of power. We should not forget that the Exodus of the ancient Israelites from Egypt (which has been a central theme of liberation theology and a paradigm of God's preference for the poor and rejected) was followed by their conquest of Canaan. Believing that God had instructed them to take the Promised Land from the indigenous population, they mercilessly slaughtered the Canaanites. This is the danger of the transfer of authority from one group to another.

It seems to me that what is far preferable is to recognise the danger of any form of authoritarian control, whether by elite minorities or by the persecuted masses. In its place, I would advocate the elimination of any kind of authoritarianism. In my book *The Future of Judaism*, I argue that in the future the Jewish religion should be based on the principle of personal autonomy. Such a conception, I believe, would free individuals to select those features of the faith which they find personally significant. Such a Copernican revolution, I contend, is consonant with the nature of contemporary Jewish life, despite the efforts of the religious establishment to coerce Jewry into specific patterns of belief and practice.

The central feature of this conception of Judaism, which I refer to as 'Open Judaism', is the principle of personal liberty:

> Open Judaism would allow all individuals the right to select those features from the tradition which they find

spiritually meaningful. This approach is not an innovation —
it has always been a tenet of Reform Judaism, for example, that members of the community are at liberty to practise those observances which they find significant. Yet the
principle of autonomy has not always been carried to its
logical conclusion; instead, throughout the history of the
Reform movement, reformers sought to impose their
religious views on others. Adherents of Open Judaism, on
the other hand, would be actively encouraged to make
up their own minds about religious belief and practice.
No one — no rabbi or rabbinical body — would be
allowed to decide what observances are acceptable for
the community as a whole.[11]

You say that people of good will can still throw their energies into
creating an inclusive understanding of authority. But I think that
it would be much more healthy for all forms of authority to be
dismantled; this would result in an individualised process of
decision-making in which respect and tolerance are expressed for
the choices made by each person.

Dan

4.7 *17 September 2003*

CONSCIENCE AND THE RIGHT TO FREEDOM

Dan,

I can imagine that this was a very poignant time to be in the
USA. When our personal lives intersect with history it can be a
searing experience. In the Gulf War of 1990 I was in India, in
Rajasthan, and spent each evening gathered around a feebly burning fire in the courtyard of a small hotel with a group of fearful
Indians watching the TV news. They felt themselves to be the
innocent victims of a conflict not of their making. This brings me
to your critique of my plea for authority from the underside of
history. Of course it was not meant to be as crude as you seem to
have picked it up! I'm aware that as far back as Plato there has
been a fear of mob rule (*ochlocracy*, he called it, or literally, the rule

of the mob). Poverty can be both degrading and dehumanising, as we both know, and there is no automatic authoritative voice arising from victimhood. What I argued for was structures of 'circles of interdependence' where all voices and levels of society find a hearing. And yet, I cannot leave this point without referring to the often repeated reference of the liberation theologians to the powerful witness of the poor communities they worked with. These communities offer us an integrity that has eluded the more sophisticated. This passage I quote has been used in the context of El Salvador as well as referring to Dalit women in India: what these poor communities offer is:

> Community instead of individualism, simplicity instead of opulence, helpfulness instead of selfishness, creativity instead of enforced mimicry, celebration instead of mere enjoyment, openness to transcendence instead of pragmatism, wisdom instead of information and naturalness instead of artificiality.[12]

These words often ring in my ears as I see the perpetuation of excluding structures. But now, moving to your response, you advocate the individualised process of decision-making, 'in which respect and tolerance are expressed for the choices made by each person' (16 September). This seems to me to be rooted in the post-Enlightenment respect for the individual and to suffer both the positive and negative fall-out from it.

Clearly, respect for each person is a crucial point in the development of social thought. But you must be aware that it took a long time, following the original Declaration of Human Rights, for the definition of exactly who constitutes a human person to move beyond the 'white, propertied male'. Women, black people and diverse ethnic groups simply were not factored in. Second, history shows us that the authority of the individual is rooted in community identity. Your reference to the catastrophe of September 11th 2001 shows that, in the willingness to commit suicide, it was the well-being of the Muslim group as a whole and not the survival of the individual that really mattered. In my view, the entire tragedy points to the lack of valuing of a subordinate group in US society.

But all of this rests on a bedrock of conscience of the individual and conscience of the group. The teaching of the second Vatican council was that, in the last resort, an individual was justified in following his or her own conscience.[13] This was within a theology of the whole Church as the people of God and a stress on communion between all sections. Indeed, Lawrence Kohlberg identified the more mature conscience in the ability to move beyond conventional morality and even the law. An Australian theologian, Eric D'Arcy, even wrote a controversial book, *Conscience and the Right to Freedom*.[14] But this, surely, does not mean that the individual is free to arbitrarily disobey the law? Surely, before any person comes to such a position, their situation must be deeply rooted in a community of faith, from which the conviction arises that the authentic authority of law and tradition of the community itself is being violated by the current regime? So I am arguing for an autonomy rooted in community relations, as well as a right to radically disobey this authority when it has betrayed its validating source. Then, the individual stands alone and appeals to a higher authority. But always in the name of the community. Anything you and I write seeks freedom and validity through rootedness in this sense of community. I remember my theology supervisor in Louvain, Belgium, years ago, saying: 'You think you stand alone before God: but you have a very long tail, because the whole of humanity stands behind you!'

Mary

4.8   *20 September 2003*

SLAYING THE DRAGON

Mary,

Your last letter, I believe, reflects your commitment to Catholicism. Repeatedly you stress the importance of communal loyalty. It is community, you write, rather than individualism, which should serve as the basis for restructuring society along more egalitarian lines. If I were an Orthodox Jew, like the Chief Rabbi, I would agree with you. Traditional Judaism emphasises the significance of group solidarity, enshrined in the principle of *klal Israel* (the community of Israel). It is for this reason, for example, that on Yom Kippur the entire congregation asks for forgiveness. The Day of Atonement supplications are for Israel as a whole, rather than individual sins.

As I have noted previously, a central belief of Orthodoxy is the conviction that God revealed the Torah to Moses on Mount Sinai: the Law was given to the people of Israel and is binding on each Jew. The covenant was established with the Jewish nation — every Jew is thereby compelled to keep all the *mitzvot*. Such a sense of communal responsibility pervades Jewish life. Traditionally no person is permitted to isolate himself or herself from the congregation of Israel. Personal responsibility and communal obligation are inextricably linked.

What this means in practice is that Jewish law constitutes a religious system which rules over all aspects of life. It is not simply the 613 commandments in Scripture which regulate Jewish existence, but rather the Code of Law (*Shulkhan Arukh*) consisting of thousands of rules covering all areas of daily life. From the moment one arises in the morning until one goes to bed, the legal code regulates one's entire life. In the eighteenth century, the founder of Hasidism, the Baal Shem Tov, stressed that cleaving to God (*devekut*) can be accomplished throughout the day as one carries out these multifarious divine commandments.

As a Reform Jew, however, I wish to disassociate from the totalitarian character of traditional Judaism. As contemporary Jews, we are no longer confined to a ghetto existence. Since the Enlightenment in the eighteenth century, Jewry has broken free of the fetters of the past. Today, we are free to subject the Jewish heritage to criticism. This has been the great contribution of Reform Judaism: no longer is the Jewish religious establishment able to coerce Jews into observing the Law under the threat of severe penalty.

This is not to say, however, that the non-Orthodox branches of Judaism are without institutional structures. On the contrary, Reform, Conservative, Reconstructionist and Humanistic Judaism support communal and rabbinical bodies. None the less, the principle of individuality is a central feature of all these Jewish movements. In all cases, individual Jews are at liberty to decide for themselves which features of the faith have spiritual significance. Such freedom, I believe, is of the utmost consequence. After centuries of authoritarian control, individual Jews are free to decide for themselves how best to integrate the tradition into their lives. You emphasise in your last letter the importance of individual conscience. I agree with you: individual Jews must be free to determine for themselves how to live religious lives.

But you also stress that the authority of the individual is rooted in community identity. This has certainly not been the case in the past for Jews. Instead, the rabbinical establishment was determined to suppress all forms of individual decision-making in favour of communal loyalty to the legal code. Fortunately, such rigidity has now been challenged by the various non-Orthodox branches of Judaism. For millions of Jews it is now the conscience of the individual that has overcome the conscience of the group — this shift in orientation has reinvigorated the Jewish faith and provided a new foundation for belief and practice. You say that you are arguing for an autonomy rooted in community relations as well as the right to disobey authority when it has betrayed its validating source. I am arguing rather for the right of the individual to disobey both traditional authority and the sources on which it is based. Only in this way can Judaism be purified from its moral distortions and spiritual corruptions. Let modern Jews cut off the tail of the dragon which has through the ages devoured individual conscience.

Dan

4.9 *6 October 2003 — Yom Kippur*

SLAY THE DRAGON OR TAME THE DRAGON?

Dan,

The solemnity of Yom Kippur in the context of the recent suicide bombing in Israel is the context of writing this letter. Since your last letter I have been in Spain (or rather the island of Mallorca), very aware of Moorish influences and the terrible consequences of the expulsion from Spain of both Jews and Muslims in 1492, consequences that still await healing. I'm also aware, following your last exchange, of the deep divisions, even polarisations *within* faith communities themselves as well as between the diverse religions. So I asked myself about the wisdom of your dramatic motif of dragon-slaying.

Of course in Christian tradition we also have the influential legend of St George, the dragon-slayer, dominant in the sense of seeming to sanction a heroic (and violent) response to evil. But feminist theology evokes a different (medieval) memory of St Martha, sister of the biblical Lazarus, who, according to a legend, tamed the dragon with her belt instead of killing the monster. In the context of our discussion, this could offer a more pluriform response. Both our traditions have shameful memories of the crushing of progressive movements or diversity within the tradition. Christians, in particular, have consistently failed since the first few centuries to honour the resistant conscience — which theoretically they respect — of both individual and group. Thus doctrinal orthodoxy was established at the expense of the expulsion of 'heretical' groups, until first the schism with the East, and then the Reformation finally split Christendom. Of course the Reformation itself was then followed by counter-Reformations. The twentieth century is full of examples of the Catholic Church responding to a decision by the Anglican Lambeth Conference with an oppositional definition.

So I absolutely respect your assertion that conscience — properly informed — should be followed, and that unjust and fallacious bases of authority and its sources should be unmasked and denounced for what they are. The authority of truthfulness is primary. After all, the founding fathers of America fled the Divine Right of Kings as the false basis of authority in England; the recent anti-apartheid movement justified violent resistance on the basis that the South African government's basis of authority was racist supremacy. My tension with you is still over individual/community loyalty.

The theme of our conversation is reconciliation and the question becomes one of how this is achieved. You and I reach agreement on certain points partly because we both come from intellectual, academic backgrounds. I probably agree more with you than with the Chief Rabbi, for instance, but that is not the point. Mostly, thank God, our daily lives are not threatened with violence — although I confess that I'm now more nervous in India, given the right-wing violence of the governing BJP party against Christians (though the real threat is against Islam).[15] If we are serious about reconciliation, don't we have a commitment to understanding and being in conversation with other positions and other sources of authority in both our traditions? While in Mallorca I read a remarkable book by Marc Gopin, *Between Eden and Armageddon: The Future of World Religions, Violence and Peacemaking*.[16] He points out the necessity of a historical perspective on entrenched positions within religions. Fundamentalist positions on authority do not come from nowhere. They are probably based on traumatised memories of suffering and scars from the past, conscious or unconscious, which may not even be articulated let alone addressed. Simply to point out the false basis of authority — misreadings of the Bible, patriarchal pyramids of power, injustice of the caste system — fails to address both the historical reasons for the system and the centuries of suppressed community memories of trauma that keep the system going. I could also argue that change is only possible from within the system. Standing outside in isolation may be a position true to one's own conscience, but will it produce the desired social transformation? That's why I want to tame the dragon and not slay it!

Mary

4.10   *11 October 2003*

CONSCIENCE AND THE COMMUNITY OF ISRAEL

Mary,

You are right, of course, that in Judaism communal life is vitally important — as you know, we believe that all Jews are united together into the body of Israel. Despite our differences, Jews in Israel and the Diaspora are bound together by ethnic ties and a shared tradition. These tribal loyalties are illustrated by the varied ways in which Jews worldwide are cognisant of one another's activities. The image that is frequently used to express such sentiments is that of the human body: when one part is injured, the entire body suffers. As I frequently explain to my students, Jews view themselves as a diversified and extended family, united by common bonds of tradition and observance.

In the past such communal loyalties provided a framework for Jewish living. The rabbinical establishment — all male — oversaw all aspects of Jewish existence, and laid down law for all members of the community. Leadership was invested in these rabbinic authorities who ruled supreme. As I indicated in previous letters, such dominance resulted in the creation of a legal code which was viewed as divinely revealed, and thus binding on Jewry as a whole.

Since the nineteenth century, Jews have been free from the legal fetters of such traditionalism. With the rise of Reform Judaism and the subsequent emergence of a variety of non-Orthodox movements, the strict pattern of rabbinic control has vanished. Yet, with the rise of these religious groupings, the Jewish community has been divided into smaller communal units, each with its particular ideology and pattern of observance. This has resulted in the formation of separate communities with their own jurisdiction. In Reform Judaism, for example, the Central Conference of American Rabbis serves as the forum for rabbinical decision-making among the Reform rabbinate; paralleling this body, the Union of American Hebrew Congregations holds conferences each year to determine policy for the various congregations affiliated with the movement. Similar communal bodies of rabbis and laity exist within Conservative, Reconstructionist and Humanistic Judaism.

It would be misleading, therefore, to suggest that since Judaism is no longer uniform in character, individual conscience has served as the sole factor in determining the nature of Jewish existence. It has not. Instead, there are now a range of different types of Judaism with their own respective communal organisations. Nonetheless, I still wish to champion the place of personal decision-making in modern Jewish life. The tradition should certainly inform such choices, but it should not bind individuals as it has in the past. As I repeatedly emphasised, personal liberty is paramount.

It is vital that what you refer to as the 'false basis of authority' — misreadings of the Bible, patriarchal pyramids of power, as well as injustice — be exposed. In my view, it is not enough simply to tame the dragon. The Orthodox will not stand for this for they are the enemy and will refuse to be domesticated by reasoned argument. They are powerful adversaries, and will seek to crush those who stand outside the fold.

Dan

4.11 *14 October 2003*

LOOKING TO AN EMANCIPATED FUTURE

Dan,

Whether dragons should be tamed or slain is a decision that is very context-dependent. Few would argue that Hitler had to be eliminated, and conscientious Christians like Dietrich Bonhoeffer were executed because they were part of just such a conspiracy. In this conversation on 'Authority and Tradition' we have ranged through a variety of positions and various sources of authority and power. We both respect the right of an individual to follow the dictates of conscience (rightly informed?) and expose fallacious positions and fascist types of authority. We also distrust fundamentalist, authoritarian positions on biblical interpretation. I understand your position within Reform Judaism, which gives such weight to the individual's process of decision-making and seeks to be free of the legalistic control of a person's entire life.

Yet this is not to pretend to complete agreement. I think that I stress rootedness in community so much because my understanding of the human person is a relational one. I'm also aware of the limits of the model of rationality of the Enlightenment, and refuse to honour reason at the expense of emotion. I seek a more holistic model of reason. I want to press my argument further because the focus of our discussion is reconciliation. So, I want to introduce two more ideas into the discussion that might be helpful later.

The first comes from a vibrant and longstanding discussion within feminist theology on connection and difference/diversity. For some years the discussion on mutual relation has been very popular.[17] At its simplest, this discussion has considered the idea that the self is constructed out of relation, God created out of a desire for relation (you may recognise Martin Buber here), and good relational energy, or the construction of mutual inter-dependent circles of relation, is the way to heal injustice. This discourse then came under challenge from the discourse of difference and otherness. Relationality, it was said, could become an imperialist discourse, assimilating 'the other' to a position of sameness in order for him/her to be accepted in the group. Emmanuel Levinas was influential in his insistence that it was the face of the Other that evoked a response and drew an individual out of his/her isolation.[18] The relevance of this for our discussion is that if we always stay with the group with whom we agree, with whom we naturally 'fit', how do we recognise difference and the position of the other with whom we disagree? In other words, what are the criteria for choosing between one model of author-ity and the other? Simply to say that it is necessary to move away from a controlling, legalistic past, is fine: but how does one relate to those who are perfectly happy with that position? How do I relate to women who tell me that the patriarchal system is fine for them?

I think not only that we have to find points of congruence with the position of others (visions of goodness and freedom, hopes and longings for justice, for example), but to find these sources of inspiration also in the past. Then we cannot be accused of rejecting the past in favour of some overblown assertion of autonomy in the present. In order not to be accused of eclecti-cism (for example, choosing Isaiah over against Leviticus), I think the necessary hermeneutical tool is that of pragmatism. Does the chosen textual memory provide inspiration for making justice and peace now in our own contexts? If so, then we still have a 'usable past', we can still relate to liberating elements of tradition as contributing to an emancipated future.

Mary

5. Sin

~~~~~~~~~~~

5.1 14 October 2003

SIN IN THE MODERN WORLD

Mary,

So far we have looked at various theological issues, but later we will want to explore a wide range of perplexing social problems in which reconciliation is vitally important. First, however, I want to say something about the concept of sin since I know this topic is of crucial importance. In the Bible, sin is understood as a transgression of God's decree. In biblical Hebrew, the word *het* means 'to miss' or 'to fail'. Here sin is understood as a failing, a lack of perfection in carrying out one's duty. The term *peshah* means a breach — it indicates a broken relationship between man and God. The word *avon* expresses the idea of crookedness. Thus, according to biblical terminology, sin is characterised by failure, waywardness, and illicit action.

Rabbinic Judaism holds that sins can be classified according to their gravity as indicated by the punishments prescribed by biblical law: the more serious the punishment, the more serious the offence. A distinction is also drawn in rabbinic texts between sins against other human beings and offences against God alone. Sins against God can be atoned for by repentance, prayer, and giving charity. In cases of offence against others, however, such acts require restitution and placation as a condition of atonement.

Rabbinic literature teaches that there are two tendencies in every person: the good inclination (*yetzer ha-tov*) and the evil inclination (*yetzer ha-ra*). The former urges individuals to do what is right, whereas the latter encourages sinful acts. At all times, a person is to be on guard against assaults of the *yetzer ha-ra*. It is not possible to hide one's sins from God since the Omnipresent knows all things. In the words of the Mishnah: 'Know what is above thee — an eye that sees, an ear that hears, and all thy deeds are written in a book.'[1] Thus, God is aware of all sinful deeds, yet through repentance and prayer it is possible to achieve reconciliation with him.

What can all this mean for modern Jews? Obviously, for the strictly Orthodox, ritual and ethical transgressions are conceived in the same way as in past centuries. But, for the majority of Jews, the legal precepts of Scripture and the rabbinic tradition have lost their religious significance. As I have previously explained, most Jews feel at liberty to select from the vast corpus of legal pre-scriptions those which animate their lives. The notion of sin has thereby undergone a major transformation.

With the exception of strictly observant Orthodox and Hasidic Jews, there is widespread neglect of the Jewish legal tradition. The laws in the Torah as well as the legal rulings of rabbinic sages are no longer regarded as authoritative. In most cases Jews do not feel any sense of remorse if they violate the Jewish legal code. Yet the notion of sinfulness has not disappeared altogether from Jewish life. Across the religious spectrum — from the most Orthodox to the most liberal — Jews continue to express shame and sorrow for various transgressions. Yet the focus today is on ethical misconduct.

Hence, I believe a new vision of Judaism for the future requires a recognition of this change of perception. No longer does Jewry feel bound by the legal dictates of previous centuries. Instead, Jews today envisage religious duty largely in moral terms. Sinfulness, repentance and forgiveness are all conceived in terms of ethical responsibility rather than loyalty to a legal code. Such a shift in understanding is reflected in the Conservative movement's for-mulation of transgression and sin in the Yom Kippur liturgy. Here innumerable moral offences are elaborated in detail, and this reorientation of religious responsibility has become universal throughout the Jewish community:

We abuse, we betray, we are cruel.
We destroy, we embitter, we falsify.
We gossip, we hate, we insult.
We jeer, we kill, we lie.
We mock, we neglect, we oppress.
We pervert, we quarrel, we oppress.
We steal, we transgress, we are unkind.
We are violent, we are wicked, we are xenophobic.
We yield to evil, we are zealots for bad causes ...
We have sinned against you through sexual immorality.
We have sinned against you knowingly and deceitfully.
We have sinned against you by wronging others ...
For all these sins, forgiving God, forgive us, pardon us,
grant us atonement.[2]

Such determination to live ethical lives can serve as a framework for Jewish existence in the modern world, as well as a basis for reconciliation between members of the Jewish community and others.

Dan

5.2   *16 October 2003*

THE FALL — TO SIN OR FREEDOM?

Dan,

I was very tempted to respond immediately to your conclusion, that when it comes to sin and wrongdoing, the focus today is on ethical responsibility rather than the infringement of legalistic rules, a position with which I thoroughly concur. My Catholic childhood was hemmed in with such rules — even my children can scarcely believe them! And the dread of being in a state of 'mortal sin' was a threat hung over us to ensure our good behaviour. It had the effect of confusing our young minds as to what was truly morally wrong or not. I remember reading a book at the age of 12, where the author wrote: 'Of course anyone reading this book is automatically excommunicated!' I was so terrified I didn't dare tell my parents and bicycled off to my church where, luckily,

I met a sympathetic priest, who assured me I had not yet been cast into outer darkness!

But I want to take us back earlier, to your statement that in Judaism, you discern the *yetzer ha-tov* and the *yetzer ha-ra* — the principles of good and evil as tendencies in every person, because this has more to do with the differences between Jews and Christians. In contrast with the Jewish understanding, the Christian understanding of good and evil is rooted in a traditional interpretation of the Book of Genesis's account of the Fall. On this bedrock rests the whole doctrine of salvation history. St Augustine (d. 430), who is the greatest influence here, thought that in an Edenic existence in the Garden, there was no sin. All creatures coexisted harmoniously in the presence of God. There was not even any sexual desire, which he called concupiscence. (Sexual desire is suspect because not rationally controllable.) But the sin of Adam, seen as the sin of humankind, destroyed this primeval harmony and humanity was cast out of the garden.

The nature of the sin, according to Augustine, was disobedience, caused by human pride and self-will. There are two important consequences of this. The first is that traditional Christian salvation theology believes that since this primeval sin, human nature remained in a fallen state (= the punishment for sin), expelled from the Garden, unable to attain eternal bliss, until the coming of Christ.[3] Through sin, humanity had lost the state of being in *imago Dei*, created in God's image. This is the basis of faith in Christ: that in him, who took all sin upon himself — that is, the sin (Greek ἁμαρτια) and corruption of the entire world — Christians can experience forgiveness, healing and the restoration of the image.

But the second consequence of this interpretation of the Fall is the way women have been blamed for Adam's sin, a frequent accusation of early Christian texts. According to the writer of the Letter to Timothy, women must not dominate men: 'For Adam was created first, and Eve afterwards; and it was not Adam who was deceived; it was the woman who, yielding to deception, fell into sin. Yet she will be saved through motherhood …' (1 Tim. 2:13—14)

The damaging consequence of this scapegoating of women for

sin, seen in typical stereotypes such as 'temptress' or 'witch', is that the good/evil contrast, which would always permeate existence, became understood as a male/female dualism, a dualism that is expressed also in the polarities of mind/body, spirit/flesh, human/animal, nature/supernature.[4] Clearly, women are as capable as men of wrongdoing. But, given the Christian understanding of Fallen Nature, and this reading of the story in Genesis 3, it has been very difficult for women to recover from a negative understanding of female nature and the blame still for evil in society that patriarchy still ascribes to her. Helena Kennedy's book describing the unequal treatment of women in the law courts is thus aptly named — *Eve was Framed.*[5]

I would argue that it is not enough to speak of fallen humanity: indeed I see the story of the Fall as an account of broken human nature, as likely to act wrongly then as now. But it is vital not to see sin as merely an individualistic act of wrongdoing, but to identify the evil systems that set one half of humanity, or one section of humanity, against another, claiming superiority or innocence at the expense of demonising the other.

Mary

5.3 *18 October 2003*

DISCARDING ADAM AND EVE

Mary,

I wonder if our backgrounds have so profoundly affected our outlooks that we cannot detect the forces that have shaped our religious assumptions. For my part, I was not subjected to formal, legalistic rules reinforced by religious institutions. Never was expulsion from the Jewish community held over me as a threat. Nor was I troubled by images of eternal punishment for misdeeds. Yet my father was an overpowering, dominating, and demanding parent who insisted that I follow his wishes. He wanted me firmly hemmed in by restrictions that curtailed any form of rebellion. Any infringement of such rules evoked the most ferocious hostility and criticism. Today I find it difficult to use my parents' silver cutlery, which was given to Lavinia and me by my mother, because it is so inextricably connected with scenes of terror. Given such an upbringing, is it any wonder I am so determined to liberate myself from the harsh demands of a legal code? Championing freedom and self-expression is no doubt a way of casting aside the dark memories of my childhood.

I am sure that my approach to sin and transgression is coloured by these early experiences. As far as good and evil are concerned, I think the concept of a good and evil inclination constantly at war — which I described in my last letter — is a helpful model. Whether this is conceived in Jewish terms, or formulated more in line with Freudian psychology, there is no doubt that all of us are driven by internal forces. Certainly this was true of my father. He was not an evil monster but an ordinary person whose emotional outbursts were explicable given his psychological make-up. In your last letter, you emphasise that for the Christian the concept of original sin based on the Book of Genesis is pivotal. For the Jew, the sin of Adam is not perceived as the source of evil in the world. Instead, the evil inclination (however it is conceived) is seen as responsible for sin: it drives human beings to choose evil over good. I think this is a much more plausible explanation for the existence of human evil.

Certainly, the Genesis account of Adam and Eve's disobedience and eventual expulsion from the Garden has tremendous emotional force. Through the centuries, it has deeply influenced both the Jewish and Christian understanding of human frailty. For the Christian, in particular, it has served as the theological framework for explaining the existence of evil in the world. But as modern Jews and Christians, I believe we must set aside the various religious theories connected with this narrative and view it instead as a mythological and misguided account of the origin of humankind.

The ancient Hebrews who composed this story lived over three thousand years ago: it is inevitable, therefore, that many of their ideas about human nature are primitive in character. Similarly, Jewish and Christian biblical exegetes and theologians of previous centuries were limited by the circumstances of their own time. Contemporary feminists are right to be troubled by the implications of the Genesis account: negative stereotypes of women are reinforced by the presentation of Eve. In many respects the narrative of Adam and Eve is a pernicious myth which must now be discarded altogether in the quest to understand the true nature of human motivation and action: today we must accept that the Bible as well as the religious literature of the past is a cage which imprisons us and limits our understanding.

Dan

5.4   *21 October 2003*

HOW ORIGINAL IS ORIGINAL SIN?

Dan,

Would it were so easy! — to 'discard the Genesis myth altogether', as you suggest in your last letter. The nature of myth is that it has a tendency to stick around and to reassert itself in new circumstances. Your painful memories of your father are a reminder to me how confusing and difficult it can be for a child to develop a genuine sense of right and wrong in the context of an inflexible authority: in your case, your father, and in mine, the authority of the Catholic Church and the way that school, family, church together presented a united front in this area.

Where I agree with you is in the presence of the two tendencies, good and evil, in each person. (Think of the way Paul wrestled to 'do the good'.) This can mean that evil presents itself in ambiguous forms. And there are different views around as to whether the human being is fundamentally good, if given a chance. Gandhi, for example, believed that human beings committed evil and criminal violence through lack of education and proper opportunity. Where these were offered, humanity would always choose the good.

This raises the question as to whether sin is 'original' or not and leads me to the reason why I think you are mistaken to suppose we can just dismiss Genesis. For example, Christians regularly read in Paul's Letter to the Romans, as I did this morning:

> Sin entered the world through one man, and through sin
> death, and thus death has spread through the whole

human race because everyone has sinned … If it is certain
that death reigned over everyone as the consequences of
one man's fall it is even more certain that one man, Jesus
Christ, will cause everyone to reign in life who receives
the free gift that he does not deserve, of being righteous.
(Rom. 5:12)

Here you have the Adam—Christ contrast, which has been used
in anti-Judaistic ways, as you know, and is responsible for the *felix
culpa* theology — the 'happy fault' of Adam because it produced
Christ. Nowadays we know that Paul was wrong to understand
the sin as that of a particular individual, Adam, and not the generic
sin of the entire human race. We also believe that St Augustine was
wrong to suggest that this 'original sin' was handed on through
sexual intercourse. (It has been difficult for Christian theology to
develop a healthy understanding of sexuality as a consequence of
this.)

But the belief in original sin is not so easy to shake off. It has
been responsible for rushing newborn babies to the baptismal
font, because failure to wash away 'the stain of sin' would result in
the baby being denied heaven should it die. Behind the sin of our
primeval parents, says the Catholic Catechism, lies the sin of the
fallen angels, who irrevocably rejected God (Paragraph 392). But
the Catechism does admit that, even though we are all implicated
by the primeval fault, its transmission is a mystery. Only through
baptism can a Christian be reoriented to God.

The original sin myth remains powerful across cultures partly
by the symbolism of 'stain'. Paul Ricoeur in *The Symbolism of Evil*
points out that religious rituals have two axes — the defilement–
purification axis, and that of bondage–extrication.[6] Both our
traditions have dimensions of the experience of sin-as-stain and
the consequent need for cleansing, purification rituals: 'There is
blood on your hands: wash yourselves and you shall be clean …
Though your sins are scarlet, they may become as white as snow',
says Isaiah (1:16, 18b).

You only have to think of the anguished cry of Shakespeare's
Lady Macbeth, after the murder of the King, Duncan — 'All the
perfumes of Arabia will not sweeten this little hand' — to under-

stand how deep the stain symbolism of sin goes, which is one of the reasons why 'original sin' is still a vibrant reality, and purification rituals make social and religious sense.

But, *theologically*, I think we have moved on considerably. I believe that St John's Gospel is right to speak of the 'sin of the world', the ἁμαρτια, which permeates the systems, structures and even the hearts and minds of everyone. (Actually the word ἁμαρτια also carries the connotation of *missing the mark*, which is close to one of the meanings you cited.)

Into this situation the child is born. But it is the responsibility of overlapping communities, religious, social, legal and familial, to interpret the ways that sin and evil are present, and to determine the balance between individual and communal responsibility. So, sin is *unoriginal* in the sense that there are always inherited patterns and structures of evil — like the scapegoating and demonising of certain groups throughout history; but it is *original* both in presenting a myth of origins, whether we like it or not, and *original* in the ever-new ugliness and horrific ways in which evil presents its face.

Mary

5.5 *27 October 2003*

ONTOLOGY AND ETHICS

Mary,

You are right that the myths of the Bible do stick around! Even in the most liberal circles, Scripture is cited as a basis for determining how to live. That is why rabbis normally begin sermons with the Torah reading, and go on to apply the lesson of the text to daily life. This raises a fundamental problem for us both: given that ours is a Jewish—Christian conversation, and we intend to go on to look at specific social issues, how are we to use the tradition? As you have seen, I have deep reservations about the Orthodox understanding of the Bible as well as rabbinic texts. I do not believe that the Five Books of Moses were given by God to Moses on Mount Sinai, nor do I view the Oral Torah as divinely authoritative. In short, I do not accept the metaphysical assumptions of Orthodox Judaism.

But that does not mean that I wish to discard the religious literature of the past. It must not be abandoned, but reconstructed in light of modern knowledge and scientific advance. What is needed is a new hermeneutics, which can draw from the tradition those elements which continue to have religious significance for contemporary Jews. The same applies to Christian sources: they too, I believe, must be understood anew. Here I think we can agree. The question is: how are the ideas of previous ages to be recast so that they are relevant for Jews and Christians today?

If, as I have suggested, we cannot embrace the traditional notion of divine revelation, and are ultimately driven to an enlightened form of agnosticism, then religious texts must be read in a new way. They must be seen as human attempts to answer the deepest questions about life and death. The mythology of Scripture and rabbinic literature has meaning for us in that it highlights the most central human concerns, and offers a vision of a better world. In particular, our religious heritages provide moral frameworks for living. Previously Jews regarded moral virtues as grounded in God's will for his chosen people. I think we can no longer affirm this — nonetheless, the Jewish faith does contain ethical insights which are intrinsically valuable and can be applied to daily affairs.

It is in this light that stories about sin, repentance and forgiveness found in Scripture and our two traditions have significance. It is a mistake to regard Genesis as a factual account of the origin of human life, and to ground the notion of sin in Adam's act of disobedience. Sinfulness does not emerge as the result of what took place in the Garden of Eden: there was no Garden of Eden, nor were Adam and Eve historical personages. No snake seduced Eve. Nor were Adam and Eve cast out of paradise for their disloyalty to God. The Book of Genesis does not record history, but is instead a spiritual meditation on human frailty.

What we can learn from the Genesis account is that all human beings are subject to temptation, and are prone to sin. The rabbinic idea of the struggle between good and evil in each person's psyche — referred to in rabbinic sources as the *yetzer ha-ra* (evil inclination) and the *yetzer ha-tov* (good inclination) — should similarly not be understood in ontological terms, but instead can be viewed as a way of explaining the nature of human action. We are not born with original sin because of Adam's misdeed, but we are prone to sin because of our psychological make-up. Evil is present in our world, and it is our task to root it out. The religious resources of the past are valuable because they can direct us to the highest human ideals as enshrined in our two traditions ... but it is vital that we recognise that the metaphysical assumptions of previous centuries should be set aside in the process.

    Dan

5.6   *28 October 2003*

ON NOT LEAVING IT TO THE SNAKE

Dan,
As I write, the long fast of Ramadan has begun, and there are escalating attacks against Americans in Iraq. This coincidence makes it very clear to me that the causes of violence are deep-rooted in history, that the seeds are buried in deep-seated traumatic memories. This emphasises that we are both right not to discard the past, but, in your words, to 'reconstruct it in the light of modern knowledge'. I go along with you to a large extent, except I want to hang on to the belief that this is how God works in history — with the advancement of knowledge and science.

Of course I agree with you that Genesis is a story of 'human frailty' (you), and 'human brokenness' (me). In fact, a book by Harvey Cox years ago, *On Not Leaving it to the Snake*, rather sums this up: stop blaming outside factors and accept responsibility ourselves, as individuals and communities, for our own wrongdoing.[7] But I disagree with you in thinking that we only have to reconstruct the tradition in the light of modern knowledge. This ignores its flawed character in terms of sexism (as I have tried to explain), as well as the way Christians have used their sources to justify their anti-Semitism and anti-Judaism. This has even

encouraged certain Christian groups to dismiss the Hebrew scriptures altogether. Rather than merely reconstructing in the light of
modern knowledge, I think we also have to enter a discerning
process as to what is the liberating word of God and what needs
to be discarded as seriously oppressive.

Trying to discern a Christian hermeneutic of sin and evil, I
want to hone in on the call of Jesus at the beginning of Mark's
gospel to 'repent and believe in the Gospel' (Mark 1:15). This is in
the context of the proclamation of the inbreaking of the
Kingdom of God. If there is one vital concept to the Christian
hermeneutic it is that of μετανοια, repentance, change of heart,
a total orientation of the human personality towards God. I call
this Christian but it has ancient Jewish roots in the prophetic call
to the people to return to God.

This total reorientation is what grounds an authentic Christian
theology of sin and forgiveness. The Russian novelist Dostoevsky
dramatically illustrates this in his novel *Crime and Punishment*.[8] He
depicts the murderer Raskolnikov and the prostitute Sonia (who
is a redemptive Christ-figure in the novel) in a garret in St
Petersburg, where Sonia, in a trembling voice, is reading aloud
from the Gospel of John. In fact she is reading from the story of
the raising of Lazarus, where Christ is revealed as the
Resurrection and the Life. The promise of new life prompts
Raskolnikov's complete change of heart: 'Sonia, I am come to
carry the cross,' he cries the next day. This leads to public confession in the marketplace, to punishment in Siberia, where paradoxically he experiences the promise of a new life, again mediated
by Sonia. The same copy of the New Testament accompanies the
couple to Siberia.

This story expresses essential elements of a Christian ethic. A
total change of heart (genuine contrition) is insufficient without
some public — or community —acknowledgement of wrongdoing. Sin injures at both individual and communal levels. A
process is involved which entails also restitution to the person
wronged — insofar as this is possible. The process of reorientation
to the community also takes its own time, as the early Christian
community recognised in its process of the reconciliation of
sinners. And behind it all is the idea that God forgives, God takes

the initiative, and that what made Christ's ministry effective was that 'God was in Christ, reconciling the world to himself' (2 Cor. 5:19).

Mary

―◦⊙――⊙◦―

5.7   *2 November 2003*

THE SIN OF THE CHURCH

Mary,

I am glad that you agree we need a fresh approach to the understanding of sinfulness. Yet, again, I think there are important differences in our understanding of divine providence. You say that we should hang on to the belief that God works in history. Such a conviction implies that God is immanent in the world, that He is an active agent in human affairs. Yet, at various points in our conversation, you assert that the notion of divine agency should be discarded. If this is so, how can we assume that God works in history with the advancement of knowledge and science? Such a belief is not consistent with the rejection of an interventionist Deity.

The image of 'not leaving it to the snake' is appropriate if we are to assume that human beings must accept responsibility for their actions and not blame others. This, as you know, is the theme of the Yom Kippur liturgy: as individuals and communities we are to confess our transgressions and resolve to do better in the coming year. The stirring sound of the *shofar* which is blown during the High Holy Day services calls us to such repentance.

I am surprised, though, by what you say about the necessity of reconstructing our faiths in the light of modern knowledge. I am sure we concur that the Judeo–Christian tradition is flawed by its inherently misogynistic character. In previous centuries, both Jews and Christians would not have viewed the inherent discrimination against women in the way that we do today. Indeed, in our two faiths there are still many who staunchly support the traditional role of women. That is certainly the case among strictly Orthodox Jews as well as the Hasidim. But today the vast majority of Jews regard the attitude toward women expressed in the

Hebrew Bible and rabbinic tradition as outmoded and morally reprehensible. Such a shift in perspective is the result of a major change in consciousness about the place of women in society. I do not see this as a matter of discerning the liberating word of God, but rather as a paradigm shift in the understanding of gender.

Similarly, the underlying anti-Jewish attitudes of the New Testament, the hostility of the Church Fathers toward Judaism and the Jewish people, and the virulent contempt for the Jew in medieval society were products of a different age. Today, particularly in the light of the Holocaust, there has been a total transformation of attitudes within the various branches of Christianity. As you are aware, both the Catholic and the Protestant religious establishment currently seek to distance themselves from previous forms of Christian anti-Semitism. I agree that we should discard those elements of our traditions which have been seriously oppressive and destructive. But ultimately this will occur as a result of modern notions of equality and justice. While reference may be made to divine liberation in such reformulations, such a revolution in consciousness has been brought about for social and cultural reasons.

You refer to the need for repentance: I agree. For the Jew, this must be the first step in the process of healing. There must be a conscious change of heart and a determination to improve. Sinners must accept their waywardness. What is needed is a total reorientation. While the Jew cannot accept the theology of the Cross, there is much that binds us together. But where we differ — and this is of vital significance — is that it is not God who takes the initiative but the sinner. The change of heart must commence through an acknowledgement of wrongdoing. Traditional Judaism places God at the centre of such a process: divine forgiveness is to be sought by the sinner. But God's pardon is conditional upon true repentance.

We began our conversation with a discussion of the history of Christian anti-Semitism. I am sure that we both agree that what is required of all Christians today (not simply official Church bodies) is an acceptance of Christian culpability for Jewish suffering through the ages. Christians must honestly face the anti-Jewish bias of their tradition. For nineteen centuries the Church blamed the Jew for Jesus' death, and viewed the exile of the Jewish people from their homeland as a punishment for their rejection of Jesus. In Jewish eyes, this is the great sin of Christianity. For the Jew, Jesus on the cross symbolises the persecution and murder of Jewry rather than God's presence in his beloved Son. Any Jewish—Christian dialogue concerning sin and repentance must inevitably lead to this chilling conclusion.

Dan

5.8 6 November 2003

THE POWER OF SYMBOLS

Dan,

I realise that winter and long dark nights approach, daylight shrinks — but I won't surrender to the gloom that your last letter presents. Again and again you declare that 'The cross of Jesus symbolises the persecution and murder of Jewry'. On 13 July you said that the cross of Jesus is 'the Church triumphant'. On 19 July you said that the anti-Jewish bias 'is a virus that contaminates the entirety of Christian life and thought'.

I have tried to respond by condemning the sin of anti-Semitism as manifested by Christians since the death of Jesus. On 28 July I admitted that we cannot just give up the Cross to achieve reconciliation, because 'following the Way of the Cross is integral to Christian life.' *But the symbolic power and meaning of the cross can change and has changed.* I wrote in that letter:

> Jesus set his face to Jerusalem in a freely chosen path of suffering love, emerging from a being totally reconciled with God, the power and source of life and justice; a path also chosen by the community that formed and nurtured him. The struggle that appeared to end for Jesus with crucifixion was a protest against all crucifixions, against the necessity of the violent putting to death of the innocent, poor and vulnerable.

I think that symbolic changes can never be understood and accepted without genuine acts of repentance from Christians —

as you say, not only official symbolic acts, but consistent expressions of sorrow from the whole Christian people that develop
into *effective* solidarity with Jewish communities now. The acts of
leaders, however, are important because they create a new political context that can enable the wider community to move on. I
think you will agree that the present Pope John Paul II has made
great attempts to wipe out anti-Semitism, as official documents
testify.[9] But there are other Christian theologians, like Eugene
Fisher and John Pawlikowski, who have made this their life
work. I do think that the onus is on Christians, not Jews, to keep
this process of repentance alive on every level. Only then can
symbols — like the cross — move on to acquire new meanings.

It is interesting that a Jewish painter like Marc Chagall could
use the symbol of the cross to interpret Jewish not Christian
history, though I imagine that some would find this unacceptable.
I have already cited the poignant novel *My Name is Asher Lev*, by
the late Chaim Potok, where the young artist Asher Lev is flung
out of his Brooklyn Hasidic community because of his painting
of his mother on the cross-panes of a large window in a gallery,
which seems to be depicting her as a symbol of suffering on a
cross.[10]

Maybe you will say that this is artistic licence and cuts no ice
with the wider community. But symbols and metaphors exert a
profound influence on our unconscious psyches. I have already
discussed the global influence of the 'stain' symbolism of sin. But
'stain' can encourage immoveable guilt. You mentioned sin as
'missing the mark'. 'Transgressing boundaries' is another
metaphor. Both these have value but I think we need something
more powerful. We have a responsibility as theologians to identify
positive symbols that nurture reconciling attitudes. Christians —
as well as changing attitudes of responsibility for the death of Jesus
— are trying to eradicate injurious expressions of the cross that
encourage passivity in the face of suffering and suggest a cruel
Father sending his Son to a humiliating death. Sin is wrong, disordered relationship. Sin causes and prolongs alienation and
vengeful attitudes. So we need symbols that promote the process
of right, just and reordered relation. The title of Miroslav Volf's
book, *From Exclusion to Embrace*, encapsulates this kind of

process.[11] Indeed the New Testament parable of the Prodigal Son (Luke 28) embraced by the forgiving Father (think of Rembrandt's picture) is a poignant symbol of what I mean.

So whereas the past condemns us (Christians) repeatedly, God's forgiveness and grace bestow new possibilities. (That's why I believe God acts in history, not in an interventionist but agential manner, through all the process of creation.) If our dialogue is to create anything positive for our communities, we need to offer hope and the possibility of change. Both our traditions emphasise the symbol of the *changed heart* as positive — isn't that the aim of the life of faith?

Mary

5.9   *7 November 2003*

THE TERROR OF THE CROSS

Mary,

I did not mean to be gloomy: yet the shadow of the cross is the most terrifying symbol imaginable for the Jew! For the Christian, it represents God's redeeming power. But in Jewish eyes, the cross — like the swastika — is emblematic of persecution and murder. Martin Luther's diatribe against Jewry in his infamous 'On the Jews and their Lies' is representative of the type of polemic levelled at Jews in Christ's name. Images of the crucifixion evoke memories of the kinds of actions Luther recommended in this tract:

> Their synagogues should be set on fire ... Their homes should likewise be broken down and destroyed ... they should be deprived of their prayerbooks and Talmuds in which such idolatry, lies, cursing and blasphemy are taught ... their rabbis must be forbidden under threat of death to teach any more ... [12]

Justifying such actions, Luther insisted that:

> this ought to be done for the honour of God and of Christianity in order that God may see that we are

Christians, and that we have not wittingly tolerated or approved of such public lying, cursing and blaspheming of his Son and his Christians.[13]

I am not asking that you give up the theology of the cross, but rather that you recognise that Christian symbolism can be a major stumbling-block in the quest for Jewish and Christian reconciliation. You mention that Marc Chagall used the symbol of the cross to interpret Jewish history and that the novelist Chaim Potok in *My Name is Asher Lev* depicts the artist Asher Lev using the symbolism of the cross to represent his mother's suffering. These artistic and literary illustrations of Christian imagery are intriguing, but we must acknowledge that on a visceral level the Jewish community is deeply disturbed by the legacy of Christian anti-Semitism as symbolised by Jesus crucified. Nineteen centuries of hostility to everything Jewish is not easily forgotten!

You are right that symbols and metaphors exert a profound influence on the unconscious: that is precisely my point. The cross has indelibly stained Jewish consciousness. There is nothing here, I contend, which can bind our two traditions together. Instead we will need to look for other shared symbols which can illuminate our path toward hope and peace in our wounded world. In the meantime, the cross should call forth repentance from the Christian world for the suffering inflicted on the Jew. Effective solidarity can only emerge out of the types of official documents you cite and the attitudes of such thinkers as Eugene Fisher and John Pawlikowski. There are many others, such as Rosemary Radford Ruether, who similarly call upon their fellow Christians to enunciate past teachings and approach the Jewish community with sympathy and understanding. The onus falls upon the Christian to reach out to the Jew in this process. Before we can work together to create a better world for all humanity, our two communities must seek to overcome their past history and discover new symbols that can serve as a bridge to the future.

Dan

5.10 8 November 2003

THE TANGIBILITY OF REPENTANCE

Dan,

You are right. I think this is a point in our dialogue when I run out of arguments. I personally believe the feminist and liberationist view of the cross as a call to identify ourselves in compassion and justice with all suffering peoples. As Sydney Carter's popular hymn put it:

> 'The poor of the world are my body,' he said,
> 'To the end of the world it shall be ...
> My body will hang on the Cross of the world
> Tomorrow,' he said, 'and today.'[14]

But I would also say that it is not the cross but what it leads to — namely resurrection — that brings new hope, and that Christian faith is founded on precisely this. Third, it is the life and ministry of Jesus that is important — and the way that the call to repentance and forgiveness was the foundation of the ethics of the Kingdom. Indeed, his call was to boundless forgiveness, which in our own context must be interwoven with commitment to justice and restitution.

But I see that the oppressive history and meaning of the symbol of the cross for Jews is still very much alive. I can only say with Rosemary Ruether:

> The Cross and Resurrection are a paradigm for Christians, not for 'all who would be a part of Israel' or necessarily for 'all men'. That is to say, it is a paradigm for those for whom it has become a paradigm. Those who have not chosen to make it their paradigm, because they have other paradigms which are more compelling to them from their own histories, are not to be judged false or unredeemed thereby.[15]

This does not take away from my point that we still need rituals and symbols that will enable a shared process of reconciliation and that we must identify resources from our joint traditions to discern the way sin and evil are present in contemporary life. Yes, I agree that Jews and Christians need to walk the pilgrimage path together again and again so that Jews can experience Christians demonstrating authentic repentance for the past and present forms of anti-Semitism. I remember what a profound impression it made on me a few years ago to stand in prayer with Jewish leaders at the ravine of Babi Yar, outside the city of Kiev (Ukraine), site of the massacre of 6,000 Jews.

But we also need not just to identify new manifestations of sin, but to act together in response. For example, it is a positive sign that Jews and Christians could both join (with other faiths) in the Jubilee 2000 movement to eradicate the debt of poorer two-thirds world countries and against the war in Iraq. Isn't it true that our fundamental agreement is that sin is an offence against God, bringing alienation from all that is good, true and righteous? And that what we have to offer society are the fruits of two traditions that still struggle for integrity in our public and personal lives, against a culture of excessive wealth accumulation, lies and deceit?

I will end with one example that gave me hope that the pilgrimage of repentance not only symbolised contrition but was a tangible part of the process of moving on. Some years ago I led a weekend of reflection for Pax Christi. We decided to build the last liturgy (a Eucharist) around the symbol of Isaiah's Holy Mountain (Isa. 25). The 'walk to the Holy Mountain' assumed a reality I could not have imagined. (We constructed an incredible structure in the room from a huge pile of chairs, sheets, greenery and a lion and lamb!) But people began to feel they could not journey to the mountain without some kind of penitential preparation. They discarded shoes, credit cards, cheque books — even a fur coat in one case. It seemed urgent that the symbols of contemporary life that distanced them from God and a just lifestyle had to be set aside. Returning from the mountain did bring an experience of healing and new beginning.

A small example, perhaps: it will take more than constructing holy mountains to counteract the escalating violence of our times. But as you yourself wrote, symbols exert great power and it is up to us to make them work for the good.

Mary

5.11   *9 November 2003*

UTOPIA?

Mary,

There have been other sustained dialogues between Jewish and Christian theologians like ours. But what I think makes our conversation different is our continual unwillingness to agree! Often Jewish and Christian thinkers tend to paper over their differences in the pursuit of common goals. Our conversation is certainly not like that. Often we disagree over the most fundamental issues that separate our two traditions, as well as over topics that concern us individually. What I think is revealing in our discussion so far are the major religious presuppositions that divide us.

You emphasise in your last letter that you simply cannot take leave of the cross: for you it brings new hope. For me (and for the Jewish community in general) it is a deeply troubling symbol of persecution and oppression. Further, it is the life and message of Jesus that is all-important for you. But for me (and for many Jews) Jesus, though an admirable spiritual leader, is of minor importance. In my book *On Earth as it is in Heaven: Jews, Christians and Liberation Theology*, I stressed that Jews could find in Jesus' words a reflection of the great Hebrew prophets.[16] Yet, while I admire Jesus, I do not think he is superior to many of the figures of the Jewish past. His insights must be placed alongside theirs.

I imagine that your religious vision centres around Jesus, and that in everything you write he is a constant presence. All spiritual roads lead back to the path that he trod over two thousand years ago. Yet, as a Jew, this cannot be so. I do not believe Jesus to have been the Messiah, nor in any sense God incarnate. I think we will need to remind ourselves of this theological chasm as we proceed to discuss concrete areas of religious concern. None the less, I believe that we can bring the resources of our two traditions to bear on the problems that beset our world.

As far as the image of pilgrimage is concerned, I have my doubts about Isaiah's vision. His words in Chapter 2 are:

It shall come to pass in the latter days
that the mountain of the house of the Lord
shall be established as the highest of the mountains,
and shall be raised above the hills,
and all nations shall flow unto it ...
He shall judge between the nations,
and shall decide for many peoples;
and they shall beat their swords into ploughshares
and their spears into pruning hooks;
nation shall not lift up sword against nation,
neither shall they learn war any more. (Isa. 2:2—4)

This prophecy was not simply a plea for justice, but rather a messianic vision based on the belief that God would eventually send his long awaited redeemer to bring about a new age. Through the centuries, the Jewish people have longed for the coming of such deliverance. At the end of history the Jewish people will be restored to their former glory, the Temple will be rebuilt, and eventually final judgement will take place. However, you know that I do not embrace such an eschatological scheme. I believe the concept of a personal Messiah should be set aside. Modern Jews should cease to long for God's miraculous intervention into human history; instead, we should rely on ourselves to create a better world. It will not be a society filled with the kind of cosmic transformation envisaged by Isaiah and others, but ideally a world in which human beings will be able to live peacefully together. They will not beat their swords into ploughshares as the prophet predicted. But, hopefully, they will leave the world a better place. Whether this will entail discarding our material possessions, tearing up our credit cards, cancelling debts of third world countries, and overturning the structure of capitalism is something we will need to discuss as we move on from this exploration of sin and repentance to concrete problems facing Jews and Christians today.

    Dan

Part Two

6. War and Peace

6.1   12 November 2003

SWORDS INTO PLOUGHSHARES — OR INTO CLUSTER-
BOMBS?

Dan,

Your letter came to me yesterday on Remembrance Day, all the
more poignant because, although the world is in theory not at
war, we are surrounded by intractable conflicts like the Middle
East, or the aftermath of others, such as the devastation in Iraq.
Add on to this the 'war against terrorism' that involves both
Europe and the USA, and the picture is bleak indeed. Can our
religious traditions offer anything helpful, in the context of these
words of Hans Kung? 'There can be no peace among the nations
without religious peace. Constructive engagement with the other
religions of this world for the sake of peace is vitally important for
survival.'[1]

That religion could be part of the solution instead of the
problem is clearly disputable. Yesterday George Monbiot wrote in
the *Guardian* an article entitled 'Dreamers and Idiots', accusing
Tony Blair and George Bush of *avoiding* a peaceful solution in
both Afghanistan and Iraq:

> Had a peaceful solution of these disputes been attempted,
> Bin Laden might now be in custody, Iraq might be a
> pliant and largely peaceful nation finding its own way to
> democracy, and the prevailing sentiment within the
> Muslim world might be sympathy for the United States,
> rather than anger and resentment.[2]

Whether one agrees with this or not, what is beyond dispute is that both these politicians make no secret of the fact that they are committed Christians, prepared to take their countries to war, supposedly to solve 'threats to national security'. Thousands of civilians have been killed or maimed in these last two conflicts alone: clearly there is a question here both as to the role Christianity is playing, and also whether there can be such a reality as a 'just war' in this modern world.

On the face of it, it is hard to harmonise the message of Jesus with war and violence. The radical ethic of peace and justice was expressed most clearly in the Sermon on the Mount (Matt. 5—6, Luke 6). When you write to me that Jesus for you is a minor figure compared with the prophets and other great Jewish figures, I can understand, but would still argue that this teaching of non-violence and radical forgiveness is a unique contribution to the world's hopes for peace. It inspired Leo Tolstoy, Gandhi and Martin Luther King. (When you say that for my faith, Jesus is central, I would say yes, in the sense of his message, and presence in the Spirit now, but not as the man, Jesus of Nazareth.)

For the first Christians, it was undoubtedly wrong to take up arms. Tertullian, a second-century apologist, makes it very clear in the debate about whether a soldier can be a Christian:

> There can be no compatibility between the divine and human sacrament (i.e. the military oath), and the standard of Christ and the standard of the devil, the camp of light and the camp of darkness. One soul cannot serve two masters, God and Caesar ... but how will a Christian go to war? ... The Lord, in disarming Peter, disarmed every soldier.[3]

There are many such texts — but I know you will argue that this early vision was completely lost when, in 312CE, the Emperor Constantine converted to Christianity, led his troops to victory under the banner of the cross, and made the Christian religion the established faith across the Roman Empire. However, I would argue that the radicality of seeking peace with justice in a non-violent manner was never completely lost: it was retained by the Quakers, by the Mennonites, with prophetic teaching on non-violence, by the poverty movements of the Middle Ages, and in the many Communities for Reconciliation since the world wars. In the recent anti-war movement something of this radicality was glimpsed.

I think we are witnessing a retrieval of the earliest Christian vision, and harnessing it in the area of conflict resolution. I'll end with one story as example. It tells of the efforts at reconciliation of the Sant'Egidio community in Rome.[4] Ten years ago, in a garden in the Roman hills, they facilitated a reconciliation between the Transport Minister of Mozambique (Frelimo) and the guerrilla in charge of the rebel army (Renamo). The founder of Sant'Egidio, Andrea Riccardi, and his companions (including the Archbishop of Beira of Mozambique), had broken through the government's insistence on a cease-fire and the rebel insistence on constitutional changes before laying down weapons. Riccardi invoked their common African heritage, their being Mozambique patriots, and the principle enunciated by Pope John XXIII, 'Let us be concerned with seeking what unites, rather than that which divides'.

One breakthrough moment was over the menu. In Mozambique, the head of the table has the right to the head of the fish. But the Italian hosts served up two whole grilled fish so that each could have one! It was these two fish, said Riccardi, which pointed towards the parties' mutual recognition, and the moment when the facilitators became the mediators.[5]

In the near despair that surrounds, this story gives much hope.

Mary

6.2   *15 November 2003*

PACIFISM AND WAR

Mary,

When I was a rabbinic student at the Hebrew Union College in Cincinnati, Ohio — the main seminary for Reform Judaism — I had a perplexing interview with the Dean and others concerning war and peace in Judaism. Like you, I resisted the idea that conflict can be resolved through war. I was inspired then by the messianic vision of a time of peace when swords would be turned into ploughshares and spears into pruning hooks. So, when faced with the prospect of registering with the military chaplaincy, I told the college authorities that I wanted no part of it. To their astonishment, I declared that I wished to be registered as a conscientious objector.

In the history of the college, no one had made such a request. I was summoned to see the Dean. When I entered his office, I discovered that he had assembled an array of professors from the seminary as well as rabbis affiliated with the military. This panel was seated in comfortable armchairs in a semi-circle. I was told to sit on a stiff chair in front of them. I explained that I was a pacifist and was grilled by my teachers. I tried to defend my view by citing Scripture. But it was clear they were unconvinced by my arguments.

Alas, they were right. Judaism is not a pacifist religion. I had failed to reflect critically on the role of warfare in the history of the ancient Israelites. If I had, I would have observed that the Bible is full of gory detail about battles between the Israelites and their neighbours. Frequently, when war did take place, divine assistance was sought. In the Book of Judges, for example, the Israelites turned to God before engaging in battle:

> The people of Israel arose, and went up to Bethel, and inquired of God 'which of us shall go up first to battle against the Benjaminites?' And the Lord said, 'Judah shall go up first' ... and the people of Israel went up and wept before the Lord until the evening; and they inquired of the Lord, 'Shall we again draw near to battle against our brethren the Benjaminites?' And the Lord said, 'Go up against them.' (Judg. 20:18, 23)

In the history of ancient Israel, warfare was a constant feature of Jewish life: wars of the early period were religious in nature and divinely sanctioned. Steps were frequently taken to ascertain God's will, and He was seen as actively involved in the course of military conflict. Priests and prophets involved themselves in the direction of battle, and took an active role in encouraging the people. In some cases, no mercy was shown to the vanquished.

Even though peace was viewed as an ideal, warfare was seen as a necessary evil.

Given such a background, it is not surprising that the Jewish people have felt and continue to feel fully justified in defending themselves through the use of force. The history of warfare in Scripture as well as rabbinic reflections on war provide a framework for justifying violence in the face of the nation's enemies. Today Jews living in Israel as well as in the Diaspora are determined to ensure that the state of Israel survives: if this involves crushing Palestinian opposition by military means, there is no hesitation in doing so. You stress that there can be no peace among the nations without religious peace. This is a noble sentiment. But arguably, it is religion itself which has fuelled the conflict between nations.

Certainly this was the case when the Jewish nation under Joshua entered the Promised Land and devastated the Canaanite population. It was so in the West as Christians triumphally crushed those who stood in their way. Similarly, Islamic crusaders spread the message of Islam by the sword. As you note, some early Christians took Jesus' words to heart and determinedly preached the message of peace. Yet, the Church itself rejected this view, and developed a just war theory to justify its actions. You may be right that Jesus' words can serve as a model for peaceful resolution of conflict, but it must be remembered that the Christian faith has continually proclaimed its spiritual message through the use of violence. For the Jew, the Crusades and the Inquisition testify to its determination that only through the spilling of blood can the Kingdom of God be won.

Dan

6.3   *18 November 2003*

A JUST WAR?

Dan,

The story of your conscientious objection and what you faced from the Jewish authorities at the time in your rabbinic seminary is both striking and moving. But I want to ask — even challenge you — what would you do now? Could you still be a pacifist? In Israel today, when two peoples are struggling to death for the same piece of land? In a way, I want to seize the same moral high ground as you and to identify myself with the inspiring Christian non-violent traditions that I described to you in my last letter. But I know I am not being realistic. I was born during the Second World War (apparently a burning bomb went off in front of our house on that day) — but, as a baby, I had no moral choice to make over war issues. I have since made choices against war and for non-violence, but I have to confess that I have never faced the barricades, machine guns, or personal threats to my family. In my imagination, however deeply I *theoretically* espouse the cause of pacifism and non-violence, being truthful, I could really see myself killing someone who threatened the lives of my children. And that horrifies me.

Was it this kind of argument that prompted someone like St Augustine of Hippo, threatened as we know by barbarian tribes battering the gates of Rome, to develop a theory of just war? Augustine tried to limit the war killing, the inevitable carnage, by arguments like the seriousness and justifiability of the cause, by balancing the hoped-for outcome in relation to the estimated loss of life, by avoiding civilian deaths and by exhausting other means of conflict solving … and so on. His arguments have been very influential over the years and have often been appealed to. But surely, I would argue, recent events have cast doubt on whether there can ever be a 'just war' — if there ever has been one. Think about it: escalating loss of civilian life is a feature of conflicts in Iraq, Afghanistan, Northern Ireland and Palestine/Israel. We can no longer assume the hoped-for out-come will balance the loss of innocent life. As we write these letters we are both aware that the loss of American life in post-war Iraq is greater than during the war. Afghanistan is sinking into lawlessness after a brief period of what seemed — to outsiders — like relative stability.

The traditional just war arguments never envisaged a world that could inflict permanent and undiscriminating damage through nuclear weapons, and in so doing could effectively self-destruct. Even though Augustine had first-hand experience of the might of the Roman Empire, the just war theory offers neither challenge nor check to the interventionist strikes of a powerful country trying to dominate small countries to gain access to their resources. Both the biblical world and the world of Augustine are far removed from this world of globalisation, from the New World Order of President Bush. A world where the so-called 'war against terrorism' cloaks vested interests and determination to control by force any country that will not fall into line.

As I write, the anti-war coalition — which remains opposed to the Iraq War and subsequent occupation of the country — is marshalling its strength to demonstrate in London during the visit of President Bush. This brings immense hope that the good will of thousands of ordinary people is committed to peace, peace with justice. Can this good will still be resourced by our faith traditions, or must we look elsewhere?

Mary

6.4 *20 November 2003*

BEYOND THE JUST WAR

Mary,

Like you, I have never been directly faced with the horrors of war. But this does not mean that both of us cannot have opinions about war and peace. I, too, theoretically espouse a policy of non-violence despite what the Bible and the rabbis have said about the necessity of warfare. In my memoir, *What's a Nice Jewish Boy Like You Doing in a Place Like This?* (where I recounted my interview with officials at my seminary), I emphasised that I was against military action. I still am.[6]

During this encounter the professor of Jewish theology grilled me concerning my attitude. 'Let's take a little example, then,' he said. 'Let's imagine that you were at home with your mother. And you heard a terrible noise. And there was the sound of breaking glass. There in front of you stood a known murderer, holding a large axe. He then grabbed your mother and threatened to rape her. Would you stand by and let him get on with it?'

'I can't imagine there would be much else I could do,' I said.

'But let's say you had a little revolver in your pocket. Would you use it?' he persisted.

'I'd try and reason with him,' I replied.

'Good, good. Reason with a mad, axe-wielding rapist ... what if he refused to listen?'

'I'd reason more loudly,' I conjectured.

At this stage, I shifted uneasily. Things were not going well. It was clear I needed to change course. 'I see what you're driving at,' I said. 'But what you're describing isn't the same as the armed forces. I don't approve of the military. Wars don't bring peace. They just make things worse.'

I still believe this is the case. Judaism has developed a just war theory which parallels the Christian view. This theoretical framework is currently used by Orthodox rabbis in Israel in their defence of the Jewish state's actions. But, like you, I have serious doubts whether war can ever be justified. Violence seems to lead to further acts of violence, as is illustrated by the history of the Middle East over the last century. I think a distinction needs to be made between individual actions where a violent response can be justified, as in the case of an axe-wielding rapist (I would use a revolver but attempt to maim an intruder rather than kill him), and the use of organised military force. Traditional Judaism does not countenance such a moral distinction. But I think it is none the less valid.

As you note, the traditional just war theory specifies that military action should only be undertaken if the results outweigh the consequences of war. In the modern world, with the possibility of nuclear conflict, it is difficult to envisage how this could ever be the case. You make this point, and I think it is of particular importance in assessing the struggle between Israelis and Palestinians. It is well known that Israel possesses a nuclear arsenal. The danger is that the Middle East may prove to be the stage for an apocalyptic encounter between Jews and Muslims. I agree with you that the world of Augustine, as well as that of the rabbis of old, is far removed from the realities of modern globalisation and the New World Order as envisaged by hawks in the American and British governments. Today there is a massive march taking place in London against the visit of President Bush. If I weren't here in wild Wales writing to you, I would be joining the ranks of this anti-war coalition. Like those protesters, I cannot see how the onslaught against Iraq has in any way eliminated global terrorism. There are, I believe, resources in our two traditions — despite the advocacy of warfare in Judaism and Christianity — which can point us in the direction of peace.

Dan

6.5 *22 November 2003*

'THEY CREATE A DESOLATION ...'

Dan,

Even though we were in 'wild Wales' last week writing letters — among other things! — and not marching against the war in London, the reality was still with us even in the lonely hills. A few yards away from where we were both lecturing was an anti-war demonstration, calling on President Bush to 'go home'. What is striking in the global anti-war coalitions is the conviction *that war solves nothing*. It reminded me of the words of the Caledonian chieftain in the Highlands, as the Roman army advanced, describing the effects of Roman 'civilisation' to his troops before battle, as described by the historian Tacitus: 'They create a desolation and they call it peace.'[7]

It is a familiar refrain to both our traditions. Jeremiah cried, 'They cry peace, when there is no peace', a cry reiterated by Martin Luther. As we witness the daily destruction of the infrastructure of Iraq, the inability of Afghanistan to crawl back to stability after being bombed by America and Britain, the struggles in the Balkans, and the deadlocked situation in Palestine, what new resources can we bring to the situation?

I suggest that both our traditions have a rich treasury in terms of the conviction that there is *no peace without justice. Justice, Only Justice* is the title of Naim Ateek's book calling for justice for the Palestinians.[8] But if we are true to the hopes for this book, we recognise the claims on both sides. Richard Harries, the Bishop of Oxford, writes that it is very easy for Christians to condemn the Israeli government and its policies and to side uncritically with the Palestinians.[9] It would be to call on the biblical story of the small David (Palestine), pitted against the mighty Goliath (Israel), backed by the might of the United States. And there is more than a ring of truth in the analogy, especially when we factor in the daily dehumanising restrictions which define the lives of the Palestinians. But there is a danger of falling anew into anti-Semitism here. There is also a danger of ignoring the complexity of the situation. Often it is assumed to be a conflict only between Jew and Muslim — but many Palestinians are Christians, although increasingly Christians are leaving the country.

Only by recognising the suffering on both sides, the claims, struggles, losses and bereavements, is there any hope of moving forward in a situation where, tragically, there seems only hatred and despair. (I do not ignore the efforts of peace groups that fos-ter prayer, conversation and support across the divide; or the efforts of inter-faith groups in this country in solidarity with them.) In a situation where the preaching of non-violence would not be heard, how is peace with justice to be achieved? I recall that Gandhi's son was a member of the South African ANC (African National Congress) when Nelson Mandela and the other leaders took up the armed struggle. Hitherto that struggle had been non-violent. Slowly the townships were locked into a vio-lence that seemed to be interminable. Young people knew no other reality. But, as we know, this was all turned around, and from a position of despair, not only was the political situation changed, but the process of Truth and Reconciliation was initiated and led by Archbishop Tutu. It was achieved through the belief that by hearing the stories of both sides in a safe space, by a qualitative lis-tening, a new situation could be created which would enable the possibility of justice. Is this what the religions could bring? An insistence that in the midst of revenge and hatred, trust can still be established by the hearing of stories, memories and hopes? This would be the hope that *out of the desolation, peace could still be possible.*

Mary

6.6 *28 November 2003*

BARRIERS TO RECONCILIATION

Mary,

The Middle East offers a salient example of how difficult it is to reconcile competing political claims. On the Israeli side, the Zionist argument is that the Jewish people have a religious and historical right to the land of Israel. Given that the Jewish nation existed for over 1,000 years in *Eretz Israel* (the Land of Israel), Israel is the natural homeland of the Jewish people. This is what David Ben-Gurion, the first prime minister of Israel, said in Tel Aviv when he read out the Scroll of Independence on 14 May 1948: 'The Land of Israel was the birthplace of the Jewish people. Here their spiritual, religious and national identity was formed. Here they achieved independence and created a culture of national and universal significance.'[10]

He went on to stress that when the nation was exiled from Palestine in 70CE by the Romans, Jews continued to remain faithful to Israel in all the countries of their exile. In recent decades, he pointed out, Jewish pioneers returned to *Eretz Israel*, reclaimed the wilderness, revived the Hebrew language, built cities and villages, and established a vigorous community. Eventually, the Zionist Congress, inspired by Theodor Herzl, proclaimed the right of the Jewish people to national revival in their own country.

This right, he went on, was acknowledged by the Balfour Declaration of 1917, reaffirmed by the Mandate of the League of Nations, and eventually recognised by the General Assembly of the United Nations. Thus, he concluded, the Jewish people have a 'self-evident right to be a nation like all other nations in its own sovereign state'.

From the Palestinian side, however, such claims have no force. Our colleague in Lampeter, Dawoud El-Alami (with whom I have written a guide to the Palestine—Israel conflict), has accused the Jewish people of stealing land from the indigenous population and trampling on their rights. Jews, he alleges, do not have a legitimate claim to the land of Palestine since the land did not belong to them — rather, it was the possession of the majority population living there at the end of the nineteenth century. Israel, he alleges, is an apartheid state which is concerned only to protect the rights of world Jewry:

> The creation of the apartheid state that is Israel represents the ultimate victory of the extreme separatist notions pro-pounded by Nazism. Is not the very concept of a Jewish state the ultimate in discrimination ... The state built by a people who have long been victims institutionalizes a form of ethnic and religious discrimination that would be unacceptable in any other modern state. [11]

Such conflicting claims cannot be resolved through discussion and debate. Even in academic circles, this conflict cannot be discussed without emotional outbursts. At a recent forum at Nottingham University, for example, I participated in a public debate about this issue, but the Palestinian side was vehement in their condem-nation of the Jewish cause. Having no sympathy for Israel, they castigated the prime minister Ariel Sharon and his government, and refused to listen to any defence of Israel's actions in the past or present.

Is it surprising that violence has taken the place of reasoned dialogue? You write about the need for a Truth and Reconciliation Commission like that which existed in South Africa. I agree with you. There have been deeply serious faults on both sides. Yet I cannot see how either Israelis or Palestinians will be able to recognise their faults as well as the suffering of others and take steps to create a better world. Isaiah's vision of a utopian, celestial city should inspire us, but it must do more than that. We need to be shown how to repent of our past misdeeds, to forgive our enemies, and to build a future in which swords can be turned into pruning hooks, and war be no more.

Dan

6.7   1 December 2003

BEYOND DESPAIR

Dan,

I read the book that you and our colleague Dawoud El-Alami have written together. Even though I found it a very valuable introduction to the history of the conflict, I found the debate with which you finished most depressing. It did not seem as if there were meeting points at all. *Just impasse.* Your last letter conveyed the same message. As I write to you today, the Christian Church has begun the season of Advent, just as the Muslims are finishing Ramadan. As you are aware, this is a season of great hope that looks forward to the Second Coming of Christ and New Creation. The prophecies of Isaiah are reinterpreted to convey this sense of great expectation.

And this has great influence on our topic. Picking up your last sentence — 28 November — you say that 'we need to be shown how to repent of our past misdeeds'. I agree. And this is our challenge. If our interchange is to mean anything, we cannot remain at the level of impasse. Yet it seems an impossible task. Bishop Richard Harries, in the book I cited earlier, *After The Evil*, describes his attempt, at a Solidarity with Israel rally in Trafalgar Square in 2002, to maintain fairness to both sides of the conflict. He suggested that 'when an 18 year old girl straps bombs around herself to blow up herself and ordinary people going about their daily business in cafés or buses, whatever else this was, it was an act of desperation.'[12]

But the crowd booed at that point and cried 'Not despair but hate.' If, as you say, repentance is the way forward, *who repents of what?* I suggest, for starters, that Christians reflect on their support for the foundation of the state of Israel and realise the part that Christian fundamentalism and Zionism has played in the struggle. This has been around for a long time, even before the Balfour Declaration and the founding of the state of Israel — since the eighteenth and nineteenth centuries in Britain and Ireland. Canon Naim Ateek, Director of the Sabeel Ecumenical Liberation Theology Centre in Jerusalem, shows how the largest number of Western Christians base their support for Israel on their understanding and interpretation of the Bible: 'to be faithful to Israel is to be faithful to God.'[13] He shows how Christian Zionists believe that God's clock is ticking, announcing the approaching end of history. They anticipate the battle of Armageddon and the annihilation of millions of people. The great social reformer Lord Shaftesbury (a conservative evangelical) also encouraged the Jews to return to Israel on these grounds. An important figure in the 1880s was the Reverend William Heckler, Anglican chaplain in Vienna: he saw the Zionist project as ordained by God to fulfil the prophetic scriptures. Although he arranged meetings with the Turkish Sultan and the German Kaiser, it was his contacts with the British élite and ultimately Arthur Balfour that would lead to the famous declaration in 1917. Thus did Christian Zionism acquire international legitimacy.[14]

This kind of argument has little to do with the claims of the Jewish people to live in their ancient land, and much to do with imperialist versions of Christianity. As such it has been a disaster for the Christians of the Holy Land. The late Michael Prior wrote: '50,000 [Christians] were among the 750,000 Palestinians expelled from [what became] the State of Israel.'[15]

The history of Christian Zionism reveals the kinds of complex journeys of repentance needed if 'swords are ever to be turned into ploughshares'. Acknowledging complicity in the injustices of the past is a necessary step in confronting the impasse of the present. And mostly Christian churches have been silent. This is not the silence that Christians sing about on Christmas Eve, in the famous carol, but a silence of complicity and denial. A silence that will never lead us *beyond despair* and impasse.

Mary

6.8   *2 December 2003*

THE WALL

Mary,

As you may know, every year Dawoud and I stage a debate for our students: Dawoud presents his perspective and I outline the

Zionist case. Invariably we disagree over the most fundamental issues. In his view, Israelis are thieves who have stolen land from their rightful owners. To prove his point, he brings in the deeds of his family's property in the Jewish state. These documents, he insists, demonstrate that the land which has been confiscated by the Israeli government rightfully belongs to his family. Not surprisingly, most of the students are persuaded by his passionate plea for justice.

I, too, am sympathetic to the Palestinian cause, but there is another side to the argument. The Jewish people have been continually subjected to thousands of years of persecution and murder. They were a dispossessed people for nearly two millennia. Yet the land of Israel was their homeland in ancient times. The patriarchs sojourned there, and Joshua led the people there after wandering in the desert for forty years. Once they inhabited the land, they were ruled over by a series of kings for hundreds of years. And after their return from exile in the sixth century BCE, they rebuilt the Temple and dwelt in Judea for centuries until their rebellion against Roman rule was crushed in 70 CE. Thus, for over 1,000 years the Jewish nation lived in the Middle East. In subsequent centuries, Jews expressed their longing to return to Zion through prayer for the coming of a messianic redeemer.

Israel and Jewish consciousness are therefore inextricably linked: this is a fact that Dawoud and other Palestinians refuse to accept. In their view, the land belongs to those who inhabited it prior to the rise of Zionism. Despite the decision of the United Nations that Palestine was to be partitioned, Arab nations simply refused to acknowledge the right of Jewry to create a state in the Middle East. Instead, they have insisted on Palestinian rights, and castigate the Jewish community for its hard-heartedness. Suicide bombers are (as Bishop Harries pointed out) desperate. But I think the crowd was right, too: they were filled with hatred. So, too, are Israelis who have been compelled to mourn their dead because of the actions of these Muslim martyrs.

Intoxicated with anger and feelings of revenge, both Israelis and Palestinians seek to destroy one another. Rightfully fearful of Palestinian intentions, the Israeli government is currently in the process of creating a wall which will separate Jew from Arab. Its purpose is to protect Israelis from their enemies. This structure symbolises the inability of Jew and Palestinian to find a means of reconciliation. You write of the need to go beyond despair. But how is this admirable goal to be achieved given the attitudes of Israelis and their Arab neighbours?

Recently, I appeared on television with a distinguished Palestinian journalist. We were instructed to engage in dialogue with one another. But, as I began my defence of Jewish aspirations, I was cut off by the Palestinian. Vehemently he accused the Israeli government of criminality and brutality. There was no way I could interrupt this flow of venom. The presenter was overwhelmed by this diatribe. By the end of our allotted time, I had hardly said a word. Such an outburst was typical of the ways in which rational encounter is sabotaged by those who are emotionally caught up in this conflict. There is an impasse at present, and I simply cannot see any way it can be overcome. Christian Zionists certainly do not help when they defend the state of Israel on religious grounds. Their premillenialist assumptions about the state of Israel simply sidetrack the debate and in no way reassure the Jewish community of Christian aspirations.

Dan

6.9   3 December 2003

JUSTICE AND ONLY JUSTICE

Dan,

The television programme you describe must have been a really terrible experience. And very humiliating. Indeed, you are right to query my hope that it is possible to go *beyond despair*. Especially looking at the realities of ordinary life in Palestine. Here is how the 'Little Town of Bethlehem', beloved of the Christmas carol, was described by a journalist from the *Guardian* a few days ago:

> It is less than two months to Christmas and the streets of Bethlehem are empty. There are no tourists, no pilgrims. On Star Street many of the shops are closed. The market where the neighbouring villages brought their produce to

feed the town is deserted. The closures imposed by the Israeli army mean that the farmers cannot come into Bethlehem and Bethlehemites cannot leave the town. The monument to peace built to celebrate Bethlehem 2000 has been demolished by Israeli tanks. The International Peace Centre ... was used by the Israeli army as its head-quarters when it besieged the Church of the Nativity.[16]

Add to this the wall of separation (which you described in your letter) that is encroaching on Bethlehem — and don't forget this separates the Palestinians from their land, their olive groves and their water sources — and the picture is bleak indeed.

What prevents hope from being completely destroyed is the fact that other conflict situations have been overcome. The South African government *did* dismantle apartheid and succeed in carry-ing through the truth and reconciliation process. The fact that they had a statesman of the calibre of Nelson Mandela has a lot to do with it. Despite the fact that the Good Friday agreement is at present in danger of collapsing in Northern Ireland, considerable progress has been made in the decommissioning of weapons. And there is still political good will to press forward.

Justice, Only Justice is the title of Canon Naim Ateek's book, as I have mentioned.[17] He has been passionate for years about justice for the Palestinians but in a context of reconciliation of the two sides. The problem being, what could this mean — for both sides? The answers are complex, but surely faith traditions can offer some pointers. Naim Ateek calls for the rebuilding of trust and for the recognition of the principle 'love your neighbour as yourself'. We are a long way from this but I believe we should highlight steps on the way to a just peace.

First, I think it's important that we separate anti-Zionism from anti-Semitism. It is not being anti-Semitic or anti-Judaistic to oppose the occupation of the Gaza strip and the West Bank, and the continued settlements and the building of the wall. Second, we should highlight groups and personalities who are building trust and cooperation and trying to act as bridges. There are numerous inter-faith groups meeting in Israel/Palestine, sharing celebrations and faith stories across the traditions. Today's *Guardian*

carries the story of courageous Israeli pilots who have left the
army refusing to destroy innocent Palestinians, including many
children. There are irenic rabbis in Jerusalem like Rabbi Jeremy
Milgrom who grew up near Bethlehem. Here he movingly
describes a visit to a refugee camp with a Palestinian escort:

> My escort, Omar, stopped to show me a reservoir — he
> thought it was Turkish but I think it's older than that. For
> the first time in maybe twenty years I saw the beauty of
> the land, and I felt I had access to it, this time with a
> Palestinian, not as a conquering Israeli Jew, and maybe not
> so far down the road there is a possibility that we could
> explore the land together — it could happen.[18]

He gives a clue here to the future possibility of sharing the land in
peace. I know this seems a pipe dream at the moment. Then I think
we should place the impasse in the context of the wider so-called
'war against terrorism'. I know I'm over-quoting the *Guardian*
today(!), but Brian Klug, a founder member of the Jewish Forum
for Justice and Human Rights, points out that both anti-Jewish and
anti-Muslim feeling appears to be growing, exacerbated by many of
the conflicts we are discussing.[19] We have to resist both, as racism.
And a last point today: The South African process was called 'Truth
and Reconciliation'. It appealed to *truth-telling* as a necessary step.
Truth must be factored into achieving justice. Maybe we will never
know the truth behind the myths of origin of the land of Canaan.
But until Jews and Palestinians can create a *safe, violence-free* space
where they can share memories and histories of belonging to this
land in order to further their common interests and common
future, peace will continue to elude both peoples.

Mary

6.10   *5 December 2003*

BEYOND DESPAIR

Mary,
Nearly thirty years ago I was a rabbi in South Africa; many of my
congregants were rich Jews living in the suburbs of Johannesburg.

At a dinner party one evening, I met a criminal lawyer. Knowing I was interested in the racial problems of South Africa, he asked if I would like to visit a black township. After making the necessary arrangements, we set off from the lush suburbs. The township was a stark contrast. Black men, women and children roamed dirt-paved streets — there were no trees or shrubbery anywhere. Occasionally dogs with protruding ribs appeared, scavenging for food.

Following this dispiriting experience, I was determined to preach about apartheid even though I was forbidden to do so by the synagogue authorities. On Rosh Hashanah I delivered a sermon to a packed congregation in which I urged compassion for the black population. It is not enough to be rich Jews among poor blacks, I said. Our ancestors were slaves in Egypt; in each and every generation, I continued, Jews are obliged to struggle for the liberation of those who are oppressed and persecuted. As Jews, we must not become the Pharaohs of the modern world. Instead, the Jewish community must stand shoulder to shoulder with their black brothers and sisters and oppose all forms of racism.

In the days following this service, I was hounded by critics. I was told that I was an ungrateful guest. The president of the congregation informed me that my sermon was the worst he had ever heard. I was accused of insensitivity. A job offer which had been made previously was revoked. I was in serious trouble! When I left South Africa, I was convinced that one day tanks would roll through the Jewish suburbs and whites would be massacred. But I was wrong. Through an extraordinary process of negotiations between blacks and whites, truth-telling and eventual reconciliation was accomplished. I am still astounded that a revolution in South African life occurred without bloodshed. It is, as you emphasise, a shining example of the way in which bitter conflict can be overcome.

So the first thing I would say is that, despite the seemingly intractable obstacles to peaceful reconciliation, one should not despair. If a peaceful resolution were possible in South Africa, the same process could occur elsewhere: hatred can be overcome. This message of hope against hope is a central theme of the Jewish faith. The Jewish tradition points to God's kingdom as the goal of humankind: a world in which all peoples and nations turn away from injustice. This is not the hope of bliss in a future life, but the building of truth and peace among all peoples. Of course, such a notion is grounded in the theology of the past. And, as I have explained throughout our conversation, I can no longer subscribe to many of these ideas. Yet the symbol of Israel's mission to be a light to the nations can still illumine our path. In this quest, both Jews and Christians can join ranks, championing the cause of the oppressed, the afflicted and the persecuted. With regard to modern Israel, a growing number of Jews throughout the world have been deeply moved by the suffering of Palestinians; as a result, they have embarked on a process of dialogue and reconciliation. Such efforts can, I believe, serve as a model for those engaged in bitter conflicts elsewhere. This is particularly so in respect of the 'war against terrorism'. What is urgently required is encounter between the West and the Islamic world. We need to understand why we in Western countries are hated, and Islamic fundamentalists need to comprehend the ideology and value system of those they detest. So, despite my previous comments about the seemingly intractable problems of the Middle East, I do believe that progress can be made.

Dan

6.11 *8 December 2003*

RELIGIONS AND THE HOPE OF PEACE

Dan,

What a charmed life you must lead, to emerge from such threatening situations as the South African one unscathed! Daniel braves the lions' den quite frequently, it seems!

It seems from our last few letters that — despite the bleakness of the many conflict situations in the world today — we share a conviction that our religious traditions have positive resources to offer, both in their continual call to repentance, and in their visions of a harmonious just society, together with those vital moral principles enabling its attainment. I call this 'the dangerous memory of the peaceable Kingdom' — that seems often to be lost but is never completely so.

Alongside this the religions offer a precious quality — the resources to build trust. Your stories have emphasised implacable hatred based on lack of trust. It is a hatred with deep roots in a history of violence and victimisation, as the story of Israel/Palestine illustrates. The resulting level of dehumanisation makes trust impossible. But, 'Into the lives of these victimised people come religious outsiders, who in varying ways convey a sense of understanding and empathy for their fears and who have established reputations for honesty, discretion and integrity.'[20]

Without the kind of trust Archbishop Tutu was able to inspire, there would have been no possibility of even listening to painful stories in the Truth and Reconciliation Commission in South Africa. And second, the religions offer disciplines for personal transformation. They do not separate political from social and personal transformation but offer an integrated notion. The late Thomas Merton, a Trappist monk, and still an inspiration for the peace movement today, wrote that:

> The rush and pressure of modern life are a form, perhaps the most common form, of its innate violence ... The frenzy of the activist neutralises his work for peace. It destroys his own inner capacity for peace. It destroys the fruitfulness of his own work because it kills the root of inner wisdom which makes work fruitful.[21]

Both our faiths offer disciplines of prayer, contemplation, and guides to a principled life that form a steady and lasting foundation for effective action for peace. They inspire a *theocentric* love of humanity that can reach out to the other, the alien, ethnically different, and frequently hostile. And finally, they offer a symbolism that can inspire a passionate commitment to the kind of just peace and non-violence culture that each of us longs for. I'll end today with the words of a former President of Ireland, Mary Robinson, who, out of her Christian vision for reconciliation in that troubled country, invoked the ancient symbol of the fifth province:

as everyone knows, there are only four geographical provinces on this island.

The Fifth Province is not anywhere here or there … It is a place within each of us, that place that is open to the other, that swinging door which allows us to venture out and others to venture in … While Tara was the political centre of Ireland, tradition has it that this Fifth Province acted as a second centre, a necessary balance. If I am a symbol of anything I would like to be a symbol of this reconciling, healing Fifth Province.[22]

We urgently need symbols of reconciliation and leaders to embody them — in Israel, in Afghanistan, in Northern Ireland and in all war-torn places. In this Advent season of hope, may they arise!

Mary

7. The Environment

7.1 *11 December 2003*

REJECTING MARXISM

Mary,

In mystical Judaism, the expression *tikkun olam* refers to the restoration of the world. In traditional sources, it denotes the process whereby divine sparks are freed from captivity and reunited in the Godhead. Such a notion is dependent on a complex metaphysical theory concerning divine emanation and the shattering of the vessels into which light from God radiated when the cosmos came into being. In modern Judaism, the concept of *tikkun olam* is often used without such mystical connotations to designate the restoration of the natural order.

This reinterpretation provides a new framework for considering ecological issues that threaten modern society. Today, what is urgently required is a new ecological vision in which the world can be rejuvenated and restored. The dire ecological problems that threaten our planet require an urgent response. Now, some time ago I addressed these issues in a book entitled *On Earth as it is in Heaven: Jews, Christians and Liberation Theology*.[1] In the final chapter, I outlined a range of subjects which, I believed, are of crucial importance, including the catastrophic policies adopted by first world countries which have had a devastating effect on the environment.

It was my view then that modern society requires the incorporation of a socialist order based on Marxist principles. Referring to the writings of Christian liberation theologians (primarily of South American origin), I noted that these writers believe that Marxism can help them to understand the nature of exploitation:

in their view, class struggle is a dominant feature of modern life. To those who see life from below, conflict between classes is a social reality in which major forces are polarised. To be oppressed means to be in a situation of dependency; denied the opportunity of being architects of their own destiny, the weak are economically, politically and culturally subservient.

I went on to explain that if Marxism is seen as an instrument of analysis — a tool of social science — there should be no objection to its being employed by both Jews and Christians as a methodology of understanding oppression. Rather than distort our two faiths, the incorporation of a Marxist viewpoint in the social sphere can help to illuminate social reality. Today, however, I am not convinced that I was right. I wrote my book before the collapse of the Soviet Union and the widespread disillusionment with Marxism in former Communist countries. I think I was naïve in my evaluation of Marxism as a system of social analysis, and it was largely for this reason that I abandoned the socialist perspective of liberation theology. In the light of what we now know about the terrible abuses of power that occurred in Russia and elsewhere, it would be a mistake to perceive Marxist socialism as an ideal.

I wonder if you agree. From what I have read, it appears that you still subscribe to socialist principles and regard the world's problems as a result of capitalist forces and the insidious values of a market economy. Am I right that you seek to restructure society along socialist lines in order to remove what you see as the oppressive forces of capitalism and its exploitation of the world's poor? You often speak of a spiritual pilgrimage to a better world: is this one in which capitalism has been replaced by a more just and benevolent world order?

Dan

7.2   *12 December 2003*

NOT MARX — BUT GANDHI!

Dan,

First I want to say how inspired I am by the vision of *tikkun olam* — many people of all faiths see it not only as mystical (the divine spark in each human being) but also as capable of being opened up to include all creation, all living creatures and life forms. It is not unlike the vision of the eighth-century Orthodox St Maximus, who believed that there was a divine 'logos' or principle (but it could be a spark!) in all forms of life.

But in being so inspired I don't want to duck your challenge. I can see why you have moved beyond Marxism. Indeed, most Latin American liberation theologians have also moved beyond Marx, especially the women. Isn't it very striking that one of the leading theologians, Leonardo Boff, in his post-Earth Summit book, *Ecology and Liberation — A New Paradigm*, tried to move liberation theology on from its Marxist roots to an ecological framework?[2] It is now recognised that liberation theology initially factored into its analysis neither women nor the earth.

So when we speak about the market, it is not trading itself — as old as civilisation — but the current system of unregulated global capitalism that I oppose strongly.[3] Not only does this — and I mean specifically the World Bank, the International Monetary Fund (IMF) and the World Trade Organisation (WTO) — impoverish millions by its restrictions and 'structural adjustment' programmes, but because it is exclusively profit-oriented, it cannot afford any loyalty to place, or to the needs of the locality. How many times do you read of factories being relocated to yet another part of the world, when it becomes unprofitable to stay where they are? But it is not only the people of the two-thirds world who suffer in this way. Let us just look at this picture of the working conditions of employees in Silicon Valley in California — where they dump 6,000 PCs *a day*:

> In Silicon Valley workers get $8 an hour and are forced to live 75—100 miles away [from their place of work]. Work is temporary and insecure: Hewlett Packard are hostile to unionisation. Packers have double the usual accidents and complain of respiratory illnesses caused by dust and toxic toners.[4]

What keeps the market going in this seemingly unstoppable fashion is a compulsive, insatiable desire to consume material goods. Just look at our high streets at this time of year! Mammon can never be satisfied — the system depends on us acting on our unquenchable desires. All must be commodified, even life itself. But the earth and her resources are limited and if we continue in this way we are on a path of self-destruction. We already know that groundwater will run out in some areas by 2015.

That's why we need a different model, beyond Marxism and beyond socialism. It was Gandhi who pointed out that there is enough for each man's need, but not for each man's greed.

All religions carry warnings against human *hubris*, pride that defies divinely ordained limits. What I seek is an organic model for civilised life on earth, not a profit-oriented model. Or rather, I want to redefine profit, to mean something that will benefit the whole web of life, not merely the ambitions of an elite few. I want, like Gandhi, to recouple economics from its present narrow basis to ethics, an ethic of flourishing for all, especially vulnerable forms of life. Economics should be about the νομος (rule) of the οἰκια (household), only here the household means the well-being of the entire earth. It is not that I want to turn the clock back and turn us all into peasant farmers who spin our own clothes — as Gandhi did. Life has moved on. But we need to rethink our common lifestyles to live more sustainably, justly and — I believe — more joyfully. Gandhi had a talisman: in any action you take, *think of the poorest person you know and ask how this decision will affect him/her*. I would add to this — think, too, how it will affect the earth.

I believe both our faiths have much inspiration for the task. Tonight, here, we are celebrating an 'Alternative Nativity' — called *Alternativity*. Everything has to be locally sourced or fairly traded — and vegetarian. And the style is modelled on a *seder* supper, with prayers and blessings. It meant that the shopping was complicated — but if we are to change the present system, it will not only be hard work, but require huge leaps of imagination!

     Mary

7.3   *14 December 2003*

BEYOND MARX?

Mary,

Given the collapse of Communist regimes in the former Soviet Union, contemporary liberation theologians are right, I believe, to examine more critically the role of Marxism in their analysis of society. Yet, from what you say, I am not entirely convinced that you have gone beyond Marx in your evaluation of the relationship between the first and the third world. In pleading the case of the poor, liberation theologians previously focused on the plight of the oppressed in third world countries. The underdevelopment of these countries, they pointed out, is the consequence of the development of other countries. As Gustavo Gutiérrez noted in *A Theology of Liberation*: 'The dynamics of the capitalist economy lead to the establishment of a centre and a periphery, simultaneously generating progress and growing wealth for the few and social imbalances, political tensions, and poverty for the many.'[5]

In this work Gutiérrez stresses that authentic development can only take place if the domination of the great capitalistic countries is eliminated. A transformation is needed, he states, to change radically the conditions in which the poor live — the gradual conquest of true freedom, he argues, leads to the creation of a new man and a qualitatively different society.

Isn't such an analysis precisely what you are describing when you refer to factories being relocated to poorer parts of the world because of their unprofitability in Western countries? Your rejection of consumerism is, I believe, tied to the kind of Marxist theorising found in works of liberation theology of earlier decades. The high streets full of Mammon, which you deplore, are the result of a capitalistic culture which fosters unquenchable consumerism. You are right that our desires are never satisfied because of the economic imperative. You stress that we need a model beyond Marxism and socialism, but what I think you are proposing is essentially a new vision of socialism for the twenty-first century (which is as critical of capitalism as Marxism was in the last century). Gandhi's statement that there is enough for each man's need, but not for each man's greed, is a reformulation of Marx's dictum: to each according to his need.

Yet I would question whether such a vision is commensurate with the kind of affluence that is required to satisfy the material needs of the human race. I cannot understand how profit can be redefined in the way that you suggest. Both manufacturing and service industries simply cannot be driven by the quest to profit society as a whole. I think Adam Smith was right that workers are not motivated by benevolence; rather it is their self-interest which is the driving force. Further, Smith was correct to view the market mechanism as dependent on the intersection of the individual self-interests of employers with those of workers.

What you consider the unstoppable fashion for material goods is, I believe, a precondition for a healthy economy. It is not a vice, but a necessary basis for general prosperity. But I think you are right that unregulated global capitalism does pose serious dangers for modern society. What our faiths have to offer are important observations about the need for governmental regulation. This is of vital significance particularly with regard to ecological excess. Here, both Judaism and Christianity provide a religious framework for understanding the need to conserve and preserve the world's resources. The well-being of the entire earth matters, and there must be a careful balance between economic necessity and ecological concern. The image of Gandhi dressed in a homespun loincloth is an arresting image, but it does not provide a sensible solution to the perplexing and complex problems of a global economy.

Dan

7.4   16 December 2003

BEYOND MARXISM AND SOCIALISM TO ECO-MYSTICISM!

Dan,

I fear we are lurching further into disagreement! Yes, you are right: I think we have both recognised the limits of Marxism —

for me, the instrumental valuing of nature as a means of production is a major stumbling-block — but I'm moving beyond socialism too. It has serious limitations, in viewing nature as needing to
be transformed by production, and in leaving out women's role in
production and reproduction. There is no sense of nature/the
earth as of value in herself and as an active and responsive agent.
Both Marxism and socialism are rooted in philosophies of nature
that see her as inert matter, the backdrop to human activity, to be
used and shaped for human profit. So not only do we need a new
form of socialism that factors nature herself into the picture; we
need a new form of liberation theology where nature is seen as
the new poor, vulnerable, and in need of exactly the forms of solidarity that the 'old' liberation theology called for. As the ecofeminist theologian Sallie McFague wrote: 'Nature is, in our time, the
new poor — oppressed, victimised, deteriorating, excluded —
and deserves our solidarity in its vulnerability. We human beings,
especially some of us, have *made* nature poor, and we are being
called to redress some of our excesses.'[6]

But how and why should we do this? Because the current con-
sumerist system does not factor the limits of the earth herself into
its insatiable demands. I agree with you that all the great faiths
insist on limiting human greed and advocate restraint. But this is
not enough. That's why I propose an approach of eco-mysticism.
This means awe and wonder — all of this. It means an attitude of
contemplation and what Sallie McFague calls looking at nature
with 'a loving eye' instead of the eye that wants to dominate and
control.[7]

But what do we see with this 'loving eye'? Not merely beauty
or even nature's vulnerability, as the forests are ruined, and species
become extinct at an increasingly rapid rate. Eco-mysticism is not
a comfortable stance. We are caught up into the wildness and
otherness of nature. Last night I had a terrible dream about the sea
— after a discussion group talking about what kind of God the
sea revealed. My dream was about the power and destructiveness
of the ocean.

I began to think about the Book of Job and God's relationship
with creation. In my recent book I discussed how in chapters
38—41 we are given magnificent poetry, wild, untamed,

unrivalled by anything else in the Bible — and we are also given a cosmology radically different from the normal reading of the Book of Genesis.[8] As opposed to apparently being the summit of creation, here humanity is toppled from pride of place. Humans are placed alongside the animals and humbler forms of life. Radically different views of freedom, justice, the wisdom of creation and the gratuitousness of God's love are presented. This is no Walt Disney view of creation: its wildness, savagery and ambiguity are poured out before our eyes.[9] Where human beings have looked through the ages to conquering the land and taming the wilderness, God gives us the image of the baby vultures being taught to drink the blood of their prey and a place for the monsters of the deep. God displays intimate knowledge of the ways of birds — even the foolishness of the ostrich has a place in creation. Dissonance is revealed not only in the text but also in reality itself. Otherness, strangeness and the savagery of animals seem to be part of God's creation. All things may be connected — but not in the comforting way sometimes presumed by romanticists. It is not that the savagery and ambiguities of creation are any consolation to those threatened by earthquake, flood and drought. But a word of warning is given to us. In the powers human beings now have at our disposal to destroy the world with nuclear bombs, to clone human beings, to manipulate the genetic structures of the plant and animal world, we have taken God's role and challenged God's control of creation. Yet God's words to Job are clear:

> Have you commanded the morning? (38:12)
>
> Have you entered the storehouses of the snow? (38:22)
>
> Do you know when the mountain goats bring forth? (29:1)

The seemingly imperious tones of God recall humanity to a proper sense of humility and place. This is a God who gives new responsibilities in the current threatened situation of creation. A call to respect wildness and the needs of wild animals, not to hunt them to extinction, and an urgent imperative to hear the cries of the victims whose land has turned to desert and wilderness because of the unjust policies of governments or the greed of corporations. The voice of God to Job from the whirlwind calls us also to respect the total ecology of place: ecological rather than exclusively economic objectives must be a priority in judging new policies.

What I am calling an 'eco-mystical' stance is a radically different way of viewing the world. In it policies of global capitalism are seen as unavoidably destructive to the planet. But an alternative is offered.

Mary

⚬⊸⊙—⊙⊶

7.5   *20 December 2003*
AN I—THOU PERSPECTIVE

Mary,

I am sympathetic to your notion of 'eco-mysticism' — certainly there are reflections of such an idea in Jewish thought. You earlier referred to the writings of Martin Buber. In his seminal theological work, *I and Thou*, he argues that there are two fundamental attitudes that a person can take up toward the world. The first, I—It, is based on a detachment of the self from others in which knowledge is objectified. But in the second type of relationship, I—Thou, there is an encounter between the subjects in which each stands over against the other. For Buber, it is through such an encounter that God is met:

> Every particular Thou is a glimpse through to the eternal Thou: by means of every particular Thou the primary word addresses the eternal Thou. Through this mediation of the Thou of all beings fulfilment, and non-fulfilment, of relations comes to them: the inborn Thou is realised in each relation and consummated in none. It is consummated only in the direct relation with the Thou that by its nature cannot become It.[10]

For Buber, God has to be approached through an I—Thou relationship with all creatures: people, animals and even trees. In *Between Man and Man* Buber recounts an incident which illustrates the nature of such an encounter:

When I was eleven years of age, spending the summer on my grand-parents' estate, I used, as often as I could do it unobserved, to steal into the stable and gently stroke the neck of my darling, a broad dapple-grey horse. It was not a casual delight but a great, certainly friendly, but also deeply stirring happening ... I must say that what I experienced in touch with the animal was the Other, the immense otherness of the Other, which, however, did not remain strange like the otherness of the ox and the ram, but rather let me draw near and touch it.[11]

According to Buber, in modern society the I—It is eclipsing the I—Thou encounter. This is tragic, Buber believes, since a fulfilled human life requires the experience of I—Thou. This is particularly the case, I think, with regard to nature. As you indicate, human beings currently exploit the natural world for their own purposes. Nature is used and shaped by human beings. We have lost the reverence implicit in the I—Thou relationship. In that respect, I agree with Sallie McFague that nature is exploited and oppressed. What is needed is a new vision of the natural world freed from humanocentrism.

Here, I believe, the Bible can redirect us to responsible action. Even though I do not accept the metaphysical assumptions of the Book of Genesis, I think the biblical writers were right to stress the importance of human stewardship. In Genesis, we read that God brought all things into being. This theocentric orientation emphasises that creation is the result of God's action. Whatever may be subsequently claimed for all creatures, including humans, can only make sense within that basic perspective. Humans are not God — they are not made gods in creation and they are not the goal of creation.

The Bible asserts that God as Creator delights in differentiated being. The world is not made just for human beings. Though humans are made in God's image, this does not mean that they are free to act as they please — rather they are to serve nature. In Genesis 2, this is illustrated by the narrative concerning Adam and Eve. Adam is to look after the garden, till it and care for it. In other words, he is to act as God's deputy. In this context, human dominion over nature does not imply domination, but stewardship. An instrumentalist and utilitarian perspective robs us of the possibility of celebrating creation.

Such reverence for the Other — for nature in its multifarious forms — is urgently required: a humanocentric perspective of the natural world should be replaced by reverence and awe. We must reject the idea that 'man is the measure of all things' and that human wants, needs and satisfactions are the goal and purpose of creation. Here, I think, we can agree. However, the question remains how such an eco-mystic vision can be used as a check against the excesses of capitalism, and in what ways it can be applied to the numerous spheres of economic activity.

Dan

7.6   *21 December 2003*

RECOVERING FROM 'COSMIC HOMELESSNESS'

Dan,

I am so glad you admire Martin Buber — he has been and is a great inspiration to me in developing my theology of mutuality and reciprocity! I know and love the story of his childhood story of the horse. I'm also glad we share an *eco-mystical* approach and realise the need to show how this can provide 'a check to the excesses of global capitalism', as you say.

The answer is multifaceted. First of all, it involves understanding how damaged is the consciousness of anthropocentrism. What we have lost by subduing the earth and distorting our relationships with all species in the web of life is a sense that we are at home in the cosmos, that *the earth is our home*. There is a wonderful passage in Dostoevsky's novel *The Brothers Karamazov* where the young monk Alyosha recovers a cosmic consciousness, and it is a vital part in his spiritual journey. He goes late at night to the cell, where his mentor or *starets*, the saintly monk Zossima, is lying dead in his coffin. There follows an intense spiritual encounter of prayer with the dead *starets*. As he leaves:

> Alyosha did not step on the steps, but went down rapidly. His soul, overflowing with rapture, was craving for freedom and unlimited space. The vault of heaven, studded

with softly shining stars, stretched wide and vast over him ... The silence of the earth seemed to merge with the silence of the heavens, the mystery of the earth seemed to merge into the mystery of the stars ... Alyosha stood, gazed, and suddenly he threw himself flat upon the earth. He did not know why he was embracing it ... It was as though the threads from all those innumerable worlds of God met all at once in his soul. He had fallen upon the earth a weak youth, but he rose from it a resolute fighter for the rest of his life, he realised and felt it suddenly at the very moment of his rapture.[12]

'Cosmic homelessness' — or believing that our true home lies beyond the universe — has had a devastating effect on Christian theology. I freely admit that Christian rather than Jewish theology is to blame. There are key historical moments forming this consciousness. They include the heritage of Greek dualisms that undervalued the physical world in favour of the spiritual and intellectual dimension, as well as the disaster of the Black Death that swept through Europe wiping out so much of its population and destroying hope in embodied life on earth. Christians placed their hope beyond 'this vale of tears' in a heaven far removed from the earth.

But the mystical dimension need not locate itself beyond, but may point to God revealed — as to Alyosha — both in the mystery of creation as well as in its homely earthiness. The ecological mystic today is not so much the beholder of bright lights and voices — was she ever? — but someone who is seized by the wholeness and interconnectedness of creation as caught up in the sustaining energy of God. The late Trappist monk Thomas Merton experienced this epiphany of connectedness in a trip to the town of Louisville:

> In Louisville ... in the centre of the shopping district, I was suddenly overwhelmed with the realisation that I loved all those people, that they were mine and I theirs, that we could not be alien to one another even though we were total strangers. It was like waking from a dream of separateness, of spurious isolation in a special world, the

world of renunciation and supposed holiness ... I have the immense joy of being ... a member of a race in which God Himself became incarnate ... There is no way of telling people that they are walking round shining like the sun.[13]

Merton's experience is confined to human beings, but eco-mysticism includes all species in its vision and is discovered across a variety of sources — such as ecofeminist spirituality and Buddhist mysticism. As the response of an entire community to creation it is a profound if hidden strand of mainstream *Christian* theology — and you agree that it is also part of Jewish tradition. The creation spirituality of Hildegard of Bingen, singing of the greenness or *viriditas* of creation and the power of the greening Spirit as the life-giving source of creation, links mysticism and the community's action of praise. But the mystic today is as involved in the political struggle as in contemplative silence, since the struggle to allow the *earth* to experience a Resurrection story — that the waste lands of the earth may blossom anew — is as much *political* as mystical.

In participating in such a process humanity recovers its rightful place in the cosmos: this is both joyful and humbling and provides a stance to challenge the destructive policies of global capitalism.

Mary

7.7   *22 December 2003*

ANIMAL WELFARE

Mary,
The key issue is anthropocentrism: we need to liberate ourselves from *hubris*, from the perpetual desire to think more highly of ourselves and to assume that our own estimation of human needs should be the main or sole criterion by which we judge the treatment of the created order. Today there is a widespread assumption that humans should dominate the earth, and that we have the unquestioned right in all circumstances to decide how certain species of life should exist, how they should live, and indeed

whether they should survive. The biblical doctrine of 'domina-tion' has been translated into notions of knowing better, or having the right to impose our own views and standards.

In all this, we have forgotten that the concept of domination in Genesis 1:26 is limited in scope. Scripture imposes obligations of stewardship, rather than providing a license for exploitation. As I have suggested, service rather than mastery is what is prescribed. This is not to say, however, that in some cases human interference in nature is desirable. Yet, what is objectionable is the prospect of ever-increasing human management, control and manipulation. There is an alternative spiritual and moral insight deeply embed-ded within our traditions: the value of letting be.

With regard to the animal kingdom, I think there are a num-ber of key elements in the Jewish tradition which are supported by biblical texts:

1. God is the Creator of all things, not just humankind, but every moving creature that has life.
2. Animals are given their own place in the world. The whole world does not belong to humankind, and humankind has no right to the whole earth.
3. Animals are under the care of humanity which exists to care for the earth.
4. Animals are intended ideally to live in peace and harmony.

Anxious to develop the theme of animal welfare, the rabbis for-mulated the principle of *tsaar baalei hayyim* (pain of living crea-tures). Although this principle is not explicitly formulated in Scripture, it is based on biblical teaching concerning the compas-sionate treatment of animals. Even though animals were used for sacrifice in ancient times and have been consumed as food, rab-binic sources stress that human beings must be compassionate in their treatment of God's creatures. Such an attitude is expressed most forcefully in Hasidic stories. A story is told, for example, about the founder of Hasidism, the Baal Shem Tov, who in his youth owned an undernourished horse that could hardly pull a wagon laden with goods. Because he was unable to afford another horse, he often descended from the wagon and pushed behind out of consideration for the animal.

Another story concerns Zussya of Anapole, who set off on a mission to collect funds for the redemption of captives. When he stopped at an inn, he found a large cage with many kinds of birds in one room. He saw that the birds wished to fly out of the cage and escape. Overcome with pity, he said to himself, 'Here you are, Zussya, walking your feet off to ransom prisoners. But what greater ransoming of prisoners can there be than to free these birds from their prison?' He then opened the cage and the birds flew away.

When the innkeeper saw that the cage was empty, he was furious and asked the people in the house who had released the birds. They replied that there was a man loitering around who appeared to be a fool. It was he that must have done this. The innkeeper then shouted at Zussya, 'You fool! How could you rob me of my birds and make worthless the good money I paid for them?' Zussya replied, 'Have you not read these words in the Psalms: "His tender mercies are over all His work"?' The innkeeper beat Zussya and then threw him out of the house. But Zussya went away serenely.[14]

Such stories emphasise that non-human creatures should be treated with kindness: they are part of the created order, and as such have their own integrity. Our relationship with them should not be expressed wholly in terms of utility and subordination. The richness of language, imagery, fable and legend within the Jewish tradition can help provoke a more imaginative spiritual engagement with animals. In our dealings with the created order, I believe, we must strive to fashion an ethical sensitivity which transcends the modern quest to dominate and control the world around us.

Dan

7.8 *Christmas Eve, 24 December 2003*

NOT ANTHROPOCENTRISM, BUT NOT
ANDROCENTRISM EITHER!

Dan,

I totally agree with you that anthropocentrism is at the root of the problem but I would go further still. Just let me pause slightly at this moment in time. It is Christmas Eve, and that has special meaning for our theme. For example, there is a medieval legend that on this evening, animals talk — or rather, they talk in a way that humans can understand. Restored creation maybe? In Christianity we also have the Christmas crib in our churches and homes, where the ox and the ass protect the cradle or manger of the Christ child. This was how St Francis used the inspiration of Isaiah:

> The ox knows its owner;
> And the ass its master's crib. (Isa. 1:3)

This not only invokes a cherished tradition, but a forgotten strand, in which animals are faithful where humans beings have strayed from the knowledge of God. It's tempting for me to pursue this strand through the lives of the Celtic saints where communication and compassion for animals is witnessed, in line with the stories you cite from Jewish tradition.

But I want to move us on to something more radical. You wrote that you want a shift of consciousness from *anthropocentrism* to recognising the value of the non-human in creation. I presume you mean plants and trees along with animals and birds? I agree but want to take it further. The problem is that you could tackle anthropocentrism (which allows dominion and domination) and still remain within a very conservative tradition as regards the earth. In fact, this is a reformist approach. I plead for a fully earth-centred approach. For this you have to recognise that anthropocentrism is built on *androcentrism* — or the male domination of the earth. This goes back to an early identification of women with nature, and with animal nature. Think how many derogatory animal names are predicated on women. Carol Adams, in her book *The Sexual Politics of Meat*, traces these links in an arresting way.[15] Think of the many texts of the Fathers of the Church who identify women with earth, sexuality, emotion and animal nature — but far from positively. Men, by contrast, are identified with culture and with transcendence. And God, traditionally, is a transcendent God, far removed from degrading matter and the embodied world. Immanence by contrast is negatively imaged, as inert matter.

THE ENVIRONMENT 155

We are speaking here of deeply rooted philosophic dualisms inherited from Plato and Aristotle, but their inheritance is powerful and still with us. When we talk of 'earth' and 'nature' it is important to clarify what we mean. Too often a disparaging of nature cloaks a disparaging of women. Nature has often meant merely the background to human (i.e. male) endeavour. To recover from this it is not enough to move on from anthropocentrism to a stewardship approach because this does not shift humanity from centre stage, and in no way addresses the links between the disparaging of nature and the disparaging of women. To move on we need a fully earth-centred approach. In a previous letter I called for an eco-mystical approach. I link this now with an *ecofeminist* approach, because this places the links between women and nature in a positive framework, calling for recognition of what that means in the context of our major global ecological concerns.

And on the night when Christianity celebrates the flesh-taking of God, that is not a bad starting point!

Mary

7.9 *28 December 2003*

ECO-MYSTICISM IN ACTION

Mary,

I am sympathetic to your quest to adopt a fully earth-centred approach in which attempts to disparage earth as well as women are eliminated. Yet it seems to me that what is of crucial importance is to bring about a revolution in consciousness. This involves a recognition of the ways in which modern exploitation of the earth's resources is causing serious harm to nature. Adopting an eco-mystical approach to the natural world, there are, I believe, practical steps that we can take as individuals to halt environmental degradation. In considering the problems facing us, let me refer to a most informative study of *Judaism and Ecology* edited by Aubrey Rose. In a chapter entitled 'Action on the Environment: A Practical Guide', Vicky Joseph, Social Issues Coordinator of the

Reform Synagogues of Great Britain, makes numerous suggestions of ways in which we can contribute to ecological balance:[16]

As householders, she writes, we can reduce energy consumption by:

1. doing more to insulate and draught-proof homes
2. choosing the most energy efficient model when replacing boilers, fridges, freezers, washing machines, and dishwashers
3. switching off lights and electrical appliances, and using low energy light bulbs
4. setting temperature at reasonable levels

As travellers, our decisions influence greenhouse gas emissions as well as air pollution. Ways to help include:

1. adopting less aggressive driving habits to save fuel
2. keeping cars well-tuned
3. choosing cars fitted with a catalytic converter
4. buying more fuel-efficient cars
5. sharing car journeys with colleagues and friends
6. using the train or bus when possible
7. walking or cycling when safe
8. using unleaded petrol

As shoppers, we can influence retailers and manufacturers. We can help by:

1. buying recycled products when possible
2. not buying over-packaged goods, or goods in packaging that cannot be recycled
3. making our views known to retailers and manufacturers
4. not purchasing goods made of scarce materials

As consumers, we can reduce the need for waste tips or for domestic incinerators by reducing our waste. We can:

1. recycle all our paper, rags, cans and glass, pressing our local authority or supermarket chain to provide better recycling facilities
2. make the most of the produce we use by reusing plastic carriers and returning egg boxes

3. dispose of fridges containing CFCs in accordance with local authority guidance
4. dispose of batteries, waste motor oil or household chemicals

As gardeners we can:

1. encourage urban wildlife with ponds, native trees, shrubs and flowers
2. use garden chemicals only when necessary
3. dispose of unwanted chemicals responsibly
4. recycle kitchen waste by making garden compost
5. choose alternatives to peat when possible
6. use bark chips or leaf mould for soil conditioning
7. buy bulbs from reputable dealers

As good neighbours we can help by:

1. keeping noise to levels that do not disturb
2. putting litter in bins or taking it home
3. keep dogs from fouling public places
4. improving the appearance of our home and garden
5. protecting the historic features of homes and streets
6. avoiding bonfires or smoking when it affects others

As investors we can:

1. seek information about the environmental practices of the companies we invest in

As responsible citizens, we can:

1. take steps to inform ourselves of the facts relating to our environment
2. join organisations active in the environment
3. involve ourselves in local planning
4. alert relevant bodies to possible breaches of planning or pollution controls
5. take care not to pollute the city, countryside, rivers or sea with non-biodegradable litter
6. encourage authorities to provide facilities for recycling
7. make our views on the environment clear

These recommendations highlight the fact that, as individuals, we can help to improve the quality of the environment. Such suggestions do not call for a radical revision of the social order. Rather, there is a recognition that modern life will continue as normal, yet by taking small steps we can make an inestimable difference to the world that surrounds us.

Dan

7.10   *30 December 2003*

WAR IS WAR ON THE EARTH

Dan,

I agree we need a revolution in consciousness — and agree that there is much we can do on a personal level to make eco-mysticism work as a lifestyle option. But what I don't agree with is that this will not involve a radical revision of world social order. I have argued already that we have lost a cosmology — meaning an awareness of being embedded in a cosmos, with myriads of interconnections. The recovery of cosmology *will* demand a changed world order. It will require us slowly and painfully to rebuild the lost connections.

Let us recall all we have said about war and peace in the last weeks. Who factors in the damage to the earth in the decision to make war? Who counts in the suffering caused by ruining the water systems, loss of food supplies — in fact the collapse of all the infrastructures, as we are now witnessing in both Iraq and Afghanistan? So has it ever been, that invaders chose moments when maximum damage would be caused to their enemies in terms of ruining their food supplies — from the wars of ancient Greece to recent wars in the Balkans. There was no harvest in Kosovo because farmers were fighting for their lives instead of sowing their crops.

The link between war and water supplies is tragically evident and water scarcity — like that I see each year in the semi-desert of Rajasthan — will provide an increasing source of conflict. Scarcity is faced in India, north-eastern China, Pakistan, much of South America, Mexico and Central America — whereas in the

Middle East and parts of Africa the threat to life increases.[17] The World Bank says that 80 countries, with 40 per cent of the world's population, suffer from water scarcity. Levels of water pollution in Eastern Europe are dangerously high and even Ireland, with plentiful supplies of rain and legendary lakes and water sources of great beauty, has had to face the fact that, within a generation, her rivers have gone 'from being almost pristine pure and clear to overblown imitations of open sewers and chemical drains'.[18]

As you are only too well aware, in Palestine water is right at the heart of the conflict. Because Israel and Palestine share the same water sources, the Jordan river with its tributaries, and the mountain aquifer fed by rainfall on the West Bank, supply one-third of Israel's needs and *all* the running water that Palestinians in the West Bank receive. Since Israel occupied the Golan Heights in 1967, it has controlled the Jordan river, destroyed the Palestinian pumps, and prevented the farmers from utilising the river's water resources by closing large areas of Palestinian farmland and imposing military orders that control Palestinian sources, thus preventing access. The Oslo agreement for a more equitable distribution has not been implemented. The resulting suffering of the Palestinian people, who have no running water for most of the year, is almost indescribable. The effects on sanitation and the running of a medical system are appalling.[19]

Making the connections between war and damage to the earth demands *both* changed consciousness and changed world order. Simply recycling our bottles and using less energy are insufficient unless they form part of our re-education and reconversion to the earth. And our churches and synagogues — all faith communities — need to cooperate in this process. We in the Christian churches have been unbearably slow in making these connections. As Leonardo Boff wrote to the churches after the Rio summit in 1992:

> We dare not deny our role as churches in the crisis which now overwhelms us. We have not spoken the prophetic word ourselves. Indeed we did not even hear it when it was spoken by others of late, including a number of scientists. Much less do we hear the cries of indigenous

peoples who have told us for centuries that modernity would foul its own nest and even devour its own children. We need to mourn and repent ... We plead for forgiveness and pray for a profound change of heart.[20]

Can we do it now? And do it together — or is it too late?
  Mary

7.11   *31 December 2003*

CHANGING THE WORLD

Mary,

You argue that there needs to be a new world order. But what is this to be? Previously you stated that we must go beyond Marx. In your view, Gandhi's philosophy of non-violence and simplicity can serve as a symbol of liberation. Yet I am sure that you do not advocate such an approach to solving the economic problems of the modern age. So you are not a socialist, nor an Indian utopian idealist. But what then are you proposing? You cite Boff's plea for a profound change of heart. Yet it is not at all clear what this will entail.

Of course you are right about the interconnection between war and ecological devastation. This is true everywhere. And the threat of nuclear war is even more terrifying than what has already occurred. However, I am not certain what we as Jews and Christians are to do about such conflict. To take the case of the Middle East, what exactly are you proposing? You are critical of Israeli policies concerning water resources for the Palestinians. All this is the result of over a century of conflict between Palestinians and the Jewish nation. Of course we should work for peace ... but what does this mean in practice? Simply citing the words of Isaiah about turning spears into pruning hooks will not remove the intractable dilemmas of the Middle East. And this applies to all current world conflicts which have brought about ecological disaster. We cannot wave a magic wand and banish the capitalistic structures that bind together the economic order of the modern world. And, even if we could do so (which is impossible!), the consequences would in all likelihood lead to impoverishment and economic collapse.

What I believe is possible, however, is for a new consciousness about the natural world to replace the anthropocentrism of the past. Increasingly there has been a growing awareness of the delicate ecological balance of which we are a part. It is widely recognised today that people are destroying the environment on which all living things depend for their existence. Many species are endangered as a result of human activity. The planetary climate may already have been destabilised. The protective ozone layer has been damaged. Forests have been destroyed. Species have been threatened or have become extinct. Pollution in various forms is widespread.

I think that we agree that, to counter these trends, humanity needs to embrace a form of eco-mysticism which regards the environment as sacred. To use Martin Buber's concept of relationship, we should see the natural world as a *Thou*, rather than an *It* to be manipulated for human purposes. Adopting such a stance, there is much we can do to develop a sensitive, caring attitude to creation. As Jews and Christians, we can support local environmental groups, arrange for an energy audit, use only environmentally friendly cleaning and building materials, avoid using non-biodegradable, non-recyclable disposable utensils, use recycled paper, etc. Moreover, we should encourage governmental agencies to review their policies and programmes to ensure that all environmental concerns are properly taken into account. By so doing, we will not bring about a new world order, but none the less we can in very simple ways bring the moral and religious insights of our two traditions to bear on the ecological problems that beset our fragile world.

Dan

8. Gender

※⟡⟡⟡⟡⟡⟡※

8.1 *New Year's Day, 1 January 2004*
BEYOND PATRIARCHY TOO?

Dan,

New Year's Day is traditionally a time of new beginnings. Isn't that what our last few letters have been calling for — in terms of altered consciousness, of changed lifestyle, of moving from anthropocentrism to an eco-centric approach that we called *eco-mysticism*? But haunting our letters has been an unexamined area — I've alluded to this from time to time and attempted to move into a more radical critique in terms of an ecofeminist approach. What I mean is, that in our attempts to move towards reconciliation, the question of relations between women and men is crucial. We do not start from a blank sheet but from a history of disordered — even diseased — relations created by the inherited patriarchal system in which both our faiths are implicated. Indeed all religions are implicated; all operate within some form of patriarchy.

There is no way of telling if the earliest civilisations were truly egalitarian — although some try to prove this. Goddess feminists for example, like Carol Christ and Merlin Stone, argue that prior to patriarchal civilisations were goddess religions, where women had a more respected position and relationships were more egalitarian.[1] Some anthropologists argue that patriarchy arose when society changed from food gathering and gardening to plough agriculture. What is uncontested is that by around 1000 BCE we have evidence of patriarchally ordered cultures where women were subjugated by men without legal status in their own right, enjoying limited inheritance rights on being widowed, where male children were preferred to female, and where women's sexuality was controlled by their husbands or male relatives. Woman's cultural role was limited: lacking education — with rare exceptions — she had no political or professional role and her value was determined in terms of procreation. This system was well established by 600 BCE. Even women's skills and achievements, the few examples of leadership and literary prowess, were usually erased from 'official' memory.

This system was reinscribed into early modern law codes and continued to define women in Europe and North America until the women's movements of the nineteenth and twentieth century.[2] But even though there have been great changes in terms of education and cultural and political involvement, in many parts of the world nothing has changed. I am about to leave for the desert of Rajasthan in just over 24 hours' time, and I am preparing for the shock I know awaits me as I see the realities of the lives of its poor rural women.

But what concerns us both is the extent to which our faith traditions are responsible for maintaining an unjust system. A system that is damaging for *both* men and women — since patriarchy, as I said, is *disordered* relation. In July we were writing about the so-called 'maleness' of God. But that is not the only patriarchal aspect of the two traditions. The image of God as patriarchal Lord sanctions the hierarchical relations of male over female, fathers over children and free men over slaves. Christianity inherited patriarchy from both Greek philosophy and the Hebrew worldview. So the limited status of women under Jewish law is carried on through the concept of male headship and superiority, where the Fathers of the Church — specifically St Augustine — doubted that woman could be created in the image of God, unless taken together with her husband.[3] So many consequences followed: as inferior beings, women are more prone to sin, it is argued, less rational and therefore more defined in terms of body and sexuality. They are certainly unworthy of spiritual leadership — as the current blocking of the ordination of women to the priesthood in the Roman Catholic Church shows.

Feminist theology challenges the idea that patriarchy is God's

will or part of the natural order. We argue that patriarchy is a construction that serves the interests of the powerful. We do not
merely argue that women have to be factored into an account of
history, politics or religion — an 'add women and stir' approach.
Rather, we argue that if we are to achieve a just society where
every woman, man, child — yes, and the non-human world
too! — has a rightful place, we have to dismantle hierarchies and
reconceive gender to make that society possible.

And that's a quite an agenda for the coming year.

Happy New Year!

    Mary

8.2   *2 January 2004*

JEWISH FEMINISM

Mary,

You are right that both of our traditions have been patriarchal in
character for centuries. It is not simply that God has been viewed
in male terms, but that the entire edifice of the Judeo–Christian
tradition has been based on the dominance of men. Today this
issue has become one of the most pressing problems in the Jewish
world as many Jewish women are attempting to reshape their personal lives as well as public institutions in the light of modern
feminism. According to these women, Jewish law discriminates
against them by exempting them from the obligation to observe
positive time-bound commandments as well as from participating
in public prayer, Torah reading and traditional study. Moreover,
such discrimination, they argue, extends to a variety of other areas
of Jewish life: marriage, divorce, sexuality outside marriage,
procreation, abortion and rape.

Some time ago, my wife and I wrote a book about the American
Jewish community, in which we included an interview with a
Jewish feminist who complained along these lines about the nature
of traditional Jewish life. Growing up in the East, she wrote:

> I had the archetypal experience, age four or five, in Coney
> Island of being taken to the corner Orthodox synagogue

and being pointed at: 'Get her out, get rid of her. She's a woman!' It really happened! I went and, as a little girl, I was allowed in the men's section with my dad. I looked three years older than I was anyway, so the day came when I had all these fingers pointed at me and my dad had to get me out of there … I know that Orthodox Judaism suits the traditional family … I certainly see the attractions for men. Perhaps if I were a man, I would be an Orthodox Jew. I think it's the only boys' club left. I mean, today you can't even segregate Elks meetings! And these guys in an Orthodox synagogue are having a great time! I think it's a racket! You have your wife waiting on you hand and foot. You're the king of the roost, and you have all these wonderful rituals. Honestly! For me it's deplorable.[4]

It is deplorable: there is simply no excuse for such discrimination in contemporary society. The Jewish tradition must be reformed, and in the non-Orthodox world enormous steps have been taken to alter such patriarchal attitudes. Over 30 years ago the first woman rabbi was ordained by the Hebrew Union College–Jewish Institute of Religion in Cincinnati, Ohio. Subsequently, the Reconstructionist, Conservative and Humanistic movements have ordained women to the rabbinate. In addition, women now serve as cantors in non-Orthodox congregations. Women also occupy positions of lay leadership within the various non-Orthodox movements. No longer are women prepared to be relegated to inferior positions within the synagogue or the Jewish community. Rightly they have pressed for equality of opportunity and for an equal role.

In seeking equality with men, these feminists demand that women be allowed to participate in all areas from which they have previously been excluded. For these Jewish feminists, all formal distinctions in the religious as well as the secular sphere between men and women should be abolished. As Susan Schneider wrote in *Jewish and Female*: 'We have been trying to take charge of events in our own lives and in every area of what we call Jewish life: religion, the community, the family, and all our interpersonal relations.'[5]

Given this impetus of liberating women from the restrictions of patriarchal structures, there is every reason for Jews and Christians to share their common concern.

Dan

8.3   *5 January 2004*

PARTICIPATION — BUT ON WHOSE TERMS?

Dan,

This letter comes to you from the ancient city of Udaipur in Rajasthan. Around this city loom majestically the deforested Aravalli Hills or mountains, and the tribal women who dwell here witness to the truth of what we have been writing in these last two letters. In the drought relief projects which we have been supporting, it is reported officially that the women did 80 per cent of the work — in addition to their domestic work and childcare. Even then, they did not receive control of what they earned, and in any case had to part with some of it to their husbands, for drink and drugs. These men, it is reported — and I have seen it myself — stand around idly most of the time.

There are historic and specific reasons for this situation —but it reveals a commonality in the grip that patriarchy holds over the lives of women. Yes, you are right it needs to be changed — but how? In Judaism, Judith Plaskow — whom I mentioned earlier — tried to insert women into the ancient Sinai Covenant, and to explore the difference this would make to Jewish theology and community.[6] But more recently a Jewish scholar, Miriam Peskowitz (and there are others), argued that this approach is too dependent on enlightenment categories as well as on Christian theologians like Paul Tillich.[7]

A diversity of approaches characterises Christian attempts too. Some divide those making such attempts into reformists and rev-olutionaries. There are examples of liberal feminists who struggle for equal rights for all in every sector of society. Separatist/radical feminists give up on the world as it is and attempt to construct a women-centred, biophilic world — Mary Daly would be an example of this. Theologically, they exchange the word 'theology' for 'the*a*logy' and call for the return of the ancient goddess — as I wrote to you in my letter on New Year's Day. Romantic feminists tend to buy into the myth that women are more caring, compassionate and relational, and work to transform public life with these 'female' qualities. Socialist feminists come closer to the views we have been expressing — in spirit rather than in literal conformism to the socialist agenda — with their call for structural justice and emphasis on human rights.

But all of these paths point to something we now understand much better, namely that gender is *constructed*, and that it is *performative*. We *perform* our gender roles, according to tradition, inherited suppositions, power positions, or a mixture of many elements. This is moving far away from the essentialist notions that have caused so much grief.

But I suspect that what we may agree on — quite apart from the struggle for human rights across the faith communities — is the kind of understanding of gender roles that are formative of the kingdom of peace and justice that is the basis of Jewish and Christian hope.

This seems to me to be the urgent task: not only to fight for women's participation in church, synagogue and society, but to work for a transformed concept of gender that helps to bring about a changed society. The current stereotypes underpin violence against women and vulnerable sectors of society. They perpetuate what Elisabeth Schüssler Fiorenza has called 'kyriarchy' or the rule of domination (*kurios* meaning lord). We have to activate the kinds of gender interplay that make 'right relation' the ethic of interchange in place of domination.

Where can we find inspiration for this from both our traditions, or indeed from any tradition? That is the issue. The day after tomorrow we are off into the Aravalli mountains, to meet with the women I wrote about at the beginning of this letter. I want very much to offer them hope.

Mary

-◦⊙—⊙◦-
8.4   *9 January 2004*
OVERCOMING PREJUDICE

Mary,

You mentioned Mary Daly's approach to feminism: the concept of a women-centred world. I have deep reservations about such a solution to the problem of gender. Let me tell you about an incident that took place a number of years ago at the University of Kent. The University had established a women's study programme, and held seminars during the lunch hour. I — as the only man — attended one of these sessions, and I was not welcome. The seminars were designed only for women, and I was viewed as an interloper. The argument was that, in order for women to speak freely and openly, it is necessary that only women be permitted to participate in discussion.

I am seriously troubled by such an outlook. For centuries men have systematically excluded women and discriminated against them. Their interests in the religious and secular spheres have been consciously overlooked. In our two traditions they have been viewed as subordinate and subservient. All this is deplorable. As a Reform rabbi, I welcome the steps that the Reform movement has made to include women at all levels of the religious life. Today it is vital that women do not themselves act in the same way they deplore.

Patriarchy of any kind should not be tolerated. Women must be liberated from the forces that have oppressed them. In Judaism, Judith Plaskow's quest to insert women into the covenant is to be welcomed. I simply cannot understand how Miriam Peskowitz and others believe that such an approach is suspect because it is based on the principles of the Enlightenment. In the eighteenth century Jewish figures such as Moses Mendelssohn and his followers were determined to free Jewry from the disabilities they previously endured. During the period of the Enlightenment, political and religious reformers pressed for the application of reason to all spheres of inquiry. On this basis, the *Haskalah* (Jewish Enlightenment) enabled the Jewish community to free itself from the barriers of a ghetto existence. In modern times, the same principles of equality have been applied to the role of women in Jewish life — today, as never before, they have been freed from the chains of the past.

I am on the side of liberal feminists who press for equal rights for all in every sector of society. This, it seems to me, is the most sensible approach. There is no reason to believe that women have a monopoly on caring and compassionate qualities; I am not persuaded that there are in fact 'female qualities'. Gender, I believe, is largely a social construct. The key issue is whether all human beings, regardless of gender, race or religion, are granted equal civic, social, educational and cultural opportunities.

You speak of a transformed concept of gender that helps to bring about a changed society. The struggle, it seems to me, should be to transcend gender altogether, so that we regard individuals as human persons with equal rights and opportunities. The rule of domination, either by men or women, must be overcome. Rather than activate gender interplay, we should seek to generate a new consciousness which regards all human beings as part of the created order. The I—Thou relationship which we have discussed in relation to ecology should equally apply to humanity. Human beings should be seen as ends, not means. This applies not only to gender, but to all categories which have led to domination and exploitation of the other.

Dan

8.5　*12 January 2004*

GENDER — A PLEA FOR A MULTI-FACETED APPROACH

Dan,

I understand your unease about separatist feminism. White women feel the same hurt when they are excluded from the discussions of black women. But I don't think you take seriously enough the importance of historically ancient wounds and memories: yet there is an ambiguity at the heart of the feminist agenda that needs to be admitted.

I have queried the overarching claims of the Enlightenment

agenda, which, I argue, have led us to an overvaluing of a narrow rationality, and eventually to the very competitive individualism that both of our faiths oppose. Yet I cannot deny that feminism was born of this very agenda. Mary Wollstonecraft, her contemporaries and followers, set the very agenda for liberalism that you espouse. Following the Declaration of Human Rights it had eventually to be admitted that women, too, were human beings and therefore deserving of human dignity. (Remember too that this was mainly a secular achievement: the Fathers of the Church had sometimes argued as to whether women even had a soul!)

Yet there is more to it. Suppose I agree that the goal is for all to achieve basic human rights, which I do; then the question becomes — how? It is not at all automatic in many parts of the world. In Euro-America, where the Enlightenment paradigm holds sway, there is far more parity between men and women. Indeed, you could say that women in our culture have more in common with men than with their third world female counterparts. Many women from the southern hemisphere have internalised the traditional view, sanctioned by religion, that they are inferior.

Let me tell you a story. As you know, I am writing to you from Rajasthan, and now from the heart of the Aravalli Hills. I am in the pilgrimage place of Ranakpur, famous for its beautiful Jain temples. At the entrance to the temple is a board that says, 'No menstruating woman may enter the temple'. What kind of message does that give? Two days ago, I was in a village meeting. We were trying to get from the women why they had no voice on their village council. But no woman would speak. Eventually the leader of the NGO we were with, an inspirational man, with exactly the same participatory agenda as you or I, said, 'Right! I will go away together with any senior man — and then perhaps you will speak!' And so it happened. As soon as he had gone, the women began to explain some of the barriers they faced. It made painful listening for me. The fact that no one would listen to women was the first obstacle. I don't need to continue: the reality is that in many contexts there is a need for 'women-only' groups to raise confidence, to build self-esteem and learn the basic economic, social and political realities and possibilities. It is an essential strategy.

But from a faith stance I agree with you, and sense that both our aspirations are for fully human and equitable communities of women and men and that separate strategies are a means to this. I cannot agree with a woman-centred universe though I think there are many experiences and even alternative senses of wisdom that come from women's contributions.

I think you go a step too far. How can we transcend gender altogether when we are far from sure what difference the gender impact on the world is and could be? When we know that yes, gender is (largely) construction but that within these constructions there is a fluidity — even, one could say, a continuum — where we participate in qualities labelled 'male' or 'female', sometimes for arbitrary reasons. Whereas you are right not to accept certain qualities, for example 'compassion' or 'caring', as essentially female, and, let us say, 'initiative' and 'rationality' as essentially male, yet this cannot mean it makes no difference to experience the world in a male or female body. (Without touching on the trans-gendered experience.)

And this is what the Italian philosopher Luce Irigaray wrestles with, as does the Bulgarian linguistic philosopher Julia Kristeva. They write fascinatingly of the female 'jouissance' — delight, pleasure, playfulness — that Kristeva says is lost by the sacrifice that has to be made to enter the (patriarchal) social contract. Glimpses of 'jouissance' are discovered in the tradition, as for example in the Book of Genesis, where Sarah laughed on being told she would have a child at her advanced age.[8] And this is exactly the point at issue. Inserting women into the social contract, the covenant or the hierarchical Church system does not necessarily disturb the basis on which these are constructed. Hence, Irigaray and Kristeva insist on returning to the foundations. Hence I plead for *not* assimilating women to men, for difference, or for what Derrida would call *différance*.

Mary

8.6   *13 January 2004*

REJECTING SEXUAL APARTHEID

Mary,

You write that I am uneasy about separatist feminism. I am not simply uneasy — I am appalled by such a stance. White women are rightly hurt when they are excluded from the discussions of black women. You must remember that I am a member of a religious and ethnic community that has been systematically excluded from the mainstream of society for millennia. Even in the twentieth century American Jews were discriminated against and excluded from elite circles of communal life. In Denver where I grew up, for example, no Jew was permitted to be a member of a prestigious country club, and there were areas of the city where Jews were not allowed to live. I am painfully aware of the wounds and memories of the past.

Such systematic exclusion has made me particularly sensitive to all situations which deny rights to any group, whether it be Jews, blacks or women. It is for this reason that I believe that feminists are wrong to insist on 'women-only' discussions. Inevitably, such meetings focus on the iniquities of men, and create a climate of suspicion and anger. It is far better, I believe, for men and women to meet together, as long as all participants are willing to listen to and learn from one another. I do not agree that it is an essential strategy to exclude men: rather, it is a pernicious error which inculcates fear and resentment.

I am also unhappy about the way in which you describe gender roles. If you really do believe that gender is a social construct, then there is no such thing as inherent male and female characteristics other than the physical differences between the sexes. It is not that there is fluidity between genders, but rather that the roles of men and women in society differ because of the ways in which male and female attitudes have been shaped by various cultures. I cannot see how we experience the world differently if we have a male or female body — our perspectives as men and women differ from one another because of the ways that various societies have understood the position of the sexes in society.

In this light, I cannot comprehend Kristeva's and Irigaray's notion of female delight, pleasure and playfulness. There is no reason to sacrifice 'jouissance' when one enters into what Kristeva refers to as a patriarchal social contract. I am not encouraging women to assimilate to men. Instead, we need to recognise that gender is ultimately a social construct: this provides a framework for reconceptualising society in such a way that human potential can be fully realised. In this regard, I subscribe to the principles of liberal feminism which continue the traditions of the Enlightenment in defining women as having essentially the same nature as men. Differences between men and women are due primarily to socialisation. What is needed is to reform the structures of society to allow women to gain an equal role with men. Radical feminists are wrong in their advocacy of separatism and female bonding by which women will be able to form counter-societies independent of males. Men and women need one another to create a better society and a more just world.

Dan

8.7 *18 January 2004*

EPISTEMOLOGY OF THE 'BROKEN BODY'

Dan,

I had not realised that this chapter would be so painful and that it would be so difficult to find common ground. For our chosen agenda of reconciliation we must find a way out of this impasse. First, I thought that we did agree on the aim of creating and living in communities of equality and justice between the sexes, and between the human and non-human. Secondly, I thought I had made it clear that as an ultimate state of affairs I cannot support a women-centred universe and find it an unhelpful concept. What I argued for, was that women of low or no self-esteem — those who have internalised patriarchy's belief in their inferiority — can be helped more effectively through women-only groups.

What has happened since the emergence of the women's

movement is the consciousness that we cannot speak of a single movement or methodology, but of a *global family of feminist theologies*, each with its own history and context. I learnt the lesson in a painful way. In 1994 I coordinated a European delegation for an International Dialogue on Violence against Women at the invitation of the Ecumenical Association of Third World Theologians' Women's Commission (EATWOT). It was held in Costa Rica. There were women from all continents each with their specific histories of suffering and oppression. But, even though our own group had powerful stories of suffering — for example, of the Women in Black from the former Yugoslavia — what burst out was the anger of the third world women against us at the long oppression of colonialism, racism and forms of neo-colonialism. Black women from the USA told of the violence of slavery;[9] from Japan and Korea came the experience of the so-called 'comfort women' for whom justice is still being sought. From the South American women came Latina theology, and from Hispano-American women Mujerista theology.

What united all these approaches was the anger at imperialism coming from Euro-American sources. And in that gathering we were the oppressors. 'It is not for *you* to call for reconciliation,' said one Womanist theologian, 'It is *we, the victims*, who will judge when the time is right.' A brilliant and spirited young theologian from Korea, Chung Hyun Kyung,[10] says that third world women come to know the world with 'an epistemology of the broken body'.[11] She means that it is on the basis of violence, or of being violated — verbally or physically — as a daily reality, that all these women make sense of their daily lives.

This is why so much of feminist theology is rooted in bodily and sexual experience: it is just not being faithful to this to reduce difference to a few biological facts. And it also perpetuates a body/spirit dualism to do so. Yesterday, I was told by an activist here in Rajasthan that she had asked a women's group if any of them had been beaten by their husbands. At first, no one answered. Then one woman put up her hand. *And then one hundred per cent of the women did.* This is a culturally condoned violence. I do not claim that such violence is universal: thank God we have made much progress in this respect in our own countries in the last decade. But one decade does not eradicate thousands of years. Hence I still argue that the damaged bodies and psyches of women — and other vulnerable groups — will need special and ongoing attention before the epistemology of the broken body is healed. The broken body and the silenced voices do not automatically recover without enabling strategies.

I do understand that Jewish history makes you suspect any strategy of exclusion. But Judaism itself treats women in a different way from men, and has excluded women from full liturgical participation —and some Orthodox women still prefer it this way. For people of faith there is no question of fostering a climate of suspicion or anger towards men: women's chosen values are relational, and it has frequently been women's role in many societies to nurture harmony in family and community. For faith communities the challenge is always to keep alive the vision of full mutuality as the goal, to resist whatever blocks this, and to act as catalyst for its embodiment.

Mary

8.8   *23 January 2004*

JEWISH ISOLATION AND FEMINISM

Mary,

I think we agree about the need for creating a world in which women have an equal place with men. Past traditions of prejudice must be set aside in the quest for the liberation of women from patriarchal structures. Yet there is a fundamental impasse in our view of the ways in which such a transformation is to be accomplished. Let me say, first, that I believe organisations such as the Women's Institute serve a positive role in society. As you may know, Lavinia my wife is a member of her local Women's Institute, and I appreciate that she and others genuinely enjoy the company of other women.

But we have not been discussing such groups; rather, our disagreement concerns the strategy of feminists who believe that they must meet together without the presence of men. My objection is that such exclusivity is pernicious. When women meet together to explore the evils of patriarchy and oppression by men, inevitably their discussions generate hostility, anger and contempt.

Arguably, the reaction of some Jews to the non-Jewish world can be instructive in this context. Secular Zionists in the nineteenth century were convinced that there is no way that Jews will ever be accepted in the societies in which they live. In 1862 the German socialist Moses Hess published *Rome and Jerusalem*, in which he argued that anti-Jewish sentiment is unavoidable.[12] No Jew, he argued, can escape from 'Judaeophobia': the hatred of Jews is inescapable. For Hess, Jews will always be regarded as strangers among the nations. In a similar vein, the Russian thinker Leon Pinsker in *Autoemancipation* maintained that the Jewish problem is as unresolved in the modern world as in former times.[13] In essence, this dilemma concerns the unassimilable character of Jewish identity in countries where Jews are in the minority. In such cases, there can be no basis for mutual respect between Jew and non-Jew.

Arguing on similar grounds, Theodor Herzl, the father of modern Israel, composed *The Jewish State*, in which he asserted that Jews will never be secure unless they have a homeland of their own. Old prejudices against Jewry, he contended, are ingrained in Western society. Assimilation will not act as a cure for the ills that beset the Jewish people — there is only one remedy for the malady of anti-Semitism: the creation of a Jewish commonwealth.

These thinkers pressed for the isolation of Jewry as a form of self-protection. They believed there is no solution to the Jewish problem. If Jews are to be safe, they will need to leave the countries where they live and create a Jewish homeland which will serve as a safe haven for the future. The state of Israel was thus established as an ultimate insurance policy, and it is not surprising that those who embrace such an ideology have been determined to protect Israel from its enemies whatever the cost.

Arguably, Jewish exclusivism — which regards the non-Jew with suspicion and hostility — is dangerous and psychologically damaging. Jewish paranoia is encouraged by the tradition itself, which continually emphasises that the Jews are a persecuted nation that will triumph over its enemies. From the beginning of their history, fear of the non-Jew has been a central feature of the faith. Thus, the Hebrew Bible recounts that the Egyptian Pharaoh sought to kill all first-born sons. However, such murderous aspirations were thwarted through God's intervention on behalf of his people. Later, the Bible records that the Jewish people prevailed over Haman's plan to exterminate Persian Jewry. The festival of Purim commemorates this victory. These stories, I believe, continue to dramatise the fear of the other, and reinforce Jewish xenophobia.

My point is that feminists who seek to exclude men from their deliberations are like those Jews who are determined to isolate themselves from the non-Jewish world. In both cases, they have created an unhealthy environment in which to rehearse their grievances and fuel their hostility and contempt. What is needed instead is for men and women to come together to examine the ways in which women throughout history have been oppressed and exploited. Full mutuality can only occur when both sexes are able to transcend issues of gender in the quest to discover their full humanity.

Dan

8.9 31 January 2004
A NEW MASCULINITY?

Dan,

I have now exchanged Rajasthan's delightful sunshine for the snow and rain of the UK and am struggling with the inevitable flu bugs on re-entry to this hemisphere. On my way home I reflected a lot on the impasse we seem to have reached. We both agree as to the kind of world we aim for, with full mutuality and egalitarian relationships between the sexes. But we differ as to the means. I do not think your comparison with isolation theories in Judaism is helpful: what I argue for is as relevant for *Jewish* women as it is for women everywhere. You are in danger of sweeping under the carpet the fact that experiences of exclusion and subordination have been shared by women globally throughout history.

There is also a strong argument that there is a process for men, too, to unravel the legacy of patriarchy as 'disordered relation'. Gender issues are not just for women! I was taught this by my male students some years ago. At the end of a course I had given on feminist theology, some of the Catholic priests present said that the values I was proposing of restored mutuality, of preferring qualities like compassion, nurture and a redefinition of power, to replace an ethic of domination, were vitally important for men too. 'But,' they said, 'you cannot do the work for us — we have to do it ourselves.' And they embarked on a process where male students were meeting together and re-evaluating the notions of masculinity they had been taught. They were trying to form a new spirituality. They felt strongly that the psyches of men too had been damaged by false notions of strength and power, by the overvaluing of rationality over emotions, by not being allowed to express emotions openly ('real men don't cry!') and by tradition's insistence on separation from the female world. (I realise that in the USA you do not have the public school tradition we still have here.) This called to mind for me the priestly training of my brothers, one of whom had been sent to junior seminary at the age of 11, and no longer shared our family celebrations at Christmas and Easter.

What I am arguing is that wrong relation is not put right automatically: it needs commitment to a long process. Rosemary Ruether has spelt out how this process differs for men and women.[14] For women, as I have been arguing, the challenge is to form an identity denied to them by patriarchy, which allowed them only a subordinated sense of self, or a self mediated by relationship with men — for example, wife of, daughter of, mother of … For women, marriage symbolised being passed from the control of the father to the control of the husband. Ruether says that anger can be a liberating grace, the 'power to break the chains of sexist socialisation', and can enable women to reclaim their own history as witnesses to an alternative possibility. Only after experiencing this anger and history of alienation can women move on to another and deeper truth. The temptation is to mimic the egoistic power-struggle and individualistic notion of the self that still dominates: what is demanded is not only the reshaping of our personal relationships, but the re-forming of our social selves and systems.

Ruether also describes the necessary male journey — although, as I said, this has to be embarked on by men themselves, in solidarity with women. In sharing household tasks and child-care in an honest way (not just with a sense that he is 'helping' his wife in *her* tasks), in being willing to express emotions — even to develop a new language of feeling — a more holistic sense of self will emerge. The ethic of superiority and domination gives way to an ethic of mutuality. Power becomes an issue of shared respon-sibility. It takes courage, perseverance, a willingness to take risks, to allow oneself to be vulnerable — but what is at stake is a new humanity, a humanity in right relation with one another, with the planet — and, I believe, with God.

Mary

8.10   *1 February 2004*

ANGER MANAGEMENT

Mary,

You will remember that the overarching theme of our conversa-tion is reconciliation: we are seeking to find ways in which reconciliation can take place at all levels in a world torn apart by conflict. Earlier I referred to the concept of *tikkun*, cosmic restoration. This is a kabbalistic notion based on the idea of the disorder in the cosmos that occurred when the process of divine contraction and emanation occurred.

The question is: how can *tikkun* take place between men and women? Given the dominance of men and the subordination of women through the ages, is there a means of restoring women to a position of equal status with men? You argue that the Jewish experience has nothing to do with this problem. I disagree. In my view, the ways in which Jews have been treated by host com-munities, and the ensuing animosity which has animated Jewish consciousness, illustrate the dangers of isolation in the face of oppression. The Jewish response to prejudice has been to wall itself off from the gentile world.

You are defending a similar form of segregation in which women are able to rehearse their grievances among themselves. You contend that men, too, must undergo a transformation of consciousness, recognising the limitations that have been put upon women by patriarchal values. You are correct that men need to be liberated from masculine attitudes which have enslaved women. In no way do I wish to sweep under the carpet women's experiences of exclusion and subordination. Rather, I believe that through a process of sharing, of reviewing past iniquities, men and women can join together in reforming society. Gender issues are for both sexes, but the process of unravelling the legacy of patriarchy should be a shared task.

I am also unhappy about the dichotomy you draw between strength, power and rationality which you appear to ascribe to men, and compassion and nurture which are attributed to women. While it is true that such attitudes have traditionally been depicted in this way, I think they are in no way gender-determined. Instead, this distinction is a social construct. What is now required is the recognition that such values are not gender-based. Today, I believe, it is vitally important to transcend the traditional concept of gender so that we can create a world in which the full range of human values can be embraced by both men and women.

You are right that women need to form a new identity. Yet I think Rosemary Radford Ruether is misguided in envisaging anger as a liberating grace. From my experiences as a rabbi I have observed that anger is a destructive force which cripples the afflicted. Ruether argues that only after experiencing this anger and the history of alienation can women move on to a deeper truth. This has not been the case with the Jewish community. By focusing on the ill-treatment they received at the hands of others, the Jewish nation has isolated itself in its ancient homeland surrounded by enemies. Intractably committed to Jewish survival, the state of Israel is in the process of constructing a wall around the Occupied Territories to deter suicide bombers from further acts of terror. The process of realisation through segregation which you champion may lead to the same outcome. Rather than integrating men and women, you may well find that a wall of resentment will be created between the sexes even if women gain the opportunities that they seek in modern society. How can reconciliation between men and women take place if women goad themselves into a frenzy of hostility and contempt?

Dan

8.11   *4 February 2004*

BEYOND ANGER AND HOSTILITY

Dan,

You are right to remind me that our goal is reconciliation, *tikkun olam*, as our last few exchanges seem to lead us deeper into disagreement! Let me clarify a few things. First, I did not mean that comparison with Jewish experience was irrelevant; rather that one form of oppression cannot be identified with another. *Sexism is not racism*, even if real experience shows the two are frequently intertwined. Collapsing the one into the other will mean we lose the specificity of both.

Secondly, you speak in seriously negative terms of women's separate spaces, where, you write, 'women rehearse their grievances', where 'they goad themselves into a frenzy of hostility and contempt.' This is a very insensitive stance! Of course, I have to admit that there are some feminist groups who refuse to budge from a stance of anger and bitterness and cannot believe that men really want to undo the damages of patriarchy. This is very hurtful for men like you who take a genuinely liberal stance. But I appeal to you, in the name of our shared purpose of greater understanding and cooperation between our two faiths, to admit that there is another way of seeing this. I have told you of my experiences in India — which can be multiplied from other contexts — where women have been so physically and psychologically damaged by harsh patriarchal structures, *often still in place*, that healing is far from automatic. It requires safe spaces, free from fear, where there is such a quality of deep listening that women find courage to break out of culturally imposed silence. There is a story, now famous in feminist theology, of such a therapeutic group of women. They had been sharing stories all week, but one woman had remained completely silent. But on the very last day she rose to her feet and, stumblingly, told her story of suffering. As she finished she turned to the women and said, in wonder: 'But you heard me before I spoke: *in fact, you heard me into speech.*' After this, hearing into speech has become a well-practised tool. Yes, you are right that 'unravelling the legacy of patriarchy' is a shared task: but in achieving this there are challenges for women and men jointly, as well as work that needs to be tackled by women or men alone.

Thirdly, I think you don't understand the role of anger in such a journey to discovery of self-esteem. This is a difficult path for women in both our traditions, because women are socialised into thinking of patience, obedience and surrender of self-will as virtues, and of anger as sin. But far from encouraging anger as a permanent state, or as incitement to revenge, many Christian feminists are now writing helpfully about the channelling of anger into positive action for justice. Beverley Harrison wrote: 'The deepest danger to our cause is that our anger will turn inward and lead us to portray ourselves and other women as victims rather than those who have struggled for the full gift of life against structures of oppression.'[15]

She argues that we are not meant to follow Christ in terms of sacrificial lives, but rather to 'live the work of radical love'. Does this sound like hostility and contempt? So, yes, I agree that we need to transcend traditional dichotomising concepts of gender, but not that we can ever transcend gender itself: if the bodies we have were not important to the way we live out our humanity, why would so many people today be seeking sex-changes? It must be that their human potential is blocked by being in the wrong body. It remains a quest for both our faiths, to grow into the kind of embodied human beings that best live out what it means to be 'created in the image of God'.

Mary

9. The Family and Community

———⊶⟨⊙⟩⊷———

9.1 8 February 2004

THE HOME

Mary,

Throughout Jewish history, family life has been of paramount significance. According to tradition, marriage is viewed as a sacred bond as well as a means to personal fulfilment. It is more than a legal contract, rather an institution with cosmic significance, legitimised through divine authority. The purpose of a marriage is to build a home, create a family and thereby perpetuate society. Initially Jews were allowed to have more than one wife, but this was banned with the decree of Rabbenu Gershom in 1000 CE.

In Judaism there are innumerable religious observances that take place in the home. According to the sages, the home is a *mikdash meat* (minor sanctuary). Like the synagogue, it continues various traditions of the ancient Temple. The Sabbath candles, for example, recall the Temple *menorah* and the dining table symbolises the altar. Most significantly, within the home, family life is sanctified. As head of the family, the father is to exercise authority over his wife and children. He is obliged to circumcise his son, redeem him if he is the first-born, teach him Torah, marry him off and teach him a craft. Further, he is required to serve as a role model for the transmission of Jewish ideals to his offspring.

Regarding Jewish women, the prevailing sentiment is that the role of the wife is to bear children and exercise responsibility for family life. According to the *halakhah*, womanhood is a separate status with its own specific sets of rules, obligations and responsibilities. In terms of religious observance, women were classed as slaves and children, disqualified as witnesses, excluded from the study of Torah and segregated from men. Moreover, they were regarded as ritually impure for extended periods of time. In general they were exempted from time-bound commands: as a result they were not obliged to fulfil those commandments which must be followed at a particular time, such as the recitation of prayer. The purpose of these restrictions was to ensure that their attention and energy be directed towards completing their domestic duties. In the contemporary world, however, a growing number of Jewish women have agitated for equal treatment; in consequence, the role of women has undergone a major transformation.

None the less, there has been a universal recognition in all branches of Judaism that the Jewish wife should continue to play a central role in the home.

Children are expected to carry out the commandment to honour (Exod. 20:12) and respect (Lev. 19:3) their parents. For the rabbis, the concept of honour refers to providing parents with food, drink, clothing and transportation. Respect requires that a child does not sit in his parents' seat, nor interrupt them, and takes their side in a dispute. The Talmud extols such treatment:

> There are three partners in man, the Holy One, blessed be He, the father, and the mother. When a man honours his father and his mother, the Holy One, blessed be He, says, 'I will ascribe (merit) to them as though I had dwelt among them and they had honoured me.'

The Jewish tradition teaches that domestic harmony is the ideal of home life. The Talmud specifies the guidelines for attaining this goal:

> A man should spend less than his means on food, up to his means on clothes, and more than his means in honouring wife and children because they are dependent on him.

Such harmony is to be attained through give and take on the part of all, as well as through the observance of Jewish ritual which serves to unify the family.

This then is the model for family life within the Jewish faith. Yet I can imagine you are grumbling about the role of women. There is no doubt that traditionally wives have played a sub-servient role to their husbands. They have been deliberately excluded from a wide range of religious activities, and denied educational opportunities. Their central task is to bear children and look after their families. Arguably, such limitations have had a profoundly negative impact on the development of Jewish women. Denied the possibility of becoming scholars, the world of Jewish learning was closed to them. They have been unable to function as religious leaders and have therefore made only a min-imal contribution to Judaism. If you look for the names of Jewish women in the *Encyclopaedia Judaica*, for example, there are rela-tively few entries. Yet, despite such discrimination Judaism has continued to flourish as a religious tradition for nearly 4,000 years: it may well be that its patriarchal traditions and rigid attitudes have enabled Jews to survive through the centuries.

Dan

9.2 *10 February 2004*

A NEW START FOR WOMEN?

Dan,

You are quite right. I am seriously worried about the traditional position of women in Judaism as you outline it — but I am also worried about your own views! You seem to me to be sheltering under traditional orthodox stances, yet in our exchanges you manifest a consistent liberalism. So how is this to be explained?

Here, as in other areas, I think we will agree on some issues but conflict on others. The Roman Catholic views on family are very similar to traditional Jewish ones. But there is one innovation that emerges from the ministry of Jesus himself. The picture you describe must have been true of families in the times of Jesus — except that we need to understand the context of Roman occupation, poverty and a growing landless population. All this has impact on family situations.

The innovative path that Jesus offered was discipleship for women as well as men. Itinerant discipleship on missionary journeys meant that women had other roles than child-rearing and household management and were accepted for different reasons. For Jesus, commitment to the Kingdom of God and its ethical demands was not only central, but facilitated a recasting of patriarchal values. When the crowd told him, 'Your mother and your brethren are waiting for you,' Jesus' response was, 'Who are my mother and my brethren? ... Whoever does the will of God is my brother and sister, and mother!' (Mark 3:32) In other words the blood ties of kinship are not constitutive of the community that is committed to the ethics of the Kingdom. The gospels tell of 'the women' who followed him and ministered to him from their own wealth and of their fidelity even in the life-threatening scenes at Golgotha (Luke 8:1; Mark 15:40). Even if patriarchal patterns quickly reasserted themselves over the next century, especially in Greek contexts, the possibility of not having to be married and valorised solely in terms of procreation and obedience to one's husband in order to follow God's dictates remains an honourable option in communities of religious sisters up till this day.

Of course I shouldn't pretend that this was a seamless web. Up till the Reformation there is abundant evidence of the authority of medieval women in monasteries — even if the Church sometimes jibbed against the freedom of women unconfined by the enclosure. St Catherine of Siena, for example, was criticized as a 'woman too much on the road'! After the Reformation the repudiation by the Reformers of monastic life again put women's traditional role — *Kinder, Kuche, Kirche* (children, kitchen, church) — centre stage. There have been exceptions, as for example women's spiritual leadership in the founding movements of the evangelical churches. In the nineteenth century there was a disastrous split between public and private space: women's role was definitely to be lived out in the latter: such qualities as gentleness, nurture and compassion were idealised, for example by the German Lutheran theologian Schleiermacher in his allegorical tale, *On Christmas*

Eve[1] — while men controlled the public space of politics and the professions. Such a split produced the myth of 'The Angel of the House', a self-sacrificing creature who opted for a shadowy notion of personhood, mediated solely by total self-abnegation in favour of husband and children. Rightly did the writer Virginia Woolf want to kill her! (Or at least kill the myth.)[2]

It is against this history of women's struggle to be valued as persons in their own right, and not merely in their reproductive role, that I approach the social and religious significance of the family.

Mary

9.3   *19 February 2004*
JESUS AND FEMINISM

Mary,

I think you do me an injustice. As I have repeatedly stated, I believe women should have the same opportunities as men. Fortunately, within the non-Orthodox branches of Judaism, such a change has taken place in the last few decades. Today there are Reform, Conservative, Reconstructionist and Humanistic women rabbis and cantors, and women occupy positions of leadership within the Jewish community. I applaud such a revolution in Jewish life. Yet I am aware that the traditional pattern of family life where women were regarded as wives and homemakers did have beneficial consequences, even though women were relegated to a subservient role and the religion was dominated by men.

As I explained in a previous letter, my wife and I wrote a book entitled *The American Jew* some time ago; in one of our interviews a non-Jewish observer of the local Jewish community had this to say about the girls in a strictly Orthodox high school:

> In a television age, it's very special that people can hang on to a tradition. I know to some of us on the outside of the *Beis Rahel* (the girls' high school) it may look inhibiting. But how can I judge? They're beautiful; they're the cream of the crop of the community, intellectually and spiritually. I admire it, I really do … I have seen young

women who are happy; young women who are not
involved in any illicit activity; young women who are not
burdens of the court; young women who are not on the
streets; who are not on drugs; who are going to raise a
family and hopefully have a happy marriage.[3]

Of course you are right that patriarchy is stifling, but you must
admit that the traditional Jewish role for women does have some
benefits, such as those suggested by this non-Jewish outsider. This
is not an inconsistency on my part, but rather an honest and
realistic appraisal.

Let me turn to your comments about Jesus. I think you are
right that he did have positive relationships with a number of
women. Itinerant discipleship on missionary journeys did provide
alternative roles for women beyond household management. But
I am not convinced that Jesus, as a first-century Jew, sought to
overturn the patriarchal patterns of the past. Patriarchy was not
suppressed, only to re-emerge in the next century. This, I believe,
is a misreading of the Gospel message. Jesus, like Paul, was shaped
by the Jewish environment in which he lived. There is no sugges-
tion that he wished to disregard biblical laws which discriminate
against women, nor is there any indication that he viewed
Pharisaic rulings concerning women as invalid. It would be comforting to believe that Jesus adopted a revolutionary stance — but
there is no evidence that he did. All that one can say is that the
Gospels present Jesus as befriending several women. In all likelihood he, like the 12 disciples, accepted biblical prescriptions and
Pharisaic interpretations of the Written Law as authoritative and
binding. The clashes between Jesus and the Pharisees recorded in
the Gospels concerned the nature of Sabbath law, rather than the
validity of the Torah itself.

While it is true that the Church has provided alternative roles
for women as spiritual leaders and mystics, the record of
Christianity is no better than that of Judaism. Our two traditions
have failed to see women as persons in their own right. And, as I
have said, despite the benefits of patriarchy, a new way must be
found to afford women opportunities of personal development
and fulfilment. Whether this can be done within the framework

of the nuclear and extended family is the question. Given the current aspirations of women, does family life have a future?

Dan

9.4   *23 February 2004*

DOES THE FAMILY HAVE A FUTURE?

Dan,

I certainly didn't intend to be unfair — far from it. But there is an irony in both our positions: we are both working for a more egalitarian partnership between men and women within traditions which — though there are progressive elements — are still extremely conservative as regards patterns of marriage. The more unstable society becomes, the more the call is heard for the re-inforcement of traditional gender roles, particularly for women to give up on career expectations in favour of full-time child care. How often is the accusation voiced that the increasing divorce rate and child crime are the fault of women preferring jobs outside the home to domestic responsibilities within?

So this is the nub of the issue — not whether Jesus overturned patriarchy or not. I largely agree with you here — as our previous exchanges have shown — that Jesus was faithful to the Torah and did not adopt a revolutionary stance; but I still maintain that he valued people for their faithfulness to Kingdom ethics and that this is the inspirational point for women now carving out roles in a changed historical context.

So, does the family have a future? I think there are at least two important points. The first is that both our faith traditions on the family clash with the modern nuclear family. Early Christian scriptures speak of extended households, extended families with a practice of hospitality, and welcoming of the stranger — I know this is a cherished Jewish tradition. In many parts of the world this is still the case: the extended family is the reality — I see this in Rajasthan — so that care of small children is not a problem, because grandmothers and other female relatives are always at hand. Of course in poor, rural, agricultural communities, women are expected to work in the fields and the children come along too. (I'm not trying to idealise a situation which is often tough on mother and child alike.)

So it is in the context of the contemporary nuclear family and single parent family, where the challenge is at its most acute. It's not a picture that the Bible reflects. But it's our task to flesh out a workable ethic in times where we respect both genders, understanding that both want to contribute to the wider society, yet have quality time together and with their children. This, I believe, is the dream of most women and men in partnership. I hope I have argued enough of the cherished value of 'right relation' to persuade you that most women do not put their own ambition and happiness before that of the relationship and entire family situation. There are still many real life situations where women have given up careers — not for their children, but to care for sick and elderly parents.

But if the family is to have a future there are tasks on many levels. I think faith communities have to accept a diversity of family lifestyles and try to give the kind of support these need. Then working patterns need to change. We are a workaholic society, valuing those prepared to give their entire lives to a job. This leaves no gap for the messy, demanding nature of childcare or the needs of the extended family, or the valuing of time just to be together. It's here that the biblical vision can be brought into play. The creation story of Genesis offers the image of Sabbath, where God rested and appreciated the wonders of creation. The Bible offers a balance between work and rest, regeneration, time for 'being'. Our society has transformed that either into longer work hours or the spending of leisure time in supermarkets or at car boot sales.

The survival of the family means creating healthy patterns of care — and the structures that enable them. Faith communities can sometimes inspire us by modelling different ways. I'll end with a story: maybe you heard Sister Frances Dominica on the radio? She is an Anglican sister, founder of the children's hospice Helen House, in Oxford. But she is also a mother — as she adopted a ten-month-old African baby who would have died of starvation. Now the boy is 16, living with his mother in a house opposite the hospice. His enthusiasm is for motorcycles, and weekend after weekend this 60-year-old nun stands in muddy fields at rallies to cheer him on! She gives quite a different picture of family life, indicating the diversity we need and the role faith can play in underpinning new patterns of care.

Mary

9.5   29 February 2004
BEYOND THE FAMILY

Mary,

In the modern Jewish world there is a universal acceptance that women should have the opportunity to fulfil themselves through a career. I have not personally heard any Jewish voices, even among the Orthodox, who maintain that divorce and child crime are the fault of women preferring jobs outside the home. Certainly among non-Orthodox Jews, domestic responsibilities are widely viewed as the obligation of both men and women.

As far as Jesus is concerned, I don't think we can know what he felt about feminist issues. The gospels are not concerned with such matters: their purpose was to illustrate that Jesus was the long-awaited Messiah who has come to redeem the world. Whether Kingdom ethics embraced traditional Jewish prescriptions about women is something we cannot establish with any certainty. I am dubious whether it makes sense for Christian feminists to cite Jesus' words as a basis for restructuring society.

Yet, as you say, the central problem is whether the family has a future. You are right that in the past families were much broader, embracing grandparents, aunts, uncles, cousins, and even in-laws. In some parts of the world this is still the case, but certainly in first-world urban centres, this has ceased to be so. Today the nuclear family has become the norm. The question is whether this nuclear unit provides the most healthy framework for individual growth and development.

Theoretically the family unit provides a means whereby infants are integrated into society. Within the home children are socialised: parents care for their offspring, feed them, protect them from danger, teach them to speak, etc. However, as you know, some of the greatest thinkers have been highly critical of family life. Plato, for example, in the *Republic*, argues that families are inherently selfish, and he maintains that it would be far better if children were taken away from their parents at a very early age and raised together by outsiders. All those born at the same time would then regard one another as brothers and sisters, and view all those who had children when they were born as their parents. For Plato, such a restructuring of social life would result in a more integrated and harmonious community.

Of course such a reorganisation of society runs counter to the values of our two traditions (even though the kibbutz in Israel was originally structured along these lines). None the less, I do believe that Plato was right: families do put their interests first, and thereby neglect the needs of society as a whole. Such parental concern is normal, but it is certainly not altruistic beyond the confines of the family unit.

The problem of family life is therefore not simply that women have been denied their full potential by being compelled to undertake domestic tasks. It is rather that both the extended and nuclear family unit have arguably had a corrosive impact on human development. We have all been conditioned to believe that the other members of our family (mothers, fathers, grandmothers, grandfathers, brothers, sisters, aunts, uncles, and cousins — and even our in-laws) deserve more concern and consideration than others simply because we are related to them by birth or marriage. Is this either sensible or morally justifiable?

Dan

9.6   *3 March 2004*

RE-VISIONING THE FAMILY

Dan,

I absolutely agree with you that the modern nuclear family, prey to the seductions of consumerism, is neither the way forward, nor the pattern advocated by Scripture! But I think the issue of women and work outside the home is only one facet of a deeper problem. I also agree that the ethic of 'blood is thicker than water' is narrow, uncharitable, unscriptural and hardly a blueprint for the future.

The challenge for both our traditions is how to move on from the dominant, exclusively approved model of the heterosexual, monogamous couple in a lifelong relationship primarily because of the procreation and rearing of children. The reality of our world calls for a *diversity of models* and both our faith communities have an urgent task to create rituals and support systems to nurture these — often fragile — relationships. First, I think that heterosexual faithful marriage is the best context for rearing children — but it is not the only one. (My story of Sister Frances and the African boy indicated this!) Secondly, men and women now do not marry solely to have children. Companionship and sexual love in a publicly committed relationship is a precious value for many; others choose not to have children because of the problem of the overpopulation of the planet and still others because their work is the chosen way of contributing to society. Thirdly, because couples are having fewer children, child-rearing does not define identity for so many years. Speaking personally, there were years when being a mother defined me more than it does now, when being a theologian/writer occupies most of my energies. Even for those couples in a traditional marriage the need to renegotiate traditional roles, to share childcare and change work patterns is urgent.

But the real diversity springs from the fact that many couples choose to cohabit without marriage; same-sex unions are increasingly publicly accepted; single parents, especially single mothers, are increasingly the norm and divorced parents who remarry become responsible for the children of two or three marriages. These last two categories bring a crucial factor into play — that of poverty. Single mothers are the most impoverished category of parents in both Britain and the USA — and this goes right across the ethnic divide.

Leaving this last category for a moment, let's just ask what should the criteria be for people-in-relationship? And isn't this where the scriptures inspire us? 'Wherever you go, I will go,' said Ruth to Naomi, and the criterion of faithful love is surely the divine prototype for the human counterpart. Humanity needs relational patterns and structures that make this faithful love possible and even though we have examples of communal living (you mentioned kibbutzes), these do not nurture and sustain the individual adequately. What is remarkable today is the quality of faithful love still manifest across generations, despite broken marriages: both mothers and fathers do skilfully negotiate care for children from several unions, and help them maintain contact with their birth parents.

Some years ago, when Nicholas and I and our children lived in Brussels, we discussed the issue of living in community seriously with like-minded friends. We were attracted by the idea that we could share domestic appliances, a car, consume less resources, encourage each other in our shared values — and so on. But we concluded that those of us who were more naturally social and outgoing would benefit and the others would suffer. (Since then I have known people who have found creative solutions to these issues.)

But the real question is whether church and synagogue will consider this diversity of models of the family as a responsibility needing new pastoral structures, or as a development to be resisted at all costs.

Mary

9.7   *8 March 2004*

RECIPROCITY IN THE FAMILY

Mary,

I agree with you that the notion of the family has undergone enormous change in recent years. Within the Jewish community, there has been an increasing acceptance of alternative forms of family life, including lesbian and homosexual relationships. Rabbi Marc Israel, Director of Congregational Relations of the Reform movement, for example, recently declared:

> I stand here today on behalf of the Union of American Hebrew Congregations and the Central Conference of American Rabbis, representing 1.5 million American

Reform Jews, to say that we fervently believe in God and the Torah, and also to state that there is no room for discrimination against, gays, lesbians, or bisexuals in our synagogues, in our communities, or in our nation.[4]

In this new context of familial relationships, it is vital that we find a framework for harmony and reconciliation. You suggest the biblical model of Ruth's dedication to Naomi. What is crucial, you write, is the concept of faithful love which is the divine prototype for the human counterpart. I would like to suggest a very different scriptural notion. In the Book of Exodus, the people of Israel assembled before Mount Sinai. Here God promises that as long as the Jewish people keep his statutes, they will be assured of a glorious future. But elsewhere he warns them of the dire consequences of disobedience.

For the ancient Israelites, God's compassionate and merciful care was dependent on fulfilling divinely appointed obligations. Otherwise, God would unleash his fury against his chosen people. Within this context, God's love was not unconditional; rather it was dependent on adhering to the terms of the agreement that had been formulated on Mount Sinai. In other words, the covenant was a binding agreement on both parties, involving responsibility on both sides.

In my view, this concept of covenant, involving reciprocal responsibility, is a much healthier framework for human relationships than is faithful love. In place of this ideal, I want to substitute the Jewish concept of reciprocity as exemplified in the biblical notion of covenant. It is neither a mistake nor morally deficient to expect others to give as well as take. This is a wholesome demand. It is the presupposition of a healthy relationship.

I want to illustrate this point by using an example drawn from my experience as a rabbi in the USA. Harold and Shirley were members of my congregation. Harold was a successful executive in a large manufacturing firm. He and Shirley and their three children lived in a large house full of expensive furnishings in one of the rich areas of the city. Although they appeared to be a successful and prosperous family, I knew that Shirley was deeply unhappy. Even though she wore expensive clothes and drove a

Mercedes Benz convertible, she was financially dependent on her husband who abused her emotionally. In addition, he was notoriously unfaithful. On several occasions, Shirley came to see me. She felt exploited and demeaned.

Harold and Shirley's marriage was typical of what all too frequently occurs between husband and wife. There is no proper rate of exchange. One partner feels oppressed and ill-treated. The relationship dissolves because the covenant of marriage collapses. In this instance Harold overlooked his wife's desires, and greedily fulfilled his own needs. For this broken relationship to be mended, the emotional equation between husband and wife has to be re-established on the basis of mutuality and reciprocity.

It would be naïve to think that marriages such as Harold and Shirley's can be easily rescued through rational discussion. But my point is that broken relationships can only be mended — if they can be mended at all — if partners are able to act responsibly towards one another. There must be an equation established between giving and taking. If one party takes all, or takes more than his or her share, then the relationship will be in trouble. And the more one takes and the less one gives, the more the relationship will suffer. Isn't mutuality a better and more realistic model for positive relationships within the context of the family than the notion of faithful, and possibly unconditional, love?

Dan

9.8   *13 March 2004*

A LIBERATION THEOLOGY FOR THE FAMILY

Dan,

Of course I was moved by your story. But I thought I had argued enough in preceding letters that what undergirds everything for me is belief in relational justice — in mutuality and reciprocity between women and men, and appropriate levels of mutuality between adults and children. And I have problems with using covenant theology to support this. As you well know, the bridal imagery in the Hebrew Bible, say, for example, in Hosea 1—3, builds on the faithfulness and forgiveness of God towards the faithless wife, the allegorical image of Israel.

But there is something quite shocking and one-sided about this relationship. The prophet is ordered by God to marry Gomer, a prostitute and 'worthless woman' with whom he has children. His faithfulness to her mirrors God's covenantal faithfulness to Israel. But then he utters violent threats towards her as she leaves him for her lovers:

> I will make her bare as the wilderness,
> Parched as the desert,
> And leave her to die of thirst.
> I will make her bare as the wilderness ... (Hos. 2:3)

The Jewish feminist writer Naomi Graetz says that even if we know from the next few verses that God (i.e. the prophet) will forgive her, take her back and show bridal love once more, this marriage imagery is based on inequality, not reciprocity. Why is it that the male prophet (allegorically representing God) is always the figure of faith and forgiveness, and the female figure (representing Israel) is always the faithless one?[5]

Furthermore, she argues that even if this is a metaphor, it is a dangerous one, given the scenario where husbands do batter wives — this until recently being considered normal in many cultures and going legally unrecognised as crime. Widen this across cultures and religions, even in Britain itself, and I see forced arranged marriages for young girls (think of the recent case of the girl who ran away from home to avoid one and committed suicide in the Lake District), forced female genital mutilations and the still high incidence of domestic violence: so, yes, mutuality and relational justice, but I cannot see that appealing to the biblical imagery of covenant will enable this.

What we seek is inspiration and support for the new situation of contemporary culture where, as I argued in my previous letter, people live in diverse forms of relationships and commitments. Never before has a culture had to face the fact that so many children are reared by a single partner — mostly women, but men also. How does the covenantal relationship help here? Often what is faced is broken relationship, with no possibility of reconciliation. The parent is facing poverty, years of loneliness, and if she is a woman, is frequently blamed for the breakdown, considered a parasite on society, in that she is forced to live on social benefit.

That's why I fall back on the faith language of liberation theology, because I believe that faithful people are committed both to God and to the flourishing of all humanity. The feminist theologian Carter Heyward writes:

> Faithful people are liberators of creation, which is the arena of all that lives. As we are shamefully, painfully aware, the creation is groaning. Lovelessness is rampant. If the work and play of creation is to make new, then the work and play of liberation is to redeem and salvage the world — that which is with us now, that which is violated, broken or lost ... Liberation requires re-membering, re-gathering and healing.[6]

How to create a liberation theology and a praxis of liberation for the family, in the many life situations and lifestyles in which the family struggles for survival today?

Mary

9.9   *15 March 2004*

BEYOND FAITHFUL LOVE

Mary,

I think you misunderstand what I mean by covenant. In the Bible, covenant is conceived as a two-way relationship with obligations on both sides. The example you cite from Hosea 1—3 is misleading. There should be nothing one-sided in a covenantal relationship. The point is that it is two-sided, involving mutual responsibilities and reciprocity. This, I believe, is often what is missing in family life, and leads to friction between parents and siblings. It is also missing in our relationships with others in community.

Let me put the matter this way: a cardinal principle of Christian ethics is that love should be unconditional, just as forgiveness should be freely given. But I believe this to be a mistake. In advocating faithful love, I assume you are referring to Jesus' message. But I believe that Jesus' moral precepts are unrealistic: they actually distort human relationships. In the gospels Jesus tells his followers that they should love all human beings, even their enemies, and that they should forgive seventy times seven. In other words, we are to be active participants, whereas others are to be the object of our concern.

Yet, paradoxically, I think that in this way we actually diminish human beings. They become faceless, one-dimensional. The Jewish philosopher Martin Buber cautioned against turning other people into objects. Yet this is precisely what Jesus encourages us to do. All of us wish to be treated as adults, and we want others to behave in an adult fashion.

But if we follow Jesus' teachings, we infantilise other human beings. If we are to love others unconditionally, and forgive them for whatever they do — and this is to serve as the basis for family life or life in the community — then these persons have ceased to be autonomous, responsible moral agents.

In my view we should abandon Jesus' ethical prescriptions about faithful love and substitute instead a more mature framework. In place of selfless giving, we should act on the principle of reciprocity. In other words, human relationships should be guided by mutual concern, give and take. All giving should be balanced by the desire to receive. We should act so that in every relationship there is an equal rate of exchange. Parents should expect their children to give as well as receive. Husband and wife should act similarly towards one another. One partner should not do all the giving, and the other all the taking. I am suggesting, therefore, that Jesus' teaching about selflessness be replaced by the principle of mutuality. If we give, we should expect to take. And if we take, we should expect to give. This should be so within the family, and within the community. Such mutuality, I believe, is a realistic praxis, and can liberate us from the illusions of faithful love.

Dan

9.10 *18 March 2004*

CARE FOR THE GENERATIONS

Dan,

I thought I had made the case often enough for mutuality! And I can concede that Hosea is perhaps not the right witness for the desired reciprocity in marriage. But we have to keep reminding ourselves that for the traditional marriage there was no question of reciprocity. Women had to agree to obey and this model is still in play in conservative circles by recourse to such texts as Ephesians 5:22:'Wives be subject to your husbands as to the Lord. For the husband is head of the wife as Christ is head of the church.'

At my own Roman Catholic wedding, where a well-known, fairly progressive priest gave a sermon, he referred to this traditional role — whereupon I made a face, and was duly reprimanded!

But I plead with you to reconsider the meaning of what Jesus said on forgiveness. I have argued with you already, on 24 July (Chapter 2), that Jesus was very aware of unjust power structures and that the forgiveness parables and injunctions are always *from the more powerful to the less powerful* and not the other way round. There is no urging that the battered woman must forgive her abuser, that land-hungry peasants must forgive rapacious land-lords. The woman from the town (Luke 7) is forgiven because she has loved much. Even Peter's famous question as to how often we have to forgive is answered in terms of the parable of the unjust servant, where the forgiveness/debt cancellation went from the powerful king to the powerless servant and not vice versa. It is very hard to sustain an argument that Jesus treated people like objects, when the evidence seems to show that encountering him was experienced as a life-giving event: 'Lord, to whom shall we go? You have the words of eternal life' (John 6:68).

But I suggest that reliance solely on a framework of reciprocity is inadequate in the current climate of family breakdown, separa-tion and divorce, as well as the fact I mentioned last time, that families are so often one-parent families. Britain has the highest divorce rate in Europe. I expect that we both agree that divorce is a just solution in the case of irretrievable breakdown and of a relationship based on injustice, violence and abuse. There has been great inequality in the allowing of divorces in the past, and reluctance to allow remarriage in church in many Christian denominations. (The Greek Orthodox do allow this — but in a spirit of penitence.)

But the danger is that in insisting on reciprocity as the model, we have nothing helpful to say to the numerous people whose reality is broken relationship, nor to the children growing up in unstable situations. I think our relationships have public as well as personal meaning and that religious communities need to be responsible for the care of future generations. How we pattern relationships matters enormously. By this I do not mean ensuring that marriages should take place within the closely knit traditional communities of the older generations (like the perpetuation of a caste system), but supporting people in a variety of relationships as they struggle to live out some kind of faithful commitment in this new pluralist world. And you cannot rule out some suffering in many situations. Relationships aim to be reciprocal and mutual — and begin this way — but life makes heavy demands. Poverty through unemployment and homelessness is responsible for so much break-up, and people in fragile relationships should be able to call out to the wider community at different times for support, loyalty, friendship, companionship, or for building bridges across diverse, even hostile communities. Within these relationships there are different power configurations — and children are frequently powerless in a context where their parents have also received poor parenting.

Children of the future desperately need icons of faithfulness: we often see them now growing up with poor relational skills after three generations of parental break-up, seeking sexual expression younger in short-lived, tempestuous encounters. But what it is all about is how love is lived and shared and how others are enabled to love. Surely this should now be the focus of the pastoral care of religious communities, who should be willing to sit more loosely to the demands of tradition, and respond more generously to the needs of the present?

Mary

❧——❧

9.11   *21 March 2004*

HEALING BROKEN RELATIONSHIPS

Mary,

I am not persuaded that the Christian notion of forgiveness is restricted to cases where the powerful should forgive the less powerful. It seems to me, on the contrary, that Christians are taught to forgive all those who transgress against them regardless who is the more powerful party. Hence, the battered wife is to forgive her battering husband; the woman who is raped is to forgive the rapist; the exploited is to forgive the exploiter. I do think that such unconditional forgiveness is one-dimensional, turning those who are to be forgiven into objects rather than persons. They are to become recipients of our forgiveness rather than persons who are culpable, obligated to feel remorse, who must resolve not to commit similar offences before they can be pardoned.

The Jewish view is very different from the Christian: offenders are to come to terms with their offence and to accept responsibility for their actions. Reconciliation is not possible unless these conditions are fulfilled. This has nothing to do with the experiences of those who confronted Jesus and were stirred by his words. Rather, it is the message itself which turns both the offended and the offender into objects.

Again, I believe that the framework of reciprocity is the only viable and realistic approach to mending broken relationships whether they are familial or social. It makes no difference whether the family is conceived in traditional terms, or is a very different kind of constellation. What is crucial is that there be give and take between the parties concerned. Even within one-parent families, there should be mutuality and a recognition of the needs of the other.

Similarly, in homosexual and lesbian relationships, the same principle applies. You refer to the notion of justice: this is at the heart of the problem. Relationships collapse because they are unjust. Mutuality demands justice and an acceptance of the needs of others. Even though life makes, as you say, heavy demands, this does not in any way rule out the necessity of reciprocity. At every level — within the family, within in the community, and within society as a whole — relationships should be based on the principle of give and take. You maintain that by advancing the model of reciprocity, we offer nothing to those who are caught in situations of poverty or who are unemployed. You suggest instead that what people need today are icons of faithfulness. I think you are right. But if such icons are derived from our two traditions, they should be examples of faithfulness based on mutual respect and care. I don't in any way dispute that our faith communities should sit more loosely to the demands of tradition and respond more generously to new patterns of family life. But this does not rule out the need to expose the reasons why relationships collapse, and to seek ways to help those in broken relationships to remedy their situation. This, I believe, can only be done through an awareness of the needs of others. In all this mutuality is the key.

Dan

10. Racism

10.1 23 March 2004

THE CHALLENGE OF OTHERNESS

Dan,

There is one theme that functions as a huge obstacle to peace and reconciliation today and that is racial difference, racially motivated violence and racial prejudice, operating on many levels. This has been a hidden factor in many of our exchanges and it can be all the more dangerous because we (i.e. society as a whole) are often in denial about it. *We are innocent liberals and count all humans equal.* I think the truth is more unpalatable. Yes, it is true that we could look at the horrendous conflicts around us today — the hunt for Osama bin Laden in Afghanistan, the assassination yesterday of Sheikh Yassin of Hamas in Palestine, the Indian—Pakistani conflict over Kashmir, or the Russian—Chechen tensions — and we would have to admit that racism would be only one factor in a cocktail of causes like conflicting ideologies, rival claims to the same land, festering historical memories of domination, and religiously motivated revenge strategies. But racial hatred is a factor that binds all of these.

Some years ago I co-authored a book called *From Barriers to Community.*[1] Addressing the Catholic Church in the main, it was an attempt to expose the roots of racism in British society and to offer some practical courses of action for schools and communities. Looking back over British history, we charted the racism that accompanied the conquest of Ireland and Wales. Hard on its heels came the racist attitudes that accompanied the British Empire in India, enabling the class structure to mesh with the Indian caste system. But it was the slave trade that revealed the worst aspects of racism: the savage cruelty that accompanied this great social evil revealed that when racial prejudice is accompanied by power and false ideology — such as the pseudo-scientific tracts that purported to prove that black people were less intelligent than whites — then we have institutionalised racism whose legacy is difficult to eradicate completely. Current attitudes to immigrants and asylum seekers are one example of this.

For, sad to report, racially motivated crimes have increased. The Home Office recorded 4,500 reported cases in 1988, and 22,000 in 1999/2000.[2] Only yesterday Lord Goldsmith, intervening to *increase* a sentence against someone guilty of a racially motivated crime, said that racism remains a cancer in our society. And this is despite better legislation, the Council for Racial Equality, and numerous attempts in many work situations to eradicate racial harassment and discrimination. As with sexism, there would seem to be something very deep-rooted about racial prejudice, something that continues to fuel the scapegoating of vulnerable groups in society. In the past it has been women (burnt as witches) or the frequent attacks on Jewish people, and the latest group is asylum seekers — or single mothers claiming social benefits. The only common fact is that the targeted group is defined as other and therefore inferior to the dominant group.

Isn't the path to reconciliation the slow unravelling and healing of the many ways we have demonised the other? Methods which did not evolve overnight. The novelist Lawrence Durrell wrote of the slow undermining of trust between Cypriot Greeks and Turks in the remote mountain village where he had settled.[3] In the Balkans War, whose tragic consequences are still with us, historical wounds affecting Serbs and Croats who had lived together as community before the conflict were deliberately uncovered to provoke hostility and turn neighbours into enemies. Michael Ignatieff wrote:

> It is not a sense of radical difference that leads to conflict with others, but the refusal to admit a moment of recognition. Violence must be done to the self before it can be

done to others. Living tissue of connection and difference must be cauterised before a neighbour is reinvented as an enemy.[4]

This means believing that what connects us is fundamentally more powerful than what divides. But to rediscover this means that racial harmony is a process for the long haul. It is a process to which both remembering and being willing to let go of certain memories belongs; where learning to respect difference and diversity is vital; and where a commitment to the well-being of the other group, whose very existence we would prefer not to acknowledge, because if we do, our lifestyle will be threatened (or so we imagine), becomes the risky path we tread. But how can this even be contemplated in the polarised world in which we find ourselves?

Mary

10.2 *26 March 2004*

RACISM AND LAW

Mary,
Your depiction of conflict in the modern world is not confined solely to antagonism between races but applies to ethnic friction and struggle. But I wonder what you mean by 'racism'. On the simplest level it refers to prejudice against members of another physical group. In the United States racism has been understood as discrimination against Afro-Americans. Growing up in the suburbs of Denver, I did come across Afro-Americans in my school, and even had some black friends. But it was unthinkable to go out with an Afro-American girl. Blacks lived in specific areas of the city and were prevented from buying houses in affluent white neighbourhoods.

Years later I worked as a rabbi in South Africa when apartheid existed. Blacks formed separate queues outside post offices, and were compelled to ride on designated buses. In Johannesburg I lived in a flat where two black maids looked after me and called me 'Master'. This was blatant racism. Both in the USA and South Africa, blacks were viewed and treated as inferior.

In modern society such racial abuse still exists, but usually on a covert level. As you point out, it is institutionally reinforced and pervades Western culture. But it is not only blacks who suffer. Other physically distinct groups as well as ethnic communities are subject to discrimination.

Of course I perceive all this from a Jewish context and cannot help but reflect on the ways prejudice has been directed at Jews. In the late nineteenth century (as I noted before), the father of secular Zionism, Theodor Herzl, wrote a monumental tract, *The Jewish State*, in which he argued that Jews will never be free of antipathy. Anti-Semitism, he maintained, is inevitable where Jews form a minority group. What is necessary, he stated, is for Jews to become a majority in their own state. In his opinion, the problem is one of power. Minority groups are destined to be victims of the majority. This analysis, I believe, not only explains the origins of prejudice against Jews, but accounts for all forms of hostility directed toward racial and ethnic groups. In the struggle between the majority and the minority, it is always the majority who will be victorious.

Is there any solution to racism as defined in the broadest terms? The Zionist answer is deeply pessimistic. The creation of Israel is a form of defeatism — solely by isolating themselves in a political ghetto can Jews protect themselves from their enemies. For Zionists, the only way to escape anti-Semitism is for Jews to become the majority in their own country. There they will cease to be victims. Yet the tragedy of the Zionist solution and its inevitable outcome is that minorities within the Occupied Territories have become the targets of the majority population.

To my mind, religious idealism can offer little to the problems of racism. Appealing to Scripture or the rabbinic tradition will not hold back the forces of malice and hatred. Ethical values will not withstand the whirlwind of prejudice and economic interest. The weak will be crushed by the strong, unless they are protected by legal restraint. It is for this reason that I regard the legal systems of modern society as the bulwark of social justice. The rights of all can only be protected by law. Law is the only restraining force against the torrent of evil that is unleashed on the weakest members of the modern world. Otherwise, the ethical and religious message of our two traditions will appear as little more than a squeak in the wilderness.

Dan

10.3 *29 March 2004*

WHEN A SQUEAK BECOMES A SCREAM!

Dan,

'A squeak in the wilderness', you say! But I argue that religious communities have far more authority than you are willing to admit. You ask what I mean by racism: in my last letter I wrote about racial prejudice in many historical contexts. This prejudice becomes racism when combined with power, power manifested by the dominant authority throughout its institutions — from the police force and judicial systems, to schools, corner shops and street gangs. Of course you are right to describe the long suffering of the Jewish people from anti-Semitism over many centuries — and we have already discussed the part that Christian theology and Church have played in this. In no way do I underestimate the weight of this, but I wonder if you are over-pessimistic in your opinion when you write: 'Ethical values will not withstand the whirlwind of prejudice and economic interest. The weak will be crushed by the strong, unless they are protected by legal restraint.'

As we wrestle with this problem, the world is still reeling from the reactions to the Israeli murder of Sheikh Yassin, the former spiritual leader of Hamas. Despite the criticism of the Israeli government for this killing, it seems that what was once persecution of the Jews is now metamorphosing into a pernicious hostility towards Islam, preventing any real understanding and dialogue, not to mention reconciliation.

But I want to argue that it is wrong to fall into extreme pessimism. I do believe that justice as well as oppression and violence is enacted in history. Within my lifetime historic steps have been taken within the Catholic Church that have brought about far-reaching changes. Don't forget that people are influenced by far

more than secular law. When I was growing up in the pre-Vatican
II Catholic Church, I am ashamed now to tell you, on Good
Friday, in the commemoration of Jesus' death, a very solemn serv-
ice, we prayed for the 'perfidious Jews'. But after the second
Vatican council such language vanished. The Council
Constitution, *Nostra Aetate* — a document I've already referred to
— ushered in a new era, as the Pope recognised Jews and
Christians as brothers and sisters in faith. This evoked a serious
and ongoing effort to rid Christian theology of anti-Judaism.
Christian—Jewish dialogue was embarked on. The present Pope
has repeatedly condemned anti-Semitism and the Holocaust and
the documents of the Church I've referred to have spelled out in
unmistakable terms that *racism is sin*. It means that no one in our
church could ever make an anti-Semitic statement with the
approval of the church. This is far more than 'a squeak in the
wilderness'!

I realise that there is always a gap between official statement and
the reality on the ground: but you must admit that, along with
the protection of law, the efforts of Christian churches — the
Catholic Church is not alone — have made modest progress. The
climate has definitely changed and this is not entirely a question
of legal restraint. But there are still two huge problems: the first is
that many people turn (legitimate) criticism of the Israeli government's actions towards the Palestinian people into continuing
anti-Semitic attitudes towards the entire Jewish people; the
second is — as I mentioned earlier — that the former racial hostility towards the Jewish people is being transferred towards the
entire Islamic world. At the moment, this might give legitimate
cause for despair.

Mary

10.4   *7 April 2004*

PIPING IN THE DARK

Mary,
I simply cannot accept your assumptions about the authority and
power of religious institutions: can spiritual ideas really change the

world? There is no doubt that religions can cause havoc, and that followers of charismatic religious figures do unleash wanton destruction. The question is whether religious ideals can curtail racism. Arguably it is a mistake to rely on liberal ideals to bring about political and social reform. Appealing to concepts of justice and equality — the principles that we have espoused throughout our correspondence — may in fact change nothing.

This certainly has been the Jewish experience. For nearly twenty centuries Jews were subject to discrimination, persecution and murder. As we have seen, the Church, on the basis of its perception of the Jews' rejection of Christ, believed that Jewry was despised by God and destined to wander the earth. Although Jewish emancipation took place in the nineteenth century, Jews continued to be subjected to constant prejudice, culminating in the Holocaust. The state of Israel was created by Jews determined to ensure that they would be protected from further attempts at genocide.

Throughout history Jewry was unable to secure just treatment by advocating moral principles. Instead, it was only through constant and determined pressure that states were compelled to grant rights to Jews which were enshrined in law. In the modern world, Jews are protected — not by appealing to moral values, but through the due process of the legal systems under which they live. You contend that I am overly pessimistic. But I am not. I am simply realistic about the inevitable failure of religious and ethical values to curb the ills of contemporary society.

You cite the case of the Catholic Church which has altered the wording of its liturgy, so that such expressions as the 'perfidious Jews' have been eliminated. You refer to *Nostra Aetate*, and the Pope's recognition of Jews and Christians as brothers and sisters in faith. All this is to be welcomed, as well as the Pope's condemnation of anti-Semitism and the Holocaust. But will it truly alter the attitude of the majority of Christians who are suspicious of Jews and contemptuous of their success? I think not. Indeed, films like Mel Gibson's *The Passion of the Christ* (based in a large part on the gospels) continue to present Jewish leaders in the most negative light and will no doubt inflame Christian passion against Jews whose ancestors cried for Jesus' death.

Officially Christians are to regard racism as a sin: this is the message of the document you cite. Yet Christian racists will, I am sure, take little if any notice of such official pronouncements. In the Middle Ages, the Church officially condemned the blood libel accusation against Jews and categorically denied the claim that the Black Death was brought about by the Jewish community. But no notice was taken of such declarations; instead, Christian mobs stormed Jewish dwellings and murdered those who were perceived as agents of the devil.

Undeniably progress has been made: Jews are not treated as they once were; women have gained equal rights in many countries; homosexuals are no longer regarded as criminals; blacks have gained protection. But, as I stressed previously, what is of fundamental importance is to ensure that legislation is passed to outlaw all forms of racism. It is not enough to cry out for justice. Justice only comes enshrined in law. The goal of religious leaders and writers should be to struggle for justice and equality under the law. Anything else is nothing more than a little squeak, a tiny piping in the dark.

Dan

10.5 *13 April 2004*

IS FUNDAMENTALISM, NOT RACISM, NOW THE REAL
ISSUE?

Dan,

Of course you are right to stress the enormous importance of law in achieving progress in social justice across a range of issues. And I realise how feeble it must sound to cite some minor liturgical changes in Roman Catholic liturgy against the horrific reality of persecutions against the Jewish people during the last two thousand years. I *could* argue, on the basis of *lex orandi lex credendi* (what we pray is what we believe), that in fact such changes do point to significant progress in attitudes — and that does offer grounds for hope.

But my real argument tackles the question as to the role of religion and faith community in fighting racism. This you seem to deny. I don't want to let faith communities off the hook. I agree that Mel Gibson's film resuscitates the ghost of anti-Semitism, even if this is not his intention, and I'm ashamed that some churches are encouraging wallowing in the sadistic violence to boost the numbers of their flagging congregations.

Just look at the facts. Whereas the doom and gloom people never fail to repeat the statistics of the emptying Christian churches — in Europe at least — glimpsed from a global perspective this is not the case. Will Hutton in yesterday's *Observer* points out that Protestant evangelism and Islamic fundamentalism are the two fastest growing religions on the planet.[5] Buddhist and Hindu fundamentalism is growing. In the US — where Protestant evangelism is at its most popular — 61 per cent of the population think life is worth living because of belief in God. Europe's reality is traceable to the effects of the French revolution and its secular principles of fraternity, legality and liberty set over against any control of religion.

Yet, as you are only too well aware, the world situation today looks grim, as the situation in Iraq continues to disintegrate. Even the two Islamic groups — Sunni and Shiite — show signs of uniting against the common enemy, the coalition forces. In practice this means one fundamentalism (Islamic) against another (Christian evangelistic). Hutton argues that because we cannot appeal to religion in Europe now, there is an ominous drift to nationalism and tribal identity, hence the reaction to immigration, asylum seekers and terrorism that everywhere in Europe is sparking atavistic and primitive responses.[6]

I think that we see old racisms assuming new forms. We read that Britain is no longer multicultural, a concept that gained much acceptance in the eighties. Ethnic diversity is gradually being perceived as a threat — although this has been consciously encouraged by right-wing and neo-fascist groups. Look at the opposition from rural communities to suggested camps for asylum seekers, an opposition that may have little to do with the truth of the people they are rejecting.

To counter new forms of fascism, ethnocentrism and racial intolerance, yes, we need a solid legal system, but we also need to be able to counter prejudice and self-seeking individualism by

commitment to diversity in community, by principles of inclusivity, by protecting the vulnerable — and yes, by showing in
practice, not only theory, that it is possible *to love the stranger.* And
that's where religious communities — if they can renounce fundamentalism — can take us beyond racist violence to respect and
the hope of harmonious co-existence.

Mary

10.6   *18 April 2004*

MULTICULTURALISM AND ASSIMILATION

Mary,

In recent weeks there has been considerable discussion about the
notion of multiculturalism. With the influx of immigrant popula-
tions, it was felt that the different communities within the United
Kingdom should have the right to inculturate the young into
different religious and cultural heritages. Yet there has been a
growing recognition that the ideology of multiculturalism has
exacerbated divisions within society and has intensified racist attitudes. To cope with this problem, the Chief Rabbi formulated a
new model to cope with the existence of social pluralism. As
reported in *The Times* yesterday, his view is that members of
minority groups (such as Jews) should seek to assimilate into the
host community while remaining loyal to their respective
traditions.

Within the Jewish community such a dualistic model was propounded in the mid-nineteenth century as Jews began to enter
into the mainstream of Western society. Across the religious spectrum, Jewish leaders encouraged their coreligionists to integrate
into the communities in which they lived while preserving the
Jewish tradition. Some Orthodox Jews, such as the religious
thinker and writer Rabbi Samson Raphael Hirsch, argued that
Jewish acculturation was possible without sacrificing Jewish
identity. His concept of *Torah im derekh eretz* (Torah with a
practical livelihood) gained widespread acceptance, becoming the
credo of modern Orthodoxy. Those of a more liberal persuasion
actively sought to reform the faith, yet they too believed that

it was possible to adhere to Judaism despite social and cultural accommodation.

This approach, I believe, is of crucial importance in contemporary society. There is no doubt that Islamic fundamentalism is a growing danger to Western societies. Since 9/11 Muslims are feared in the countries where they live. Yet the more they segregate themselves, the greater will they be misunderstood. You refer to the clash between Islamic and Christian fundamentalism, but the clash between Islamic and Western civilisations is even greater. What is now urgently needed is for Muslims to adopt the same pattern of integration that Jews embraced over the last 200 years. Only by learning and speaking the languages of the societies in which they live, and adjusting to the value system of host communities, will they be able to overcome prejudice and persecution. Cultural and religious apartheid is no solution.

Recently the former Archbishop of Canterbury, Lord Carey, criticised theocratic Islamic states for fostering terrorism. Muslim leaders were quick to respond, accusing him of Christian chauvinism. But he was right. Throughout the world, fanatical Muslims espouse hatred of the West and encourage followers to resort to violence. This clash of civilisations inevitably fosters old racisms, and leads to suspicion and contempt. As much as we might deplore contemporary forms of racism, no solution will be found without the cooperation of Muslim communities. If Muslims truly wish to overcome prejudice, they must desist from segregating themselves into Islamic ghettos. Instead of insisting that their children go to Islamic schools, they should ensure that from the very earliest age Muslim youth attend schools with non-Muslims.

The experience of modern Jewry is, I believe, instructive in combating modern forms of racism. As I have continually noted in our correspondence, the Jewish people have been detested through the centuries. It was only in the last 200 years that Jews have been able to assimilate into the societies in which they lived. This was accomplished through a process of acculturation. Rather than isolating themselves as they had done throughout history, Jews actively sought to accommodate themselves to Western culture. At the same time, they pressed for civil rights. This arguably should be the model for all minority groups who seek to overcome social and cultural discrimination.

Dan

10.7 *19 April 2004*

ASSIMILATION — INTO WHAT WORLD ORDER?

Dan,

I think it was always realised that multiculturalism was a weak word and a weak concept. But it did express a willingness to accept a wider notion in Britain and the West of who counted as British and European. Nevertheless we should not rush too fast into using words like 'assimilation' on the one hand, or into an assumed 'clash of civilisations' on the other. On this last point, we are referring to the current 'war on terrorism' which is in fact a war against Islamic extremists: but when we also refer back to Samuel Huntingdon's remark as to its inevitability, there is good reason to resist the notion.[7] In a lecture two years ago in St Paul's Cathedral, London, the Indian economist Amartya Sen argued that the West has failed to acknowledge and value Arab learning and its contribution to the foundations of European society — a fact that partly caused the angry response to George Carey's speech, to which you refer. We have pitifully short historical memories: there is a widespread amnesia as to times when Christian, Jew and Muslim managed to coexist more or less in harmony.

'Assimilation' has a terrible history for Jews, Muslims and Afro-Caribbeans in particular. I think you need a different word to express the tensions to which you refer, namely, the freedom to live and practise one's own faith and at the same time to partici-pate meaningfully and positively in a specific society. But this challenge should be made not only to minority faiths, but to all faiths. On 5 December you wrote to me: 'We need to understand why we in Western countries are hated, and Islamic fundamen-talists need to comprehend the ideology and value system of those they detest.' Only in this way can our world be protected from those who are prepared to destroy Western civilisation, and from the Allies who are intent on annihilating their enemies.

Let me cite the comparison with India, where the dominating political party is right-wing Hindu, the BJP (Bharatiya Janata Party), itself springing from an even more fundamentalist umbrella group, the RSS.[8] Since 1992, after the destruction of the Muslim mosque at Ayodha, anti-Islamic tensions have increased to the point where, in February 2002 in Ahmedabad (Gujarat), nearly two thousand Muslims were violently murdered and women raped, with devastating consequences. As this is a Jewish—Christian conversation, I'll limit this comparison to the way the situation is being compared with Germany in the 1930s. In the vision of the BJP, 'India was a sacred indigenous nation of Hindus that was weakened by the invaders of the eleventh century — that will only be restored by purification from minority foreign elements, or at least a subjugation of minorities to Hindu superiority.'[9] A textbook for 14-year-olds refers approvingly to Hitler's strong administrative set-up which gave such dignity to Germany.

Shabnam Hashmirie, who runs ANHAD (Act Now for Harmony and Democracy), and is from a Delhi-based non-believing Muslim family, says living in India now feels like living in Germany in the 1930s. Now, whereas it is true that there are more liberal elements in the BJP, and true too that Christians are also being persecuted in this systemic discrimination, the way forward — for India and for the world as a whole — cannot lie in assimilation to the dominant ideology, but to an active inclusion of opposing factions in a vision for the common good. To do otherwise is to repeat what Nazi Germany did to the Jewish people up to 1945.

We need to reflect why western society is offensive to Islam and why so many of its elements are unacceptable. Not only sexual lifestyles, extravagant materialism and consumerism, but what Islam sees as the violent neo-colonialism of America, abetted by Britain, vis-a-vis Arab countries threatens its very identity. It seems to me that the vision of Gandhi — who saw the basis of all religions as one of love, service, self-sacrifice and non-violence — has to be re-harnessed in this new situation. It was rejected in his lifetime for many reasons, and the consequences of Hindu—

Muslim violence continue to be tragic. Can Jews and Christians cooperate in this changed situation with a commitment to our mutual well-being and a changed world order?

Mary

10.8   *20 April 2004*

ASSIMILATION AND THE FUTURE

Mary,

You are highly critical of assimilation, yet I believe it is of funda-mental importance. You will remember that previously I referred to the criticisms levelled at assimilationist attitudes by secular Zionists such as Moses Hess, Leon Pinsker and Theodor Herzl. These nineteenth-century Jewish thinkers were convinced that Jews would never be accepted in the communities in which they lived. All three were themselves assimilated Jews who were deeply troubled by what they perceived as the intransigent attitudes of the non-Jewish world. Herzl, for example, witnessed the Dreyfus trial in France, and subsequently argued that the hostility toward Jews displayed during the trial illustrated the deep-seated antago-nism toward Jewry embedded in Western civilisation. In *The Jewish State*, he declared that anti-Semitism is inevitable: nowhere other than in a Jewish state could Jews be free of such prejudice.[10]

Implicit in this argument is the belief that assimilation will never help Jews. It is impossible, these secular Zionists maintained, for Jews to be accepted into the majority culture, no matter what degree of assimilation takes place. Such pessimism is at the heart of Zionist ideology. It is an attitude I fervently reject. I am an assimilationist, and I believe that by adapting to majority culture and embracing the ideology of the dominant civilisation Jews, as well as members of minority groups, will be able to integrate into the societies in which they live. This does not imply that they must sever their links to the past. On the contrary, Jews, Muslims, Hindus, West Indians and others should feel strong ties and a sense of loyalty to their respective heritages. But it is far healthier, and certainly more creative, to live what I would refer to as a double life. On the one hand, to assimilate; and on the other, to remain faithful to religious and cultural traditions. Jews, and others, should dance to two tunes simultaneously.

No doubt there are offensive features of Western society: extravagant materialism, conspicuous consumption, and consumerism. But this is no excuse for minority communities to isolate themselves from mainstream culture. As I have said, it is vital that they learn the languages of the countries in which they live, and that the young attend integrated schools. Assimilation, acculturation and integration are necessary if racism is to be combated. Multiculturalism did express good will, but as an ideology it has failed. We live in a divided world, threatened by a clash of civilisations. It is naïve to think that Islamic fanaticism is an aberration of Islam. Throughout the world it is rooted in Islamic society, and it is growing. Lord Carey was right to point out its danger and its pervasiveness. Non-violence is an ideal, but in a world beset by violence, it is meaningless without the recognition that those at the margins of society should move to the centre in the quest for recognition, equal rights and respect.

Dan

10.9 *25 April 2004*

OUT OF THE GHETTO OR PROPHETIC CRITIQUE?

Dan,

I can understand why you hold to this position so firmly. Dancing to the tune of 'civilised' society, while simultaneously holding on to a firm faith position, is *one* solid way of establishing a strong, fully accepted Jewish presence in the contemporary world. It is turning around the horrendous memory of ghetto existence, of a regime which would never tolerate even assimilation but demanded total obliteration. It is an option that is coherent with your espousal of the achievement of the Enlightenment and its privileging of rationality, but it is not the solution of all branches of Judaism.

Ghetto existence is also part of my history — to some extent. Even though Roman Catholic emancipation occurred in 1832, the history of three hundred years of persecution was certainly not speedily eradicated. Being an Irish Catholic in England was to be the butt of Irish jokes, and to be the unacceptable face of Christianity. When I was a child it was an urgent matter of identity to eat fish on Friday, to receive ashes on Ash Wednesday and so on. But I longed to be the same as everyone else. Now it's much easier in hindsight to discern what was worth holding on to, and what to discard. And, you are right, Polish Catholics — or any other group which has problems integrating — struggle with language, poverty, perhaps now the right to asylum, and usually a measure of racism. And the goal is *integration* — to me that's a better word than assimilation.

For I cannot forget that assimilation has dangerous implications. As I said to you in my last letter, assimilation policies justify violence against minority groups — I cited the right-wing ruling Hindu party in India, the BJP, and its violence towards Muslim and Christian. It is a practice going back to the demands of the Roman emperors that the early Christians sacrifice to pagan gods, and to the emperors themselves, with the threat of execution hanging over them if they refused. Secondly, assimilation has the tragic effect of internalising the standards of the dominant group: Toni Morrison, in her novel *The Bluest Eye*, depicts this ideology in the form of the little girl Pecola, whose dream is to have blue eyes like the white girl in whose home her mother works — a dream with tragic consequences for Pecola herself.[11]

In the case of Afro-Caribbeans in Britain, it is the assumption of white superiority that is the problem. In a situation where religious belief is apparently in decline, Christianity, despite the Church of England's superior position, no longer occupies the privileged status with regard to other faiths that it once held. Surely then, we are in a new situation? Our question here is how to overcome racism. As you point out, Jews are now relatively privileged compared with fifty years ago. The leader of the opposition party is Jewish and he has a good chance of being elected Prime Minister. The real danger now is Islamic extremism — and this is whipping up a dangerous level of racism against Islam. Even though you appear to be sceptical, I believe there is a new call for religions not only to lead the way in terms of tolerance, but to provide a prophetic critique of those elements of society that are fanning this racism — namely the desire to dominate, to impose a world order that fails to respect minorities, and to do so in a violent, militaristic manner. If we in the North and West can learn together to embrace and value difference and otherness, and to adopt a lifestyle that allows others to survive *in a way they have chosen* (assuming this does not threaten fellow citizens), we will painfully, with a degree of self-sacrifice, forge a way to overcome racism.

Mary

10.10 *29 April 2004*

OUT OF THE GHETTO

Mary,

Throughout the nineteenth and twentieth centuries, the Jewish people were anxious to escape from the restrictions of ghetto life. You cannot minimise the disabilities that Jews faced throughout the Middle Ages until the Enlightenment. Nowhere were they accepted as equals; instead, they were regarded as aliens and outcasts. Only the strictly Orthodox and the Hasidim rejected the opportunities offered by modern Western society. Rather than break down the barriers that separated them from the outside world, they clung to their ancient traditions, defiantly determined to follow the tenets of traditional Judaism.

This is the background to my endorsement of the ideology of assimilation. You wish to make a distinction between assimilation and integration. But integration is possible only if a minority group actively seeks to embrace the values of the dominant society. I know that you fear that such a process of inculturation will lead to the abandonment of religious values and ideals that are an inherent feature of the faith traditions of these minority groups. I don't deny this will inevitably occur, but the issue we are discussing is racism. In my view, the only way to combat prejudice is to blur the distinctions between different groups. It is far better to melt down the religious divisions that lead to contempt and persecution than to encourage acceptance and intolerance. No one will hear these pleas, and the result will simply be the continuation of hatred and misunderstanding.

The ghetto walls were broken down — not through the rhetoric of liberty, equality and fraternity, but because the Jewish community escaped from self-imposed isolation. Rather than speaking the language of the ghetto, they learned the languages of the countries in which they lived and sought to ameliorate their situation by embracing the lifestyle of the gentile world. Now, you might deplore such attitudes, but in my view shedding outmoded, backward-looking and xenophobic attitudes was an advantage. This is why I am a Reform, rather than an Orthodox, Jew. The rigidity and inflexibility of Orthodoxy continues to stifle religious creativity and reflection.

In this connection, I have just completed a new book, *The Vision of Judaism: Wrestling with God*, in which I advocate a new approach to the tradition. This is what I wrote in the Conclusion:

> In the past Jews were compelled to live isolated, self-enclosed lives, regulated by the Jewish legal tradition. In such circumstances, religious authorities were able to impose their will on the community ... In modern times, however, such a theocratic structure has disintegrated ... This study calls for a religious reorientation of religious observance. From biblical times, Jews perceived themselves as bound by an eternal covenant which was sealed on Mount Sinai. The law, they believed, was divinely revealed, and sin was understood as a transgression of God's will. Today Orthodox Jews carry on this tradition, regarding themselves as the true heirs of Pharisaic Judaism. In the non-Orthodox world, on the other hand, deviations from the legal code have been justified by an appeal to the findings of biblical scholarship. This study similarly embraces such findings, but takes the further step in advocating the principle of personal liberty. A modern approach to Jewish practice, I believe, should acknowledge and respect the rights of individual Jews to determine for themselves which aspects of the tradition are religiously meaningful.[12]

What I am advocating — which is in fact the attitude of most Jews worldwide — is the principle of personal choice. Inevitably, such a shift from the absolutism of the past provides a basis for assimilation and integration into the mainstream of contemporary society. You may disapprove. Yet I firmly believe that only in this way has Jewry become acceptable. Racism has been undermined by a conscious attempt by the Jewish people to divest themselves of attitudes and practices that brought about their isolation. My point is that racism, which is inherent in contemporary society, can only be successfully combated if minority communities recognise that by insulating themselves from the outside world, they have created a climate of suspicion and contempt. Jewish history illustrates that by ceasing to be the Other, minorities can be accepted on equal terms.

Dan

―◦―◦―

10.11 *1 May 2004*

LOVE, JUSTICE, MERCY

Dan,

Our interchange on racism has been carried on against the background of a deteriorating situation both in the Iraqi conflict and in Palestine. My son Stephen, a journalist, has just returned to Iraq after a gap of five weeks, and poignantly describes the growing hostility to the coalition troops even within this space of time.[13] During this exchange you have repeatedly asserted that the comparatively improved situation of Jews in many countries — not everywhere, surely? — is because of deliberate attempts to come out of the ghetto and assimilate with the dominant culture, a policy not espoused by Orthodox Jews. I have to accept what you say, but only want to plead with you to see that on a worldwide and universal level you cannot advocate this policy exclusively.

For black South Africans under the apartheid regime it was not a question of integration — they *were* integrated but on supremacist white terms. It was a question of justice and dignity on *black* terms that was at issue. Again, in the example of India I quoted earlier, it is not an issue of assimilation: the BJP government is only too happy that Muslims, Christians and tribal people assimilate to the dominant Hindu majority without their own basic human rights being respected. An Indian journalist has compared the BJP with both Israel's right-wing Likud party and the US Republican party in its extraordinary mix of politics and religion.[14]

As I write today it is 1 May and the European Community is being enlarged to admit ten new countries. Concerns are being expressed about the status of asylum seekers already in the UK whose situation will change with the expected influx of people from the countries newly admitted to the EU; while at the same time it is feared that there may be racist reactions to these newly arrived people seeking jobs and a new life.

You are right to insist on good legislation. But in this final exchange on racism I want to appeal for a multi-strategic approach in this changed world situation. The recent conference in Israel, 'Challenging Christian Zionism: Theology, Politics and the Palestine-Israeli conflict' (attended by 500 people from 40 different countries) drew attention to the growing *political* power of Christian (fundamentalist) Zionism, with its apocalyptic disaster-dominated scenario.[15] One speaker, a Palestinian Christian lawyer, Jonathan Khattab, argued that the central issue was 'love, justice and mercy' and that the battle must be fought on concrete, human terms.

I think this is the heart of the issue. Yes, we need just legislation and policies that integrate diverse communities into our societies, while respecting their identities. But for this we need inspiration that is generous enough to reach out to alienated groups, with mercy, love and forgiveness — and the humility to ask for their forgiveness for past rejections. As I said earlier, *we are all recovering racists* ... New situations bring hidden prejudices to light and send us scurrying to protect and defend our territory.

But we must never lose hope even in the most desperate of situations. I'll end with a story from Rajasthan. At the marriage of the daughter of one of our partners in Jodhpur, the parents chose to ignore the fact that they had broken a caste boundary in the choice of husband. Their own family was furious, refused the wedding invitation, and would not accept the future son-in-law. So the parents invited the humble people from the villages whom they were helping — even the poor street children were invited.

Like the gospel story: if the invited guests will not come, go out into the highways and byways ... (Matt. 22:1—10) There was a sense that transgressing what was a racist custom meant a new sense of inclusive and generous community was possible. Is that not what we mean by the ethics of the Kingdom of Heaven?

Mary

11. Crime and Punishment

─◦⟨౷⟩◦─

11.1 *5 May 2004*

PUNISHMENT IN JEWISH SOURCES

Mary,

So far we have discussed a wide range of moral issues and their consequences for modern society. I want to turn finally to the concept of punishment. As you know, the Bible prescribes a wide range of penalties for those who transgress the law. The central purpose of such punishments is to purge evil from the midst of the people. This action is not so much directed against the offender, but is a demonstration of disapproval. By legislating judicial punishment, such conduct is condemned. Punishment is thereby inflicted on offenders not so much for their own sake, but to deter others. Thus Deuteronomy 21:22 decrees that an offender should be impaled on a stake after having been put to death so as to proclaim the execution. In addition, Jewish law seeks to ensure that the individual offender will be prevented from committing further crimes. Finally, punishment was executed to bring about the restoration of the status quo by inflicting on the criminal the same injury as he had caused.

Capital punishment was prescribed in ancient times for a series of crimes including kidnapping, murder, idolatry, desecration of the Sabbath, blasphemy, adultery, incest and other sexual offences. Two forms of capital punishment are mentioned in Scripture: stoning and burning. In Talmudic times two additional forms of execution

—slaying by a sword and strangling — were added. Nonetheless, Talmudic law severely circumscribed the court's ability to convict those accused of criminal offences. Capital crimes could only be tried by a court of 23; conviction could only be obtained on the testimony of two eyewitnesses; circumstantial evidence and hearsay were inadmissible; witnesses related to each other or the accused by blood or marriage were disqualified; and conviction could not be obtained unless the accused was warned in advance.

The Bible also prescribes flogging as a biblical command, as well as for a person who refuses to fulfil a positive commandment. A maximum of 40 lashes is stipulated. In Talmudic times sages levied fines as a substitute for penalties prescribed by Scripture. The court could also confiscate property as a means of ensuring compliance with the law. Although imprisonment was not decreed by Scripture, a person could be held in custody until the court could ascertain punishment. Rabbinic courts were also able to excommunicate those who gravely violated Jewish law or failed to comply with the decrees of local rabbis. Of course, all this legislation governed by rabbinic law has been superseded in modern times by recognition that punishment is to be made by secular authorities. The general principle in Judaism is that the law of the land is the law: as a consequence, Jewish courts no longer function as they did in previous centuries. Nevertheless, Jewish teaching about punishment — enshrined in biblical and rabbinic legislation — provides a framework for understanding the Jewish attitude to punishing offenders. Those who have violated the moral code are to be censured and punished for their offences. Penalties are viewed as necessary so that the community is protected from crime and wrongdoers are to be brought to judgement.

Dan

11.2   *5 May 2004*

AN EYE FOR AN EYE?

Dan,
You are right, this is a serious area and we have not discussed it. But whereas I am glad you give me the official Jewish position, I

miss your own gloss on it. And this has been such a lively part of our interchange that I feel sure it is important — so, what do you really think? I'm all too aware that we are discussing punishment in the safety of our studies, when the news has just broken of the abuses inflicted on Iraqi prisoners by American and British soldiers. My son Stephen — a journalist in Baghdad — was on Radio 4 yesterday giving terrible details. So the legitimacy of inflicting punishment is far from being an academic exercise.

As you know, Christianity began as a small sect in opposition to the Roman Empire. At first, official crime consisted — in the eyes of the Romans — in opposing the Roman emperor and the punishment was death, including being thrown to the lions in the arena. Then Christianity, under the Emperor Constantine, became the established religion (312 CE) and became itself the arbiter of what was legally right or wrong. The Church's sphere of authority has ranged from secular power, where right through history it has punished groups it defined as 'enemies of Christianity' — including the expulsion and killing of faith groups like Jews and Muslims — to its own internal jurisdiction via the ecclesiastical courts. Thousands of women have been burnt as witches, their 'confessions' exacted by torture.[1]

Yet the official position appears moderate enough: 'the traditional teaching of the church has acknowledged as well-founded the right and duty of legitimate authority to punish malefactors by means of penalties commensurate with the gravity of the crime, not excluding, in conditions of extreme gravity, the death penalty.'[2]

But, as you know, this area is a painful one for Jewish—Christian relations. For Christians have interpreted key passages of the New Testament in anti-Judaist ways. For example, in Matthew's gospel (5:38), Jesus says: 'You have learnt how it was said: eye for eye, tooth for tooth. But I say this to you: offer the wicked man no resistance. On the contrary, if anyone hits you on the right cheek, offer the other as well.'[3]

The context is where Jesus appears to radicalise certain areas of traditional Jewish teaching. (Other examples are in the areas of adultery and divorce.) But this particular example has been taken out of context, and used to proclaim a Christian God of love over

against a Jewish God of wrath and vengeance. Even if this interpretation is now never used, and 'an eye for an eye' is understood
as damage limitation, *only an eye and no more*, this contrast between
God of love and God of wrath has not completely disappeared,
and lurks in the psyches of many Christians.

The tragedy is not only that Christians do not show much
inclination to adopt a non-violent stance (if that is what this text
is advocating), but that in practice throughout history we have
shown neither restraint nor mercy towards criminals. The Church
officially states that punishment is meant to redress the disorder
perpetrated by the offender, and when accepted by the offender,
takes on the character of expiation.[4] But isn't the real problem that
Christians, along with the rest of humanity, in fact frequently
regard punishment as *revenge*, as legitimate *vengeance* for wrongdoing? And this is what we are dealing with, whether in Iraq,
Palestine, or in the UK itself, where Myra Hindley went to her
grave without being released from prison, because no one would
admit that she had been punished enough.

Mary

11.3   *13 May 2004*

UNACCEPTABLE PUNISHMENT

Mary,

You refer to the fact that Jesus appeared to reject traditional Jewish
teaching about punishment when he said: 'You have learnt how it
was said: eye for eye, tooth for tooth. But I say this to you: offer
the wicked man no resistance.' From this and other sayings, some
Christians (particularly in the early Church) espoused a doctrine
of non-violence. But there is no doubt that Jesus' apparent radi-
calisation of Jewish teaching did not serve as the framework for
the Christian understanding of punishment. Even Paul appears in
Romans 13 to accept the validity of capital punishment.

As in Judaism, corporal punishment was also accepted by the
Christian community as a valid penalty for transgression, and
flogging was inflicted for such crimes as robbery with violence
and sexual assault. Since the Church acknowledged that civil gov-

ernment was a necessary institution for society, the structures for punishing transgressors were embraced by the authorities. From the time of Constantine in the fourth century through the Middle Ages, Church and State were united into one commonwealth: the distinction between them was seen largely in their separate hierarchies and the systems of law they administered. After the schism between East and West, there were essentially two commonwealths of this kind, and at the Reformation the Western Church was divided into a variety of national churches; yet there was a common acceptance throughout Christendom of the validity of civil legislation, and this attitude has endured to the present day.

Hence, there is considerable common ground between the Church and the Synagogue about the necessity for punishment. Nonetheless, I think both of us have serious reservations about various aspects of this shared tradition. Regarding capital punishment, I think we would both agree that there is no substantial evidence to demonstrate that this form of punishment actually deters offenders. Further, if reformation is seen as a crucial justification for inflicting punishment, the death penalty does not allow for such change of heart to occur. Are we in agreement? I think we would also concur that retribution should not be the aim of punishment. If crime is a sickness to be cured rather than punished, therapy rather than judicial proceedings should serve as the remedy.

Currently we are witnessing terrible scenes of torture and violence in Iraq. The United States and Britain are being accused of maltreating prisoners, and Islamic fanatics have challenged the occupying forces in Iraq by beheading an American. Such actions on both sides are fuelled by contempt and hatred, yet the perpetrators seek to justify their actions by appealing to principles of justice. What we are witnessing is a gross distortion of ethical values in the pursuit of political ends. Yet both Christianity and Judaism, I believe, can provide an alternative model for formulating a rational approach to human misconduct. In our violent and war-torn world, such a task is of the greatest urgency.

Dan

11.4   *17 May 2004*

FROM VENGEANCE TO RESTORATIVE JUSTICE

Dan,

I completely agree with you — and this seems a rare occurrence! To my shame, it appears that the brutality inflicted on Iraqi prisoners was sanctioned by US politicians who are committed Christians. Yet, as you say, both our faith traditions offer alternatives to vengeance and retribution.

One of the stumbling-blocks to peace is that the global violence targeted against Islam is given justification as revenge for the events of September 11th 2001, when Muslim terrorists hijacked planes and destroyed the Twin Towers in New York with appalling loss of life. Violence against Iraqi prisoners is one example of scapegoating — even demonising — an entire group of people because of the murderous actions of a small minority. But scapegoating as a way of coping with evil has a long history: René Girard's life work has been devoted to this. He shows how feuding groups can unite in venting anger on the scapegoat, thus ensuring harmony in the community.[5] So nations split by internal wrangling can still unite against the common enemy. As Quaker activist Tim Newell writes: 'Part of the "criminology of the other" is the assumption that the offender (or "criminal") is the common, internal enemy. As such, the criminal is required to assume the same identity as ... the scapegoat.'[6]

But, as the Russian novelist Solzhenitsyn pointed out in his Nobel speech, it is not so easy to draw a fine line between the totally innocent and the evil-doers: 'If only there were evil people somewhere insidiously committing evil deeds, and it were necessary only to separate them from the rest of us and destroy them. But the line dividing good and evil cuts through the heart of every human being. And who is willing to destroy a piece of his own heart?'[7]

The problem is that facing our own complicity and responsibility in a violent situation is far from easy. Yet we must face this challenge: doing so will empower a community to consider punishment not in terms of vengeance or retribution but in terms of rehabilitation and restorative justice.

In the document *Evangelium Vitae*, Pope John Paul II argues for an increasingly rare use of capital punishment. (Of course his arguments have been criticised, mostly because the motivation on which they are based is self-defence.)[8] But perhaps more importantly, he has been responsible for four documents calling for a theology of peace to promote a culture of peace. In his most famous statement, 'Message for World Peace Day 1991', the Pope begged the world to include the earth in building this culture: 'In our day, there is a growing awareness that world peace is threatened not only by the arms race, regional conflicts and continued injustices among peoples and nations, but by a lack of due respect for nature, by the plundering of natural resources and by a progressive decline in the quality of life.'[9]

There are many Roman Catholics — like the social activist Dorothy Day, the Cistercian monk Thomas Merton, and the Berrigan brothers, both priests — who tried to resist structural violence in a non-violent way. In Christian tradition since the Reformation it has been the Quakers who have been at the forefront of both the peace movement and prison reform. The 'Great Experiment' of William Penn (1644—1718) in governing Pennsylvania, USA, in the 1670s, during which he abolished capital punishment, was the earliest example of Quaker thought in action.[10] But it is not only the Quakers, but also the Anabaptists since 1632 who have pioneered a non-violent response to war. Their successors, the Mennonites, are tireless today in seeking for non-violent methods of conflict resolution.[11] Joseph Montville sums up the influence of religious communities:

> If one single quality has to be chosen to account for the influence that religiously-identified third parties have, it would be their ability to inspire trust. One might think this is an obvious answer ... but in ethnic and sectarian conflict people have endured aggression and loss simply because of their membership in an identity group ... Into the lives of these victimised people come religious outsiders, who in varying ways convey a sense of understanding and

empathy for their fears and who have established
reputations for honesty ... discretion and integrity.[12]

Is there any hope that such religiously inspired groups of integrity
can initiate a breakthrough in the situation that is so dangerously
volatile today, or is religion to be viewed only as a force that
continues to fuel further aggression?

Mary

11.5 *19 May 2004*

CATHOLICISM AS VILLAIN

Mary,

I am afraid that when I read about the ways in which Catholics
are portrayed as resisting violence in a non-violent way, I am
reminded of the dark history of the Church in which Jews were
treated as the 'Other'. Let me rehearse what I have repeatedly
stressed throughout our discussion. 'Judaeophobia' did not origi-
nate with the emergence of Christianity; rather Jewish hatred was
common in the Hellenised world. None the less anti-Jewish
sentiment intensified within the Christian community. Jesus'
Messiahship was understood as ushering in a new era in which
the true Israel would become a light to the nations.

Christian animosity was fuelled by the gospel writers, who
depicted Jesus attacking the leaders of the nation. Further, the
Church taught that what is now required is circumcision of
the heart rather than obedience to the law. In proclaiming the
good news, Paul emphasised that the Hebrew people had been
rejected by God: Christ is the true eternal Temple in opposition
to the early cult in Jerusalem. Such a contrast is also to be found
in the fourth gospel, which differentiates between the spiritual
universe of Christianity and a fallen world represented by the
Jews.

The New Testament served as a basis for the early Church's
vilification of the Jews. According to the Church Fathers, the
Jewish people are lawless and dissolute. Because of their rejection
of Christ, the Jewish nation has been excluded from God's grace

and is subject to his wrath. During the Crusades, Christian mobs massacred Jewish communities: Jews were charged with killing Christian children to use their blood for ritual purposes, blaspheming Christ and Christianity in their sacred literature, and causing the Black Death. Throughout the Middle Ages Jews were detested, and the image of the satanic Jew became a central feature of Western iconography.

This terrible legacy of Christian hatred championed by Roman Catholic leaders through the centuries is at odds with your idealistic presentation of Christian values of tolerance and acceptance. For me — and for the vast majority of Jews — the Catholic Church has been the great enemy, and I find it difficult if not impossible to transcend 19 centuries of hostility and contempt of everything Jewish. I know you do not share the attitudes I have depicted, and I applaud the change of heart which you describe. But I think you fail to comprehend the ways in which Jewish consciousness has been scarred by the events of the past. Please do not preach to me about the virtues of the Catholic Church and its espousal of non-violence and restorative justice.

Dan

11.6   *21 May 2004*

REMAIN LOCKED IN THE PAST - OR MOVE ON?

Dan,
That was an unkind accusation! I have never "preached the virtues of the Catholic Church" but was agreeing with you, as you wrote in a previous letter that "therapy not retribution" should be the response to crime. In my previous letter (11.5), I was responding to your statement on 13th May, that:

> "both Christianity and Judaism can provide an alternative model for formulating a rational approach to human misconduct".

In our correspondence I have repeatedly condemned anti-Semitism, the crimes of Christianity in the past, the many forms of anti-Judaism in Christian theology and any new forms of anti-Semitism. I also understand the complexities around the whole area of forgiveness, and have called on the churches to undertake an ongoing journey of repentance. I am aware that we cannot undo the crimes of the past. What I attempted was — in response to your challenge – to trace an alternative strand in Christianity to enable us to move forward. That's why I ended my letter with the plea:

> Is there any hope that such religiously inspired groups of integrity can inspire a breakthrough in the situation that is so dangerously volatile today, or is religion to be viewed only as a force that continues to fuel further aggression?

My conviction that religion *does* have a positive role to play was stressed in another context this week. I have been listening to an Anglican priest, Donald Reeve, founder of *The Soul of Europe* charity, talking about reconciliation in his work in war-torn Bosnia. Here the context is not simply Jews and Christians (there are small communities of Jews), but Serbian Orthodox, Croatian Catholic and Muslim communities. You are well aware of the Serbian atrocities against Muslims, but there are also terrible crimes that Catholics have committed under the Ustase regime. In the town of Banya Luka – where *Soul of Europe* is focusing its efforts at the moment — all the mosques have been destroyed. A huge amount of denial is present – Serbs denying that the atrocities have taken place and that there were any concentration camps. The parallels are obvious. What Donald is attempting is to get all the faith communities to talk together – and to work together in rebuilding one of the mosques, Ferhadija, there to establish a Centre for Economic Development and Reconciliation.

Like the Jewish communities, the Bosnian Serbs have terrible memories of crimes inflicted on them: when the former President Milosevic tried to claim Kosovo in 1989, he was deliberately recalling the shameful defeat of the Serbians by the Turkish empire (Muslim) five hundred years earlier in 1389, when the hero Prince Lazzar was killed. He became seen as a Christ-like figure and memories of him are still powerful. Even in the two meetings I attended this week these memories were powerful and their recall provoked resentment. My point in citing this example is to say – how do we deal with painful memories of past crimes, in order to move forward?

It is absolutely essential that the perpetrator tells the truth and admits responsibility. Forgiveness can only come from the person or group wronged, and only as part of a long process of reconciliation, where trust is worked for between all parties, and restitution and justice are genuine dimensions. That's why I called for restorative justice as a theoretical foundation for punishment: religions *can* call us forward into a new space, new possibilities, because they are committed to the well-being of their adherents. Where communities are locked in bitterness and revenge there can be no genuine flourishing.

Do you remember the film *Babette's Feast*? A Danish community was locked in bitterness and tension. Babette – a French cook spent her entire inheritance on a wonderful, totally over the top meal, which the people enjoyed together. They came out into the starlit night and experienced a wonderful renewing harmony. I do not for one minute suggest that solutions are so simple. But I do passionately believe that a way has to be found to respect deeprooted historical memories of suffering and oppression that allow wronged communities to move forward into mutual respect and harmonious co-existence with other groups. It is certainly *not* forgetting the memories — that would not honour those who were killed and are still dying today in the unjust conflicts around us. But it is about acknowledging that revenge keeps us inextricably locked into a bitterness that fuels unending killing.

Mary

11.6   *24 May 2004*

OVERCOMING REVENGE

Mary,

Perhaps I overreacted to your last letter. I know you deplore the terrible actions of the past. We both believe the Church was culpable for heinous crimes. We seek to move forward. Yet, as a Jew, I remain sensitive to the legacy of previous centuries. In a post-Holocaust world it is difficult to transcend these feelings, but you are right that we must move on. The question is: How is this to be done? Throughout our correspondence, we have stressed that both our traditions offer resources for *tikkun olam*. No more is this so than in considering the problem of revenge.

Turning first to the Bible: the verse in which it is stated that it is wrong to take revenge is the same as that in which love of neighbour occurs: 'Thou shalt not take vengeance nor bear any grudge against the children of thy people, but thou shalt love thy neighbour as thyself: I am the Lord' (Lev. 19:18). The meaning here is that love of neighbour is to be expressed by refusing to take revenge.

A rabbinic comment in the Talmud *(Yoma* 23a) on this verse draws a distinction between taking revenge and bearing a grudge. If a person asks his fellow to lend him his sickle and he refuses and on the next day the second asks the first to lend him his axe, and he replies: 'I will not lend it to you just as you would not lend me your sickle' — this is revenge. But if a person asks someone to lend him his sickle and he refuses and on the next day the second asks the first to lend him his robe, and he replies: 'Here it is, I am not like you' — that is bearing a grudge.

The twelfth-century philosopher Moses Maimonides added that the wise will refuse to take revenge because worldly things are simply not worth making a fuss about. To feel a sense of outrage because one has been refused the loan of a sickle is to magnify the importance of a sickle. Furthermore, Maimonides understands the prohibition against bearing a grudge to be a means of avoiding the more serious offence of taking revenge. All this, he concludes, is the proper attitude to be cultivated if society is to be well established and social life possible. A later thinker, Moses Hayyim Luzzatto, in his *Path of the Upright*, urges fellow Jews to avoid in all circumstances any semblance of revenge and bearing a grudge.

This is the ideal, and we should strive to incorporate these biblical and rabbinic principles into our daily lives. Yet this will not be a simple task. It is very easy to be overcome by feelings and memories. This is what Luzzatto himself wrote about the difficulties of overcoming such negative attitudes:

Hatred and revenge. These the human heart in its per-
versity finds it hard to escape. A man is very sensitive to
disgrace, and suffers keenly when subjected to it. Revenge
is sweeter to him than honey; he cannot rest until he
has taken his revenge. If, therefore, he has the power to
relinquish that to which his nature compels him; if he can
forgive, if he will forebear hating anyone who provokes
him to hatred; if he will neither exact vengeance when he
has the opportunity to do so, nor bear a grudge against anyone; if he can forget and obliterate from his mind a wrong
done to him as though it had never been committed;
then he is indeed, strong and mighty.[13]

I agree that religion can have a positive role to play. Such sentiments as these, deeply woven into the fabric of the Jewish
heritage, can guide us in our dealings with others in seeking to
create a better world.

Dan

11.7   *31 May 2004*

WHOSE REVENGE? WHOSE JUSTICE?

Dan,
Yesterday Christians celebrated the Feast of Pentecost, a feast with
Jewish roots, which now symbolises both the end of the Easter
period and specifically the gift of the Holy Spirit to the Church.
Some call it the birthday of the Church. What I find significant is
that the focus of Easter/Pentecost is the Risen Jesus bringing the
gift of peace to his followers. And with the gift of peace comes
the commission to forgive. As the Gospel of John puts it: 'Peace
be with you. As the Father has sent me, so I also send you. And
when he had said this, he breathed on them, and said to them,
Receive the Holy Spirit. If you forgive the sins of any, they are
forgiven; if you retain the sins of any, they are retained' (John
20:21—3).

   In the context of this chapter, it is clear that forgiveness of sins
does not form any official part of our secular criminal system. I

have already cited the case of Myra Hindley, who repented yet received no mercy from the criminal system. Your last letter emphasised the necessity of being able to move away from revenge and grudge-bearing — and you cited strong witnesses from Jewish tradition. Both these elements suggest that our religious traditions recognise the necessity for a change of heart to prevent further crime and to call a halt to the cycle of vengeance.

But there is a further dimension. Both forgiveness and letting go of grudge-bearing are frequently interpreted on an individual basis. Yet most of the violent incidents threatening to overwhelm us at the moment are group-based, and related to historical conflicts, recent or long-seated — the Middle East, Sudan, Northern Ireland, Kashmir, Iran, Iraq and Afghanistan ... How to change the *collective* commitment to revenge is the issue. Even if the British justice system were prepared to set Myra Hindley free, such was the degree of hatred and desire for revenge of ordinary people here that it was not considered possible.

We have to acknowledge the power of the long history of a penal system that is steeped in punishing the offender commensurately with his or her offence. Timothy Gorringe, in *God's Just Vengeance*, has traced the roots of this to certain interpretations of Christian Atonement doctrine.[14] He is particularly strong in showing how theories of rehabilitation alternated with notions of retribution in the development of the prison system. I have also explored the way in which blame for crime has been disproportionately laid on women.[15] Even now, although the proportion of women in prison is *one-fortieth* that of men, they receive far severer sentences.[16]

This points to the need to seek other fundamental strands of our faiths to appeal to the wider society. When we appeal to justice, for example, the retort will be 'Whose justice?' In my earlier letter to you I appealed to the notion of *restorative* justice: but this is ambiguous where there are competing claims for the same land or territory. Christopher Marshall has helpfully described several categories of justice. He speaks of 'natural and rough justice, distributive and remedial justice, poetic and practical justice, each of which is inevitably partial and fallible'.[17]

I suggest to you that, in our frequent appeals to mutuality and reciprocity in this correspondence, if we are to move forward to reconciliation, we have to bring these into the public discourse and see them as vital tools in our efforts for peace between conflicting communities. Both justice *and* mutuality *and* love are privileged values for both our faiths: how can they be harnessed to break us out of cycles of revenge?

Mary

11.8   *7 June 2004*

COMMUNAL HATRED AND VENGEANCE

Mary,

You are right that revenge is normally viewed in individual terms. Both of our traditions contain spiritual insights that can help believers to come to terms with hatred of the other. But what can be done to remedy the determination to commit acts of collective revenge? This has become an increasingly pressing problem, given recent world events. It appears that we are now living through a clash of civilisations. Following the terrible events of 9/11, the West is determined to root out terrorism whatever the cost. No doubt, the horrific incidents that we are witnessing in Iraq are rooted in the quest to punish terrorists for acts of inhumanity. Conversely, a significant number of Iraqis seem equally committed to driving foreign powers from their country, regardless of the consequences for innocent civilians.

You may be aware that the Chief Rabbi, Jonathan Sacks, recently published a book about religious pluralism, *The Dignity of Difference*, in which he argues that in a multifaith society, we should view other traditions with tolerance. In his view, God is manifest in all the world's faiths, and therefore, believers should strive to discover spiritual riches outside their own religious heritages. Only in this way, he maintains, can we overcome contempt and hatred. The same point is repeatedly made by the Christian theologian Hans Kung, who contends that there can be no world peace without religious sympathy and understanding.

In our conversation, I think we have both struggled in our different ways to highlight the importance of such a stance.

Despite the terrible legacy of the past, Jews and Christians can find common ground and unite in the quest to create a better world. Yet arguably there cannot be healing when there is injustice. This is at the heart of Islamic resistance to the West. For Osama bin Laden and his followers, the West is culpable for horrendous crimes. In an interview given to Al-Jazeera television several years ago, he chillingly castigated Americans and the Jewish people and encouraged Muslims to wage a holy war against the enemies of Islam:

> Our duty is to incite the jihad against America, Israel and their allies ... With the grace of God we have established [common cause] with a large number of brothers in the International Islamic Front to confront Jews and Crusaders. We believe that the affairs of many of those are moving in the right direction and have the ability to move widely. We pray to God to grant them victory and revenge on the Jews and Americans.'[18]

To the terrorist mind, there is no justice in the modern world. Pious exhortations about renouncing vengeance are meaningless to those who see themselves as freedom fighters, struggling to overcome Satanic powers that have crushed the powerless. Do we have a message for those who view the world in such terms?

Dan

12. What Have We Learned?

—◦◦◦◦—

DOES GOD ACT?

Dan,

We have been writing to each other for almost a year. Neither of us can pretend that the world has changed in that time, nor did we expect it to. Violence continues in the same places — and has even broken out in a few more. But we need to pause a little and ask — what have we learnt from our interchange? From my own perspective, quite apart from the stimulus of our correspondence I think there are some clear lessons to be learnt. Let's begin to tease these out.

I want to begin with something I find very difficult in your thinking. In our exchanges, beginning with the first chapter on 'God', you have made it clear that you do not believe that God acts in the world. Neither of us believes in an interventionist God — or a patriarchal God: I think you are convinced by the sheer weight of radical evil, and especially by events like the Holocaust, where God clearly did not intervene on behalf of the Jewish people, that this idea of God acting in history is nonsensical.

While agreeing with you about the capricious nature of inter- ventionism, I want to maintain faith in a God who acts through the processes of creation, who loves and cherishes creation, who is vulnerable to some of its manifestations and who has given creatures such a measure of freedom that they are now capable of self-destruction and destroying the planet. I recognise that your arguments have solid rational weight, but I want to hang on to this faith in a God of love, because of what it offers to people in terms of hope. If God does not act in love, what is the point of prayer and worship? There are numerous stories from both Jewish and Christian sources, often from imprisonment experiences, where faith in God sustains people even where the situation seems hopeless.

I feel this even more strongly now, where, as we are repeatedly stating, the cycles of violence seem to admit no crack, no opening up to compassion for the 'other'. I want to increase the grounds for hope by appealing to a God who can act by increasing our compassion, our perseverance, our imaginations and our longing for a reconciled world. According to Martin Buber, prayer is one of the great angels stalking history — but prayer is to and in the presence of God. To me that is one of the greatest resources in the pathway to reconciliation.

Mary

⁐

12.2   *12 June 2004*
DIVINE ACTION

Mary,

At the end of our correspondence, we are returning to the issue we discussed at the outset: God's action in the world. I am familiar with the position you outline. You do not believe that God intervenes in the world — He is not a causal agent, affecting everyday affairs. By implication, you have rejected the conception of a God which is central to Jewish and Christian theology. In other words, you cannot accept the picture of divine action as portrayed in the Bible and in Jewish and Christian sources. Yet you believe in a God who affects the world. You say that God cherishes creation, is vulnerable to its manifestations, and is a loving Deity.

What I fail to understand, however, is how you can be certain what God is like if He does not act. Surely you cannot know his nature through his actions since you do not believe He intervenes in the world. So, how can you be sure that He cherishes the world, that He is loving, that He increases our compassion, our perseverance, our imaginings, and our longings to create a reconciled world? Repeatedly I have asked you for evidence to support such claims, but I don't think you have given any. Rather, I think you make such statements simply because this is what you believe God to be.

In making such claims you have not explained away the problem of evil. Instead of confronting the perplexities of human suffering, you have retreated into repeated affirmations of God's compassion and care. You contend that God wills that we bring about God's kingdom on earth without explaining how He could have created a world in which there is so much evil and suffering. In other words, you do not offer a coherent theodicy as the basis of your desire for peace and reconciliation. I myself have not sought to provide a defence for theism. Instead, I have argued that our two traditions provide us with a moral framework for reconciliation. There are rich resources embedded within our two faiths which can serve as a basis for mending broken relationships.

But, as we have both noted throughout our discussion, we must be selective in isolating those moral values which are applicable in the modern world. It would be a mistake to swallow whole the entire ethical code contained in the Bible, rabbinic literature, and Christian sources. In making this selection, we will have to be guided by our consciences, not by what we believe God wills. As I have stated, I am an intuitionist — my ethical values are ultimately based on an intuitional apprehension of morality. And I believe you are the same, despite what you say about the nature of God. In the end, I think you are using moral values which you intuit as true to judge the religious tradition you have inherited. You maintain that it is God who is the source of such values, but I think you are projecting on to a God who does not act those values you believe He ought to have. A simple example are the many comments you make about patriarchy. You reject the patriarchal depiction of God in the Bible and in Christian literature because you assume, a priori, that God is not like that. This is because you reject patriarchy on ethical grounds. The argument is thus as follows:

(1) Theological assumption: God is good
(2) Ethical assumption: Patriarchy is morally unacceptable
(3) Therefore: God is not patriarchal

Your conclusion is thus a conflation of theological and ethical assumptions rather than an argument based on observations about the nature of God and His action: the theology you offer is thus a projection of your own ideas on the world, rather than a reflection of the way things are.

Dan

-⟳—⟳-

12.3   *14 June 2004*

A PRESENCE THAT CALLS TO ACCOUNT

Dan,

I liked your challenge and thought it was justified. But I hope I am less muddled in thinking than you accuse me! And what I believe is deeply embedded in both Jewish and Christian *practice* — don't forget there are many ways of understanding the action of God, and you and I approach this issue after a few thousand years of theorising about this.

To begin with your concluding syllogism: Yes, it is true that wisdom as to the injustice of patriarchy comes from non-religious, *extrinsic* sources, contemporary secular wisdom, you might say. But no one ever claimed that the Bible had the sole claim to wisdom! There is a solid body of thought that moral convictions experience a steady process of growth, influenced by many sources, including the secular. (Think of the Wisdom sayings.) The prophets, whom we both cite, had deep convictions concerning justice — which we believe change and develop in the light of changing circumstances.

Let me address your main anxiety: you write to me today:

> How can you be sure that He cherishes the world, that He is loving, that He increases our compassion, our perseverance, our imaginings, and our longings to create a reconciled world? Repeatedly I have asked you for evidence to support such claims, but I don't think you have

given any. Rather, I think you make such statements simply because this is what you believe God to be.

My answer to you is that this is simply the life of faith — which Jews and Christians share. I cannot give you empirical, verifiable proof — your very request emerges from a perspective that I recognise from Oxford positivist philosophy. *Produce evidence verifiable according to sense-data!* Repeatedly through our correspondence I have tried to express the belief that faith in the God of Judaism and Christianity impacts on daily life. In prayer, hope, faith, we interpret all that happens. I experience the power of God in love, compassion and even judgement in thousands of ways in my life and the life of my community. It's not so simplistic as the 'Please God send me a bicycle for Christmas' mode. In fact, when prayer is directly answered, it can come as a total shock. It's more that life is lived in the presence of a God who hungers for justice and is all too aware of the blockages in achieving it. (Remember my words on vulnerability?)

I'm aware that it is very difficult — almost impossible — to reconcile a loving, compassionate God with the horror of the Holocaust. This has been in both our consciousnesses as we wrestled with the issue. We are not so far removed from the event and stories of suffering still emerge. There is no way that I would attempt to 'solve' the dilemma where facile solutions have only added to the pain. It's more that belief in God entails life lived in a presence, a sense of being called to account, to witness, to a life where all acts of love and justice find place in an all-embracing scheme of harmony and peace for all creation.

The fact that I cannot 'prove' all of this in the way that you demand throws me back to the problem of the Enlightenment. We are both 'children of the Enlightenment' in a certain sense — in our belief in education and in human rights, as well as in the need for rational explanations. I know that feminism was made possible by the Enlightenment. But there the similarity ends. I look for more than an agenda of equal rights and suspect deeply the privileging of reason at the expense of other dimensions of the human person. The Enlightenment has given birth to the competitive individual of contemporary times and ultimately to the whole agenda of globalisation. This has made the values of faith communities seem outdated and old-fashioned. I think this tension has been underlying in much of our discussion.

Mary

12.4   *17 June 2004*

GLOBALISATION AND CHANGE

Mary,

I have been aware throughout our correspondence that you are deeply troubled by the effects of globalisation (which you attribute to the Enlightenment). Frequently you argue that a new economic structure must replace the current system. Only in this way will the corrosive and corrupting values of the modern world be overcome. In the last decades of the twentieth century, liberation theologians — particularly in third world countries — made the same point. Even though these writers did not accept Marxism as an all-embracing framework, they believed that the insights of Marxism could help them to understand the nature of contemporary exploitation.

Now, I know that you do not see yourself as a Marxist. Yet it does appear that you share the same perspective as such thinkers as Gustavo Gutiérrez, Leonardo Boff, José Miranda and others. Like them, you denounce the evils of the capitalistic world, and would seek to banish those multinational institutions that enslave the poor. Am I right? Previously you endorsed Gandhi's simplicity, and called for a revolution in consciousness. Am I correct that you would wish to see a new world order emerge, based on humane values rather than those of crude consumerism?

In my opinion, however, such a view is based on a misguided understanding of economics. In *The Wealth of Nations*, the eighteenth-century economic theorist Adam Smith argued that the public good is best served through a free market in which all participants seek their own self-interest. This mechanism, which he referred to as the 'invisible hand', is the central regulatory principle of the marketplace. According to Smith, it is not benevolence that drives individual workers, but self-interest.

I think Smith was right about this. Individuals work for wages, not for the common good. This might appear to be a wholly selfish motive, but it is in fact the driving force of a healthy economy in which prices are naturally regulated by competition, and wages are determined through the same forces. Human needs — whatever they might be — are met through the interplay of these factors, and society benefits from economic growth and expansion.

I fear that if you had your way you would wish to interfere with this delicate mechanism. In our correspondence, you repeatedly denounce the materialism and selfishness of modern life. But I think you fail to appreciate the numerous ways in which those of us who live in first world countries have benefited from a flourishing economy. We live in well-equipped houses with central heating, running water, indoor plumbing; we are able to travel by car, and fly by airplane around the world; we benefit from highly efficient healthcare. In so many ways, we are better off than our ancestors. All this is the result of the modern market system. It is an unrealistic, and arguably pernicious dream to wish to return to the simplicity of the past. What we need to do instead is raise the living standards of the third world. This will not be accomplished by dismantling multinational companies, but by expanding opportunities for work throughout the world. Impoverishing the poor even further will not be a way to bring about God's Kingdom on earth.

Dan

12.5 *17 June 2004*

NEW WORLD ORDER?

Dan,

You are absolutely right that I denounce the injustices of unregulated global capitalism. I have seen too much of the misery inflicted on poor countries through the debt crisis, the damage inflicted on the environment through profit-driven policies and the wretchedness of the very poorest groups of people whose livelihood has been taken away by World Bank projects, to doubt this for a minute. But you are also right, I'm not a Marxist, but I do believe in a kind of reconstructed socialism that puts the well-being of the poorest sectors of society first. And yes, I'm inspired by Gutiérrez, Bonino and so on, and more so by women theologians like Aruna Gnanadason at the Women's Desk, the World Council of Churches in Geneva, who put such a theology into practice.

But it's not only the liberation theologians who cast doubt on whether global capitalism can solve the world's problems. I am now impressed by the work of Joseph Stiglitz, formerly Chief Economist of the World Bank, and a key member of President Clinton's economic team.[1] He is now exposing how the conditions laid down by the IMF (International Monetary Fund) actually exacerbate the very poverty they are meant to be alleviating!

Are people really motivated only by self-interest, as Adam Smith wrote? The welfare state, whatever difficulties it is running into now, was inspired by a concept of sharing — and the practice of sharing is now found in the poorest of communities, rather than the richer. Ask Christian Aid or any large charity where their greatest contributors live: they will tell you that they come from the poorer parts of Britain — like around Liverpool. It seems that the richer you are the more corrupted by wealth you become.

I know I am inspired by the simplicity of Gandhi, and his belief in the essential goodness of human nature. And I also know we act from mixed motives and there will be always an element of self-interest. I have to admit I enjoy writing these letters, for example. Nor do I believe in turning the clocks back, *per se*. It is easy to ridicule Gandhi's simplicity — but his advocacy of spinning and local crafts, *in context*, meant restoring sustainability to village economies, as well as reawakening pride in India's traditions. But I do believe that there is an appropriate level of technology to be striven for, if more people are to participate in what in religious terms we call the 'feast of life'. Of course I'm grateful for the level of comfort we enjoy, but I want more people to enjoy it! When I stay in Delhi I look out of hotel windows to see homeless people either huddled in blankets, or trying to light a fire with a few twigs to keep out the cold. And I feel angry: it shouldn't be like this! We could still have a happy life with less choices of ice-cream in the supermarkets, for example, and more fairly traded goods.

I think you will agree that religions have a role to play in advocating the practice of restraint in enabling our neighbour, the stranger, the 'other' to lead a life of dignity. And what draws us together above and beyond all these differences, whether God is an interventionalist or, as Dorothee Soelle believed, an 'intentionalist', is the ideal of the Kingdom of God: whether you believe it is coming at the end of time, when the Messiah comes, when Jesus comes again, is this not a meeting point where we can agree that such an ideal, vision, or ethical programme for peace and justice is exactly what Jews and Christians can offer today to our violent world?

Mary

12.6 *18 June 2004*

ECONOMIC DEVELOPMENT AND POVERTY

Mary,

I wonder what kind of world you really want. You argue that it is the poor who are anxious to share, rather than the rich. There is no doubt that Marxist ideals have been championed by the underprivileged. But I don't believe this was due to altruistic motives. Rather, the poor struggled to bring about a restructuring of society so they would be able to benefit socially and materially. The Communist revolution in Russia, for example, was spearheaded by many disenfranchised Jews who were convinced that by restructuring society they would be able to benefit from a new social order. More recently, we have witnessed the collapse of the Soviet Union due to mass discontent with the corruption of the socialist system and the lack of economic progress in the Communist world. It was not altruism that brought about such an upheaval, but rather deep-seated discontent and the desire for a higher standard of living.

You must admit that it is unregulated global capitalism that underpins your own life here in Britain. Every material object you own is produced through a complex web of interconnected manufacturing industries. The petrol you use for your car (as well as petrol used on planes that take you from country to country) is extracted, shipped and transported through a complicated, inter-related industrial system. The component parts that are used to manufacture your computer are dependent on the existence of multinational companies. Your everyday life is supported at every turn by the market system that you deplore. There is no place for the kind of simplicity extolled by Gandhi in the modern world. No one — not even you — would really wish to turn the clock back to an age devoid of the goods and services supplied in the first world. What is an appropriate level of technology? Would you be happy to live without a telephone, car, fax, computer, microwave, or central heating? Would you prefer not to be able to travel by plane? Would you wish to live like those in the third world?

Global capitalism is here to stay, and despite the vulgarity and crassness of modern materialism we are privileged to live in the twenty-first century. The feast of life that we experience is under-standably envied by those who are bereft of our advantages. You are right to despair when you look out of the windows in Delhi and see homeless people. But against whom is your anger directed? You say that if we reduced the choice of ice-cream in supermarkets and introduced more fairly traded goods, the imbalance between East and West could be improved. I don't see a correlation between ice-cream products and mass poverty. What is needed instead is a vibrant world economy, a market system that operates without restraint so that it can improve the lives of all. Inevitably those living in underprivileged areas will only gradu-ally be able to emerge out of poverty, but I believe the gap between the rich and the poor will eventually narrow. Our two traditions will not solve the problems of the world. Yet I do think they contain spiritual resources for improving life and paving the way toward reconciliation — it is this limited goal that I have attempted to highlight throughout our correspondence.

Dan

12.7   *24 June 2004*

ANOTHER WORLD IS POSSIBLE!

Dan,

I think you may recognise these words. They were the inspiration of the World Social Forum at Mumbai (Bombay) in January of this year, 2004. One hundred thousand people came together — activists, faith groups, NGOs — all believing that a different world order is possible, one that allows the world's poorest communities a life of dignity.

Of course you are right that my own life is compromised by the system of global capitalism. There are very few innocents around! Of course you are right that I value and appreciate some of the comforts of this century — and I want them for others too. But I won't give in to a system that intrinsically privileges only those who can pay their way to comfort. To investigate whether people are acting from altruism or not is beside the point — what matters is that they act *for* justice and not against it. And justice means that people are not forced systemically to live in dehumanising poverty.

When I attended the American Academy of Religion a few years ago, Gustavo Gutiérrez — often called the founding father of liberation theology — brought out a biography of Bartolomé de los Casas, a sixteenth-century Mexican priest and hero of his, who blazed a trail for liberation theology. He was asked by well-known theologians present if anything had changed in his lifetime in the issues that he had worked so hard for. He replied, 'The poor are even poorer and the rich care even less.'

It is inherent in the market system that it has to create desires that demand satisfying, hence unbridled consumerism has to be sustained whatever the cost. Of course humans have always had markets since we learnt to barter, but never has there been a system that privileged profit *whatever the cost* and valued people according to their spending power.

But where you might agree with me, since we both want a system that respects the earth, is in the need to control the furious exploitation of resources. You mention cars and air travel, and I fully agree that we should work for a culture that limits petrol consumption. But global capitalism depends on a massive over-consumption of resources. Many countries will experience water-stressed situations by 2015, *and Asia will experience a 90 per cent shortage.*[2] Here is where we can both draw on faith resources, where water is considered precious, a gift of God. Longing for water is like longing for God, as Scripture says, and this should be a warning against privatising water and other precious commodities needed for sustaining life — again another way that makes it difficult for poor communities to survive.

I do believe *another world is possible*, and that there are already small groups and communities creating spaces where they can live to another kind of truth. You laugh at Gandhian simplicity, at my example of ice-cream (only one example out of hundreds), but my point is that we can all work for food and clothes to be fairly traded, for alternative energy sources (the Methodist Church has just committed itself to find alternative energy sources for its London churches), for affordable public transport that avoids excessive use of cars, for more earth-friendly ways of dealing with waste, and so on. When food is fairly traded, the growers and producers are enabled to live in dignity; when water consumption is reduced, the groundwater is allowed to be renewed by rainfall, and our ecological footprint becomes lighter.

I think this is what we gain from faith sources, the trust that another world is possible and the strength to keep on trying to make this belief a reality. The flourishing of earth and all her creatures is part of God's dream for the earth — that's why believing another world is possible can provide momentum for changing what is destructive about our lifestyles.

Mary

12.8   *24 June 2004*

A PROPHETIC VISION

Mary,

What is intriguing about our conversation is the fact that religion and politics are so frequently intertwined. Obviously, there are many areas where we differ, yet I think we can both agree that our religious traditions offer spiritual riches that can help to achieve reconciliation in the modern world. It is clear that we cannot agree about economic policy, nor about numerous other issues. Nevertheless, I think we are united in our determination to create a better world, one free of discrimination and injustice. In this regard, as a child I was moved by the eloquent ethical message of the prophets of ancient Israel as recorded in the synagogue liturgy. In the evening service for the Sabbath, I remember reciting the following responsive reading:

> May the righteous of all nations rejoice in Thy grace and exult in Thy justice.
> Let them beat their swords into ploughshares and their spears into pruning-hooks:
> Let nation not lift up sword against nation nor learn war any more.
> Righteousness exalteth a nation, but sin is a reproach to any people.
> Treasures of wickedness profit not but righteousness delivereth from death.
> Thou shalt not hate thy brother in thy heart:
> But thou shalt love thy neighbour as thyself.
> The stranger that sojourneth with you shall be unto you as the home-born.
> For ye were strangers in the land of Egypt.
> What mean ye that ye crush My people and grind the face
> of the Lord, saith the Lord.
> I know that the Lord will maintain the cause of the poor,
> and the right of the needy.[3]

Throughout history, the Jewish people have seen themselves as God's suffering servant, yet inspired by this vision of God's reign on earth they have been able to transcend their own misfortunes. In the contemporary world where Jews are often comfortable and affluent, the prophetic message of justice and freedom can too easily be forgotten.

But the Passover festival in particular reminds us of our history and our duty. It is a symbolic exaltation of freedom. Jews are to rejoice in the liberation of their ancestors, in which each of them takes part. Year by year this festival has awakened the spirit of the people to the significance of human freedom. The Passover *seder* is a symbol of Israel's vocation as a people. It was not only in ancient times that enemies rose up against the Jews; enemies have arisen in every generation. All this points to the ultimate redemption as prophesied by Isaiah — of the day when the wolf would dwell with the lamb and the world would be as full of the knowledge of the Lord as the sea is of water. The Passover ceremony thus unites the Jewish people with their ancestors who endured slavery and oppression in Egyptian bondage. Remembering the divine deliverance of the ancient Israelites, we Jews today can work for the emancipation of all those who are enslaved. The biblical motif hence contains a reservoir of meaning for Jews in the struggle to create a better world. The Passover — by symbolising the primal act of liberation — points to a future and ultimate redemption of the human family. Of course, in saying all this I cannot accept the theological underpinning of the biblical account, nor the religious assumptions of rabbinic commentators. But I do believe that the ethical imperatives embedded in the Passover Haggadah in the prayer book are of vital significance. The quest for *tikkun olam* (repairing the world) remains a focal point of the tradition: it is a bond that unites our two faiths whatever new world order is envisaged.

Dan

12.9   *25 June 2004*

COMMUNITIES THAT HOPE

Dan,

I was moved by your recalling the promise of Passover traditions. Isn't it true that one of the texts for the celebration is the Song of Songs? This speaks to me not only of the celebration of human love (or the allegory of divine—human love, as it is often interpreted in Christian circles), but of the sense of flourishing of earth and people in a redeemed creation.

So I think we both share the hope that liturgies can keep alive the hopes for reconciliation. Especially where hospitality, generosity and inclusivity are manifest, and offered beyond the immediate narrow group. (And we both frequently experience the opposite!) In Christian practice it is the Eucharist that has the same potential, yet it can also be the place of experiencing great exclusion — witnessed by black communities in Britain, to give one example among many.

As you know, the Eucharist builds on Passover memories as the context for remembering Jesus' offering of his life. Connecting with the themes discussed between us, for Christians there must always be a dimension of repentance as to how this death has been used in anti-Jewish interpretations. So the first priority is to be aware as to how the ongoing eucharistic liturgies can continue anti-Jewish prejudice — for example in simplistic reading of the scriptures that fails to acknowledge Jewish experience. The Eucharist is a place of remembering: for us the historical dimension of suffering and injustice that we have inflicted on innocent people, and continue to do in some parts of the world, is a vital part of this journey of repentance.

But there are wider dimensions of liberation that we can also share. Writers like Tissa Balasuriya, in *The Eucharist and Human Liberation*,[4] have highlighted the fact that from its origins, this celebration focused on social justice, seeing that care for poor communities and structures of justice flowed from the ministry of Jesus' life, which in turn inherited the prophetic vision to which you refer. Not only does the reverence given to the raw elements of creation — bread, water, wine, salt, oil — call the community to awareness as to the realities of these in the world (famine, water scarcity, the price of oil); but it evokes the Jewish Hasidic tradition of the 'hallowing of the everyday' — which Martin Buber has made so popular. But the 'hallowing of the everyday', the sacred quality of ordinary living, is enacted in times when the earth herself is threatened. This is why the liturgy becomes a place of recommitment to sustaining the basis of life.

But exactly in the way you have outlined, it can be a place of recommitment to building a civilisation of mutual respect, of peace and justice between the nations. Here is where we can share the dimension of eschatology. Taking the prophetic vision seriously, whether the Jewish Holy Mountain (Isa. 25) or the Christian Feast of Life, means becoming communities of hope. Even if we will not live to see the fulfilment of our hopes, it means committing ourselves to breaking down divisions and creating the kinds of communities that keep hope alive, even in the teeth of bitterness and despair. The tenor of our letters has sometimes created a mood of near despair: it is hope that kept us writing, and an unquenchable hope of a peace with justice, embodied and lived in community, is the least we can offer to the victims of violence, past and present.

Mary

12.10 *27 June 2004*

THE PROPHETIC VISION

Mary,

Of course, for the Jew eucharistic theology cannot serve as the basis of moral sensitivity. For me it is the prophetic message — which echoes throughout the Jewish tradition — that serves as a clarion call to action. As I have indicated previously, the ancient prophets were passionate about the ethical demands made upon human beings. For sins of personal greed, social inequality, and deceit, the prophet in God's name denounced the Jewish nation and threatened horrific catastrophes. The voice of the prophet was continually charged with agony and agitation. The eighth-century prophet Amos, for example, stressed that the nation would be destroyed because of its disobedience. Israel had sinned, he stated:

> because they sell the righteous for silver,
> and the needy for a pair of shoes —
> they that trample the head of the poor in the dust of the
> earth,
> and turn aside the way of the afflicted. (Amos 2:6—7)

His contemporary, Hosea, lamented that the nation would be punished because of what they had done iniquitously:

> You have ploughed iniquity,
> you have reaped injustice,
> you have eaten the fruit of lies. (Hos. 10:13)

Later, the sixth-century prophet Habbakuk declared:

> Woe to him who heaps up what is not his own ...
> Woe to him who gets evil gain for his house ...
> For the stone will cry out from the wall,
> And the beam from the woodwork respond.
> Woe to him who builds a town with blood,
> and founds a city on iniquity. (Hab. 2:6, 9, 11—12)

Such shrill denunciations of iniquity were the result of the prophetic conviction that people must be stirred from their spiritual slumber.

Now, arguably, the ethical intensity of the prophetic message has been largely absent from our correspondence. Instead, we have fiercely debated with each other, and have often found no possibility of harmonising our divergent views. It is paradoxical that we have found it so difficult to establish common ground, even though our intention has been to explore the ways in which our two traditions can contribute to reconciliation. Yet, despite our differences — and they are many — I think we do share the conviction that it is possible to improve society. Prophetic concern is a central feature of both Judaism and Christianity, and I think we do share the same commitment to free the oppressed and liberate the enslaved. We are both in our different ways liberationists, although we cannot agree about the liberationist programme. We can only hope that the prophetic vision which is embedded within our two faiths can awaken Jews and Christians to the task of *tikkun olam*. The Jewish tradition points to God's Kingdom as the goal and hope of humankind: a world in which all peoples and nations shall turn away from iniquity and injustice. This is not the hope of bliss in a future life, but the building up of the divine kingdom of truth and peace among all peoples.

Dan

12.11 *29 June 2004*

PURSUING THE DREAM

Dan,

It is now just over a year that we have been writing these letters
and it is now time to lay down the metaphorical pen. We began
with energy, enthusiasm and hopes of reconciliation, and in one
sense it seems we have failed. We tried to be attuned to world
events, and have been consistently concerned about violence, terrorism and the yawning gulfs between nations, and conflict
between faith communities. We began writing just after the Iraq
War, and yesterday saw a historical moment when power was
handed over by the occupation forces to the Iraqi interim government. But the violence continues and security on the streets
will be an immense challenge for the new government. We still
remain anxious and troubled about events in Palestine and the
killing of innocent people on both sides of the struggle: there has
been no progress in the course of our writing, and in other parts
of the world new conflicts have begun.

As we tried to build bridges, yet more chasms appeared. There
have been moments when I almost gave up. But something always
made me keep going, some intuition that reconciliation is worth
struggling for. Perhaps the honesty and truth-telling we tried to
maintain, our refusal to paper over the many cracks for the sake of
harmony, has proved a sound strategy, and at least not compromised integrity. But, in the end, we both agree that reconciliation
is not an end but a process. We are both convinced that it is a
matter of truth-telling, and listening with sympathy and empathy
to opinions that are painful to each of us. In that sense, our disagreements could be seen as a form of reconciliation, in that we
were able to communicate honestly with one another and to see
where the chasms were in our vision of the future.

Again, positively, I do think you are right that we share faith in
the ethical intensity of the prophetic message of peace and justice:
by a felicitous synchronicity the Amos text you cited yesterday
was the prescribed reading for the day in my lectionary. We can

both point to communities where the prophetic message takes on a new life, and inspires resistance to injustice in the name of a different vision for the world. But I think we share more than this. Prophecy and knowledge will pass away, said St Paul (1 Cor. 13:8). What abides, in his words, is love. And this, in my belief, springs from mystical faith. This is the hope and trust that despite all the evidence against, and storm clouds threatening, there will be peace and reconciliation between Christians and Jews — but maybe we will not live to see it. Dorothee Soelle, the German political theologian, who died last year but who continues to inspire many people, wrote that 'To sing of peace in the midst of war is, I believe, the secret of the people in the New Testament.'[5]

Continuing to sing of peace and justice in the midst of violence and military domination is the hallmark of *all* peoples of biblical faith: this is the song that sustains hope for a different world order. It is *one* way of pursuing the dream. Our correspondence may be ending but commitment to singing and *pursuing the dream* will carry on. And if so, this activity has not been in vain.

Mary

Further Reading

Bayfield, Tony; Braybrooke, Marcus (eds), *Dialogue With a Difference* (London: SCM, 1992)

Collection of essays by British Jewish and Christian scholars focusing on important issues in Jewish–Christian dialogue.

Beck, Norman A., *Mature Christianity: The Recognition and Repudiation of the Anti-Jewish Polemic of the New Testament* (Philadelphia: Associated Universities Press, 1985)

This work explores the most pressing themes of the Christian agenda. The author argues that the Church needs consistent help from New Testament specialists in order to reach a new consensus and disseminate its findings to those responsible for liturgy and worship.

Bemporad, Jack; Shevack, Michael, *Our Age: The Historic New Era of Christian–Jewish Understanding* (Hyde Park, NY: New City Press, 1996)

This book, written by two rabbis, depicts the efforts by Catholic and Protestant churches to refute the falsehoods of the past.

Berkovits, Eliezer, *Faith after the Holocaust* (New York: Ktav, 1973)

An important discussion of the Holocaust by a leading Orthodox theologian who uses the free-will argument to explain the tragedy of the Nazi era.

Boys, Mary C., *Jewish–Christian Dialogue: One Woman's Experience* (New Jersey: Paulist, 1997)

Explores the contribution of a serious and sustained encounter with another religious tradition as one of the most important factors in forming healthy religious commitments.

Boys, Mary C., *Has God Only One Blessing? Judaism as a Source of Christian Self-Understanding* (New Jersey: Paulist, 2000)

Explains why commitment to the way of Jesus cannot come at the expense of deprecating the Jewish people.

Bradshaw, Paul F; Hoffman, Lawrence A., *The Making of Jewish and Christian Worship* (Indiana: University of Notre Dame Press, 1992)

Two scholars explore the origin and growth of Christian and Jewish liturgies from the first century.

Braybrooke, Marcus, *Time to Meet: Towards a Deeper Relationship between Jews and Christians* (London: SCM, 1990)

A leading British Christian theologian explores the nature of Jewish–Christian encounter in the modern world.

Braybrooke, Marcus, *Christian–Jewish Dialogue: The Next Steps* (London: SCM, 2000)

Surveys the changing relationship between Judaism and Christianity reflected by Jewish scholars' interest in Christianity and Christian scholars' appreciation of Judaism.

Burrell, David; Laundau, Yehezkel (eds), *Voices from Jerusalem: Jews and Christians Reflect on the Holy Land* (New Jersey: Paulist, 1992)

A Jewish–Christian dialogue concerning the Holy Land.

Cargas, Harry James, *Shadows of Auschwitz: A Christian Response to the Holocaust* (Indiana: University of Notre Dame Press, 1987)

A Catholic scholar considers the Nazi era from a Christian perspective.

Charlesworth, James H. (ed.), *Overcoming Fear Between Jews and Christians* (New York: Crossroad, 1992)

This series of essays focuses on the courage demanded for Jewish–Christian encounter.

Cohn-Sherbok, Dan, *Holocaust Theology* (London: Lamp, 1991)

An examination of significant theological responses to the Holocaust by a number of Jewish writers.

Cohn-Sherbok, Dan, *Holocaust Theology: A Reader* (Exeter: Exeter University Press, 2002)

A collection of the writings of Jewish and Christian thinkers who explore the religious impact of the Holocaust.

Cohn-Sherbok, Dan, *The Crucified Jew: Twenty Centuries of Christian Anti-Semitism* (New York: HarperCollins, 1993)

A history of the development of Christian anti-Semitism through the centuries.

Cracknell, Kenneth, *Towards a New Relationship: Christians and People of Other Faith* (London: Epworth, 1986)

The author seeks to present a Christology and spirituality for inter-faith encounter.

Croner, Helga (ed.), *Stepping Stones to Further Jewish–Christian Dialogue* (New York: Stimulus, 1977)

A collection of key documents from Catholic and Protestant sources dealing with Jewish–Christian encounter.

Croner, Helga (ed.), *More Stepping Stones to Further Jewish–Christian Dialogue: An Unabridged Collection of Christian Documents* (New York: Stimulus, 1985)

An important collection of sources.

Croner, Helga; Cohen, Martin A. (eds), *Christian Mission–Jewish Mission* (New York: Stimulus, 1982)

A collection of essays providing an overview of the varied uses and meaning of the term 'mission' for Jews and Christians.

De Gruchy, John, *Reconciliation: Restoring Justice* (London: SCM, 2002)
Christian biblical and theological perspectives on reconciliation from the experience of the South African Truth and Reconciliation Commission.

Eckhardt, A. Roy, *Elder and Younger Brothers: The Encounter of Jews and Christians* (New York: Schocken, 1973)
The Methodist scholar Roy Eckhardt expresses disillusionment that the Christian churches remained silent for twenty years about the Holocaust and continue to dismiss contemporary Jewish existence.

Eckhardt, A. Roy, *Jews and Christians: the Contemporary Meeting* (Bloomington: Indiana University Press, 1986)
A stimulating attempt to depict and assess the contemporary encounter between Christians and Jews.

Eckhardt, Alice; Eckhardt, Roy, *Long Night's Journey into Day: A Revised Perspective of the Holocaust* (Detroit: Wayne University Press, 1987)
This study reflects on the task now facing Christian theology in the light of the Holocaust.

Edwards, John, *The Jews in Christian Europe 1400–1700* (London: Routledge, 1987)
Survey of a critical period in the rise of anti-Semitism.

Ellis, Marc, *Faithfulness in an Age of Holocaust* (New York: Amity House, 1986)
The author argues that Holocaust theology has failed because of its inability to analyse the modern use of power.

Ellis, Marc, *Beyond Innocence and Redemption: Confronting the Holocaust and Israeli Power* (New York: Harper and Row, 1991)
The author criticises various themes within Holocaust theology including suffering and empowerment, innocence and redemption, and specialness and normalisation.

Evans, Craig; Copan, Paul (eds), *Who was Jesus?: A Jewish–Christian Dialogue* (Louisville: Westminster/John Knox, 2001)
A collection of essays revolving around the discussion between Jewish New Testament scholar Peter Zaas and the Christian writer William Craig.

Fackenheim, Emil L., *The Jewish Return to History: Reflections in the Age of the Holocaust and a New Jerusalem* (New York: Schocken, 1978)
Here the author seeks to interpret the significance of survival rather than the death camps. In his view, God and Israel are still in relationship.

Fackenheim, Emil L., *To Mend the World: Foundations of Future Jewish Thought* (New York: Schocken, 1989)
A discussion of the theme that the Shoah has not undermined the Jewish faith experience.

Feld, Edward, *The Spirit of Renewal: Finding Faith after the Holocaust* (Woodstock, VT: Jewish Lights, 1994)
The author argues that religious belief must be reconstructed in a post-Holocaust world.

Fisher, Eugene J., *Faith Without Prejudice: Rebuilding Christian Attitudes Toward Judaism* (New York: Crossroad, 1993)

A book designed for Christians to help them translate the spirit of *Nostra aetate* and other Vatican statements into action.

Fisher, Eugene J., *Homework for Christians: Preparing Christian–Jewish Dialogue* (New York: National Conference of Christians and Jews, 1989)

A study guide for small groups addressing the New Testament, conversion and persecution, the crucifixion, anti-Semitism and the Holocaust.

Fisher, Eugene J., *Interwoven Destinies: Jews and Christians Through the Ages* (New York: Paulist, 1993)

A collection of pairs of essays by four Jews and four Christians concerning Jewish–Christian relations through history.

Fisher, Eugene J. (ed.), *Visions of the Other: Jewish and Christian Theologies Assess the Dialogue* (New Jersey: Paulist, 1994)

These essays illustrate that both Christians and Jews can come to terms with theological problems.

Fisher, Eugene J.; Rudin, James; Tanenbaum, Marc (eds), *Twenty Years of Jewish–Catholic Relations* (New Jersey: Paulist, 1986)

A collection of essays by Jewish and Catholic scholars concerning a range of topics including liturgy, the Bible, Israel, and religious education.

Friedlander, Albert A, *A Thread of Gold: Journeys Towards Reconciliation* (London: SCM, 1989)

An autobiographical account exploring the nature of Jewish–Christian dialogue and reconciliation.

Friedlander, Saul (ed.), *Probing the Limits of Representation: Nazism and the 'Final Solution'* (Cambridge, MA: Harvard University Press, 1992)

An important study of Hitlerism by a leading Jewish scholar.

Fry, Helen (ed.), *Christian–Jewish Dialogue: A Reader* (Exeter: Exeter University Press, 1996)

An excellent collection of readings from leading writers covering a range of central issues.

Gager, John, *The Origins of Anti-Semitism: Attitudes Towards Judaism in Pagan and Christian Antiquity* (New York: Oxford University Press, 1983)

This work by a leading New Testament scholar offers an extensive account of anti-Jewish attitudes prior to the emergence of the Church.

Gold, Judith Taylor, *Monsters and Madonnas: Roots of Christian Anti-Semitism* (Syracuse: Syracuse University Press, 1999)

The author argues that the depiction of Jews in the gospels is the result of Christian anti-Semitism.

Gopin, Marc, *Between Eden and Armageddon: the Future of World Religions, Violence and Peacemaking* (New York: Oxford University Press, 2000).

A Jewish scholar with vast experience in international diplomacy argues that religion — in constructing global communities of moral commitment and vision — can play a great role in conflict resolution.

Grey, Mary, 'To Struggle with a Reconciled Heart: Reconciliation and Justice', in *New Blackfriars*, 85, January 2004, pp. 56–73.
A rethinking of feminist ideas of sacrifice in the context of justice and reconciliation.

Hall, Stanley G., *Christian Anti-Semitism and Paul's Theology* (Philadelphia: Fortress, 1994)
A useful survey of the field.

Hargrove, Katharine T. (ed.), *Seeds of Reconciliation: Essays on Jewish–Christian Understanding* (North Richmond Hills, TX: D. and F. Scott Publishing, 1996)
A collection of essays written by leaders in Jewish–Christian encounter.

Harrelson, Walter; Falk, Randall M., *Jews and Christians: A Troubled Family* (Nashville: Abingdon, 1990)
A positive evaluation of Jewish–Christian encounter by a Christian biblical scholar and a rabbi who explore a wide range of issues.

Harries, Richard, *After the Evil: Christianity and Judaism in the Shadow of the Holocaust* (Oxford: Oxford University Press, 2003)
A sensitive approach to contentious issues such as forgiveness, suffering and the Palestinian issue.

Helmick, Raymond; Petersen, Rodney L. (eds), *Forgiveness and Reconciliation: Religion, Public Policy and Conflict Transformation* (Philadelphia: Templeton Foundation Press, 2001)
A range of scholars from different global contexts engage with the contextual issues of conflict resolution, justice and peacemaking.

Heschel, Susannah (ed.), *On Being a Jewish Feminist,* (New York: Schocken, 1983)
One of the first collections of essays by Jewish women scholars encountering feminism through the eyes of Judaism.

Hilberg, Raul, *The Destruction of the European Jews* (New York: Holmes and Meier, 1985)
An early study describing the events of the Nazi period.

Isaac, Jules, *The Teaching of Contempt: Christian Roots of Anti-Semitism* (New York: Holt, Rinehart and Winston, 1964)
A classic account of the Christian background to the development of hostility toward Judaism.

Kessler, Eduard; Pawlikowski, John T.; Banki, Judith H. (eds), *Jews and Christians in Conversation: Crossing Cultures and Generations* (Cambridge: Orchard Academic, 2002)
This collection includes contributions from important theologians from the USA, Europe and Israel.

Klein, Charlotte, *Anti Judaism and Christian Theology* (London: SPCK, 1975)
This work by a German Roman Catholic nun who converted from Judaism reveals the ideas of those who contrast law and grace in Pauline theology.

Klenicki, Leon (ed.), *Toward a Theological Encounter: Jewish Understandings of Christianity* (New Jersey: Paulist, 1991)
Contains contributions from Norman Solomon, Elliott Dorff, Walter Jacob, David Novak, Michael Wyschogrod and Daniel Breslauer.

Klenicki, Leon; Wigoder, Geoffrey, *A Dictionary of Jewish–Christian Dialogue* (New Jersey: Paulist, 1984)
Contains brief articles on key theological concepts.

Langmuir, Gavin I., *History, Religion and Anti-Semitism* (Los Angeles: University of California Press, 1960)
A historical account which seeks to explain the oppression of the Jews in European history.

Lapide, Pinchas E., *Hebrew in the Church: the Foundations of Jewish–Christian Dialogue* (Grand Rapids: Eerdmans, 1984)
A work which examines attempts made by Christians to translate the New Testament and Christian liturgy into Hebrew for evangelistic purposes.

Lodahl, Michael E., *Shekhinah–Spirit: Divine Presence in Jewish and Christian Religion* (New Jersey: Paulist, 1992)
The author wrestles with three theological difficulties: exclusivism, evil and eschatology.

Lohfink, Norbert, *The Covenant Never Revoked: Biblical Reflections on Christian–Jewish Dialogue* (New Jersey: Paulist, 1991)
This collection contains a series of theses providing a new approach to the New Testament texts on Judaism.

Lubarsky, Sandra B., *Tolerance and Transformation: Jewish Approaches to Religious Pluralism* (Cincinnati: HUC Press, 1990)
The author elucidates the concept of veridical pluralism, the view that there is more than one tradition that conveys religious truth.

Maduro, Otto (ed.), *Judaism, Christianity and Liberation* (Maryknoll: Orbis, 1991)
This volume contains important essays by Jews and Christians about the theology of liberation.

Maybaum, I., *The Face of God after Auschwitz* (Amsterdam: Polak and van Gennep, 1965)
The author sees God's providence in the events of the Nazi era.

McGarry, Michael B., *Christology after Auschwitz* (New Jersey: Paulist, 1977)
According to the author, the main condition for fruitful dialogue is the Christian repudiation of supersessionism.

McInnes, Val A. (ed.), *New Visions: Historical and Theological Perspectives on the Jewish–Christian Dialogue* (New York: Crossroad, 1993)
This collection of essays focuses on the early centuries of Jewish–Christian encounter.

Merkle, John C. (ed.), *Faith Transformed: Christian Encounters with Jews and Judaism* (Collegeville, MN: Liturgical Press, 2003)
Contains essays by Walter Harrelson, Alice L. Eckardt, Eva Fleischner,

Franklin Sherman, Norman A. Beck, Clark M. Williamson, John T. Pawlikowski, Eugene J. Fisher, Michael McGarry, Mary C. Boys and John C. Merkle.

Mussner, Franz, *Tractate on the Jews: The Significance of Judaism for Christian Faith* (London: SPCK, 1994)

The author emphasises the Jewishness of both Jesus and Paul and their relationship to the Law.

Neusner, Jacob; Chilton, Bruce, *The Intellectual Foundations of Christian and Jewish Discourse* (New York: Routledge, 1997)

The authors argue that the Judaic and Christian heirs of Scripture adopted Greek philosophical modes of thought and argument for their own ends.

Neusner, Jacob; Chilton, Bruce, *Jewish and Christian Doctrines: The Classics Compared* (New York: Routledge, 1999)

An introduction to the foundations of Judaism and Christianity.

Novak, David, *Jewish–Christian Dialogue: A Jewish Justification* (New York: Oxford University Press, 1992).

A Jewish scholar argues for the theological validity and necessity of dialogue between Christians and Jews.

Oberman, Heiko A., *The Roots of Anti-Semitism in the Age of the Renaissance and Reformation* (Philadelphia: Fortress, 1981)

Written by a Dutch scholar, this work summarises the findings of much detailed research.

Oesterreicher, John M., *The New Encounter Between Christians and Jews* (New York: The Philosophical Library, 1985)

Contains Roman Catholic perspectives on Jewish–Christian dialogue.

Parkes, James, *The Conflict of the Church and Synagogue: A Study in the Origins of Anti-Semitism* (New York: Athenaeum, 1969)

An important study of the conflict between Christianity and Judaism.

Pawlikowski, John T., *What are they Saying about Christian–Jewish Relations?* (New Jersey: Paulist, 1980)

The author treats the central issues concerning Jewish–Christian dialogue.

Pawlikowski, John T., *Christ in the Light of the Christian Jewish Dialogue* (New York: Paulist, 1982)

The author reformulates Christology and mission in the light of Jewish–Christian encounter.

Pawlikowski, John T; Wilde, James A., *When Catholics Speak About Jews: Notes for Homilists and Catechists* (Chicago: Liturgy Training Publications, 1987)

A helpful resource which provides detailed suggestions for teaching, preaching, writing and praying.

Peck, Abraham J. (ed.), *Jews and Christians after the Holocaust* (Philadelphia: Fortress, 1982)

This collection contains contributions by leading Jewish and Christian theologians.

Pulzer, Peter, *The Rise of Political Antisemitism in Germany and Austria* (London: Peter Halban, 1987)
An appraisal of the extent of Christian responsibility for the Final Solution.

Rahner, Karl; Lapide, Pinhas, *Encountering Jesus–Encountering Judaism: A Dialogue* (New York: Crossroad, 1987)
A leading Christian theologian and a Jewish writer discuss Jesus' life and work.

Rausch, David A., *Fundamentalist-Evangelicals and Anti-Semitism* (Philadelphia: Trinity Press International, 1993)
The author argues that theological triumphalism and supersessionism fosters contempt for Judaism.

Rubenstein, Richard, *After Auschwitz: Radical Theology and Contemporary Judaism* (Indianapolis: Bobbs-Merrill, 1966)
An important work which argues that the traditional concept of God must be jettisoned in the light of the events of the modern period.

Rubenstein, Richard, Roth, John, *Approaches to Auschwitz* (Louisville, KY: Westminster/John Knox, 1987)
A collection of material summarising most of the positions discussed in treatments of the Holocaust.

Rudin, A. James; Wilson, Marvin R. (eds), *A Time to Speak: the Evangelical–Jewish Encounter* (Grand Rapids: Eerdmans, 1987)
The evangelical position is treated in this discussion. Topics include Scripture, theology and history.

Ruether, Rosemary Radford, *Faith and Fratricide: The Theological Roots of Anti-Judaism* (New York: Seabury, 1974)
The author argues that anti-Jewish attitudes in the New Testament were related to the development of anti-Semitism.

Sanders, Jack, *The Jews in Luke–Acts* (London: SCM, 1987)
The author argues that Luke–Acts represents the most serious polemic against the Jews.

Sandmel, Samuel, *We Jews and Jesus* (New York: Oxford University Press, 1965)
A contemporary understanding of New Testament research about Jesus.

Saperstein, Marc, *Moments of Crisis in Jewish–Christian Relations* (London: SCM, 1989)
A rabbi's brief treatment of the central turning points in the history of Jewish–Christian relations.

Shermis, Michael; Zannoni, Arthur E. (eds), *Introduction to Jewish–Christian Relations* (New Jersey: Paulist, 1991)
A collection of articles on key issues of dialogue. Basic essays on Scripture, Holocaust, Israel, anti-Semitism, and Jesus.

Spong, John Shelby; Spiro, Jack, *Dialogue: In Search of Jewish–Christian Understanding* (Haworth, NJ: St Johann Press, 1999)

268   FURTHER READING

A discussion of Jewish–Christian relations by a rabbi and a leading Christian thinker.

Standhal, Krister, *Paul Among Jews and Gentiles* (Philadelphia: Fortress, 1976)
The author examines the New Testament in the light of his work and involvement with interfaith relations.

Swidler, Leonard, *Bursting the Bonds: A Jewish–Christian Dialogue on Jesus and Paul* (Maryknoll: Orbis, 1991)
Contributions from leading thinkers about Jesus and Paul.

Thoma, Clemens, *A Christian Theology of Judaism* (New Jersey: Paulist, 1980)
The author assesses biblical and systematic theology in the light of the Jewish–Christian dialogue.

Thoma, Clemens; Wyschogrod, Michael, *Understanding Scripture: Explorations of Jewish and Christian Traditions of Interpretation* (New Jersey: Paulist, 1987)
Jewish and Christian biblical scholars consider issues raised by both their traditions' claim to the Hebrew scriptures.

Thoma, Clemens, Wyschogrod, Michael (eds), *Parable and Story in Judaism and Christianity* (New Jersey: Paulist, 1989)
A collection of essays about the art of storytelling common to Christians and Jews.

Ucko, Hans, *Common Roots, New Horizons: Learning about Christian Faith from Dialogue with Jews* (Geneva: World Council of Churches, 1994)
The author reflects on his worldwide experience.

van Buren, Paul M., *A Theology of the Jewish–Christian Reality* (Lanham, MD: University Press of America, 1995)
A systematic theology which reinterprets the Christian tradition to see Judaism and the Jewish people as partners on the same way.

von der Osten-Sacken, Peter, *Christian Jewish Dialogue: Theological Foundations* (Philadelphia: Fortress, 1986)
The author envisions a transformation of Christian theology in light of its encounter with Judaism and the Jewish people.

Wigoder, Geoffrey, *Jewish–Christian Relations since the Second World War* (Manchester: Manchester University Press, 1987)
The author surveys the development of Jewish–Christian relations since the Second World War.

Wiles, Maurice, *Christian Theology and Interfaith Dialogue* (London: SCM, 1992)
A Christian scholar focuses on the central question whether Christian theology is able to develop a positive view of other religions.

Williamson, Clark M., *A Guest in the House of Israel: Post Holocaust Church Theology* (Louisville, KY: Westminster/John Knox Press, 1993)
Discusses anti-Jewish teachings within the Church, and argues that Christians should reconsider the doctrines of the faith.

Zannoni, Alfred E. (ed.), *Jews and Christians Speak of Jesus* (Philadelphia: Fortress, 1994)
A stimulating collection of essays concerning Jesus.

Notes

1. God

1. Dan Cohn-Sherbok, *Modern Judaism* (London: Macmillan, 1996), p. 83.
2. *Union Prayer Book* (New York: CCAR, 1960), p. 12.
3. Ibid., pp. 14–16.
4. See Brian Davies, *The Thought of Thomas Aquinas* (Oxford: Clarendon Paperbacks, 1992).
5. This is an extremely condensed version of Alfred North Whitehead's view of God.
6. A rough translation of this is:

    > There was a young man of Dijon,
    > Who didn't like religion.
    > He said, 'Goodness me,
    > How funny, these three,
    > The Father, the Son and the Pigeon!'

7. Martin Buber, *I and Thou* (Edinburgh: T. & T. Clark, 1939).
8. See Etty Hillesum, *Etty: An Interrupted Life* (New York: Washington Square Press, 1985).
9. Melissa Raphael, *The Female Face of God in Auschwitz* (London and New York: Auschwitz, 2003).
10. Phyllis Trible, *God and the Rhetoric of Sexuality* (Philadelphia: Fortress, 1978), p. 45.
11. Kwok Pui Lan, 'God Weeps with our Pain', in John S. Pobee (ed.), *New Eyes for Reading* (Geneva: WCC, 1986), pp. 90–5.
12. Steven Jacobs, *Rethinking Jewish Faith* (Albany: State University of New York Press, 1994), pp. 119–22.
13. Richard Rubenstein, *After Auschwitz* (Indianapolis: Bobbs Merrill, 1966), p. 153.
14. Judith Plaskow, *Standing Again at Sinai: Judaism from a Feminist Perspective* (San Francisco: Harper and Row, 1990).
15. This story has been attributed to various authors, including Elie Wiesel.
16. Edward Feld, *The Spirit of Renewal* (Woodstock, VT: Jewish Lights, 1994), pp. 140–3.

2. Jesus

1. 'Nostra Aetate: Declaration on the Relation of the Church to Non-Christian Religions', 28 October 1965, in *Documents of the Second Vatican Council* (New York: Costello Publishing, 1974).

2. *Catechism of the Catholic Church* (London: Geoffrey Chapman, 1994), p. 135.

3. Rabbi Harold Kushner, *When Bad Things Happen to Good People* (New York: Bantam Doubleday, 2004).

4. Rosemary Radford Ruether, *Faith and Fratricide* (New York: Crossroad, 1974), p. 248.

5. Beverley Harrison, 'The Power and Work of Love', in Carol Robb (ed.), *Making the Connections* (Boston: Beacon, 1986), pp. 18–19.

6. Leslie Griffiths, *The Aristide Factor* (Oxford: Lion, 1997), p. 73.

7. Dan Cohn-Sherbok, *On Earth as it is in Heaven: Jews, Christians, and Liberation Theology* (Maryknoll: Orbis, 1987), p. 51.

8. This is highlighted by Katherina Kellenbach, *Anti-Judaism in Feminist Writings* (Atlanta: Scholars' Press, 1994).

9. See Mary Boys, *Has God only One Blessing? Judaism as Source of Christian Self-understanding* (New York: Paulist, 2000), pp. 163–5.

10. Ibid., quoting Larry Hurtado, *One God, One Lord: Early Christian Devotion and Ancient Jewish Monotheism* (Edinburgh: T. & T. Clark, 1998), p. 82.

11. See Chaim Potok, *My Name is Asher Lev* (London: Penguin, 1973), pp. 287–8.

12. Cited in Boys, *Has God only One Blessing?*, p. 239.

13. Mary Grey, *Sacred Longings: Ecofeminist Theology and Globalization* (London: SCM, 2003), p. 109.

14. Moses Maimonides, *Yad*, Yesode Ha-Torah, 1.7.

15. Cited in Louis Jacobs, *A Jewish Theology* (New York: Behrman House, 1973), p. 28.

16. Wells for India is a small NGO, of which I am a co-founder, working in desert areas of the drought-prone state of Rajasthan in north-west India.

3. The Bible

1. *Catechism of the Catholic Church* (London: Geoffrey Chapman, 1994), pp. 112–14.

2. See John Sawyer, *The Fifth Gospel: Isaiah in the History of Christianity* (Cambridge: Cambridge University Press, 1996). Despite the title, this illuminating book does not fall into the trap but is descriptive of the process.

3. Moses Maimonides, *Commentary to the Mishnah*, Sanhedrin, X, I.

4. Pittsburgh Platform, in Dan Cohn-Sherbok, *Modern Judaism* (London: Macmillan, 1996), p. 83.

5. Ibid.

6. The text quoted is from *Dei Verbum* 11 (*Constitution on Revelation* from the second Vatican council).
7. Phyllis Trible, *Texts of Terror: Literary Feminist Readings of Biblical Narratives* (Philadelphia: Fortress, 1984).
8. See Elizabeth Schüssler Fiorenza, *Bread not Stone* (Boston: Beacon, 1984).
9. Judith Plaskow, *Standing Again at Sinai* (San Francisco: Harper and Row, 1990), p. 25.
10. Lieve Troch, 'A Method of Conscientisation: Feminist Biblical Study in the Netherlands', in Elizabeth Fiorenza (ed.), *Searching the Scriptures* (London: SCM, 1994), pp. 351–66.
11. See Musimbi Kanyoro, *Introducing Feminist African Biblical Hermeneutics* (Sheffield: Sheffield Academic Press, 2001).
12. Dan Cohn-Sherbok, *On Earth as it is in Heaven: Jews, Christians, and Liberation Theology* (Maryknoll: Orbis, 1987), p. 91.
13. Toni Morrison, *Beloved* (London: Vintage, 1997).
14. Adrienne Rich, 'The Desert as Garden of Paradise', in *Time's Power: Poems 1985–1988* (New York: W. & W. Norton, 1989), pp. 30–1.
15. Mordecai Kaplan, *The Meaning of God in Modern Jewish Religion* (Detroit: Wayne State University Press, 1962), p. 76.

4. Authority and Tradition

1. The phrase is from Letty Russell (ed.), *Feminist Interpretation of the Bible* (Philadelphia: Westminster Press, 1985).
2. Elisabeth Behr-Sigel, *The Ministry of Women in the Church* (California: Oakwood, 1991), p. 19.
3. This last is citing *Lumen Gentium*, The Vatican Council Constitution on the Church, 12.
4. For the historical arguments see John Wijngaards, <www.women-priests.org>.
5. Mishnah, 1.1.
6. See Julie Clague, 'Authority', in Isherwood and McEwan (eds), *An A to Z of Feminist Theology* (Sheffield: Sheffield Academic Press, 1996), pp. 14–16.
7. St Ignatius of Loyola (1491–1556) was the founder of the Jesuit order. His spirituality, or *The Spiritual Exercises*, is extremely popular today.
8. Pittsburgh Platform, in Dan and Lavinia Cohn-Sherbok, *A Short Reader of Judaism* (Oxford: Oneworld, 1996), pp. 135–6.
9. Letty Russell argues this in 'Authority', in Letty Russell and J. Shannon Clarkson (eds), *Dictionary of Feminist Theologies* (London: Mowbray, 1996), pp. 18–19; *Household of Freedom: Authority in Feminist Theology* (Louisville, KY: Westminster/John Knox, 1987).
10. Audre Lorde, *Sister Outsider: Speeches and Essays* (Trumansberg, NY: Crossing Press, 1984), pp. 110–13.

11. Dan Cohn-Sherbok, *The Future of Judaism* (Edinburgh: T. and T. Clark, 1994, p. 190).

12. Dr Sanjay Paswan, Dr Pramantha Jaideva, *Encyclopedia of Dalits in India*, Vol. 9, *Women* (Delhi: Kalpax Publications, 2002), p. 158. Also cited by Rodolfo Cardenal, 'The Crucified People', in Mary Grey (ed.), *Reclaiming Vision: Education, Liberation and Justice*, (La Sainte Union: Southampton, 1994), p. 17.

13. Declaration on Religious Liberty, *Humanae Dignitatis*, 7 December 1965, 3, Section 2, p. 801: 'He is bound to follow his conscience faithfully in all his activity so that he may come to God, who is his last end. Therefore he must not be forced to act contrary to his conscience.'

14. Eric D'Arcy, *Conscience and its Right to Freedom* (London: Sheed and Ward, 1961).

15. Since May 2004 the BJP has been replaced by the Congress Party.

16. Marc Gopin, *Between Eden and Armageddon: The Future of World Religions, Violence and Peacemaking* (Oxford: Oxford University Press, 2000).

17. See Carter Heyward, *The Redemption of God: A Theology of Mutual Relation* (Washington: University of America Press, 1982); Mary Grey, *Redeeming the Dream* (London: SPCK, 1989).

18. Emmanuel Levinas, 'Ethics as First Philosophy', in Séan Hand (ed.), *The Levinas Reader* (Oxford: Blackwell, 1989), pp. 82–4.

5. Sin

1. Mishnah.

2. *Mahzor* for Rosh Hashanah and Yom Kippur, Rabbinical Assembly (2000), pp. 371–7.

3. It must be noted that the Orthodox Church has a different theology. It believes that human beings did not lose the image of God, *imago Dei*, but only the 'likeness'. The journey of faith is therefore the journey of growing into the likeness once more.

4. See Rosemary Ruether, *Sexism and God-Talk* (London: SCM, 1983), pp. 160–1.

5. Helena Kennedy, *Eve was Framed* (London: Chatto and Windus, 1992).

6. Cited in Harvey Cox, *The Seduction of the Spirit: the Use and Misuse of People's Religion* (London: Wildwood House, 1974), p. 284.

7. Harvey Cox, *On Not Leaving it to the Snake* (Toronto: Macmillan, 1969).

8. Fyodor Dostoevsky, *Crime and Punishment* (London: J. M. Dent, 1911). I have discussed this at greater length in Mary Grey, *The Wisdom of Fools?* (London: SPCK, 1993).

9. See 'Nostra Aetate' (1965), 'Guidelines and Suggestions for Implementing Nostra Aetate' (1974), *Catholic Jewish Relations: Documents from the Holy See*, intro. Eugene Fisher (London: Catholic Truth Society, 1999).

10. Chaim Potok, *My Name is Asher Lev* (London: Penguin, 1973), pp. 287–8.

11. Miroslav Volf, *Exclusion and Embrace: A Theological Exploration of Identity, Otherness and Reconciliation* (Nashville: Abingdon, 1996).

12. Dan Cohn-Sherbok, *The Crucified Jew: Twenty Centuries of Christian Anti-Semitism* (Grand Rapids: Eerdmans, 1997), p. 73.

13. Ibid.

14. Sydney Carter, 'Said Judas to Mary', in Peter Smith (ed.), *New Orbit* (Galliard, 1972), No. 49; cited in Marcus Braybrooke, *Time to Meet: Towards a Deeper Relationship between Jews and Christians* (London: SCM, 1990), p. 71.

15. Rosemary Ruether, *Faith and Fratricide* (New York: Crossroad, 1974), pp. 250–1.

16. Dan Cohn-Sherbok, *On Earth as it is in Heaven: Jews, Christians, and Liberation Theology* (Maryknoll: Orbis, 1987).

6. *War and Peace*

1. Hans Kung, *Global Responsibility: In Search of a New World Ethic* (London: SCM, 1990), p. 75.

2. George Monbiot, 'Dreamers and Idiots', *Guardian*, 11 November 2003, p. 23.

3. Tertullian, *Treatise on Idolatry*, 19, cited in John Helgeland, Robert J. Daly and J. Patout Burns, *Christians and the Military: the Early Experience* (London: SCM, 1985), p. 23.

4. See Mario Marazitti, 'A Miracle of Two Fish', *The Tablet*, 28 September 2002, p. 6.

5. Ibid.

6. See Dan Cohn-Sherbok, *What's a Nice Jewish Boy Like You Doing in a Place Like This?* (New York: O Books, 2003), pp. 31–2.

7. Tacitus, *Agricola*, ed. E.V. Rieu (London: Penguin, 1948), p. 80.

8. Naim Ateek, *Justice, Only Justice: a Palestinian Theology of Liberation* (Maryknoll: Orbis, 1989).

9. Richard Harries, *After The Evil: Christianity and Judaism in the Shadow of the Holocaust* (Oxford: Oxford University Press, 2003), p. 217.

10. Paul Mendes-Flohr, J. Reinharz (eds), *The Jew in the Modern World* (Oxford: Oxford University Press, 1995), p. 319.

11. Dan Cohn-Sherbok, Dawoud Al-Alami, *The Palestine Israeli Conflict* (Oxford, Oneworld, 2002), p. 186.

12. Harries, *After The Evil*, pp. 218–19.

13. Naim Ateek, 'Christian Zionism: the Dark Side of the Bible', in *Cornerstone* 30 (Winter 2003), pp. 1–3.

14. Revd Donald Wagner, ibid., p. 4. This text originally appeared in the *Beirut Star* as part of a series, 9–13 September 2003.

15. Michael Prior, 'The Holy Land and the Scandalous Performance of the Churches', ibid., p. 6.

16. Ahdaf Soueif, 'The Waiting Game', *Guardian*, G2, 24 November 2003, pp. 2–5.

17. Ateek, 'Christian Zionism'.

18. Garth Hewitt, *A Candle of Hope* (Oxford: The Bible Reading Fellowship, 1999), p. 61.

19. Brian Klug, 'No, anti-Zionism is not anti-Semitism', *Guardian*, 3 December 2003, p. 23.

20. Joseph Montville, 'Looking Ahead: Toward a New Paradigm', in Douglas Johnston and Cynthia Sampson (eds), *Religion, The Missing Dimension of Statecraft* (Oxford: Oxford University Press, 1994), p. 332.

21. Thomas Merton, *Conjectures of a Guilty Bystander* (London: Burns and Oates, 1995), p. 86.

22. Cited in Fergus Finlay, *Mary Robinson: A President with a Purpose* (Dublin: The O'Brien Press, 1990), p. 156.

7. *The Environment*

1. Dan Cohn-Sherbok, *On Earth as it is in Heaven: Jews, Christians and Liberation Theology* (Maryknoll: Orbis, 1987).

2. Leonardo Boff, *Ecology and Liberation — a New Paradigm* (Maryknoll: Orbis, 1995).

3. I realise you are quoting my views in *Sacred Longings: Ecofeminism and Globalisation* (London: SCM, 2003).

4. Graham Carey, unpublished paper dedicated to the memory of peace activist Rachel Corrie, 'World Out of Control and the Inevitable Revolution', 2003, p. 9.

5. Gustavo Gutiérrez, *A Theology of Liberation* (Maryknoll: Orbis, 1973), p. 84.

6. Sallie McFague, *The Body of God* (London: SCM, 1993), pp. 200–1.

7. See Sallie McFague, *Super Natural Christians: How we Should Love Nature* (Minneapolis: Fortress, 1997); also *Life Abundant: Rethinking Theology and Economy for a Planet in Peril* (Minneapolis: Fortress, 2000).

8. Mary Grey, *Sacred Longings: Ecofeminist Theology and Globalization* (London: SCM, 2003), Chapter 7.

9. See Bill McKibben, *The Comforting Whirlwind* (Grand Rapids: Eerdmans, 1994).

10. Cited in Dan Cohn-Sherbok, *Fifty Jewish Thinkers* (London: Routledge, 1997), p. 26.

11. Martin Buber, *Between Man and Man* (London: Fontana Library, 1947), p. 41.

12. Fyodor Dostoevsky, *The Brothers Karamazov* (Baltimore: Penguin, 1963), pp. 426–7.

13. Thomas Merton, *Conjectures of a Guilty Bystander* (London: Burns and Oates, 1995), pp. 156–7.

14. Richard Schwartz, *Judaism and Vegetarianism* (Marblehead, MA: Micah, 1988) p. 25.

15. Carol Adams, *The Sexual Politics of Meat* (New York: Continuum, 1990).

16. Aubrey Rose (ed.), *Judaism and Ecology* (London: Cassell, 1992), pp. 121–4.

17. Sean McDonagh, 'Water is Life', in Clare Amos (ed.), *Thinking Mission* (London: United Society for the Propagation of the Gospel, 2001), pp. 5–14.

18. Ibid., p. 11.

19. For more information, see Jad Isaac, 'The Water Conflict in the Holy Land', in Amos (ed.), *Thinking Mission*, pp. 15–19; Yehezkel Lein, 'Disputed Waters: Israel's Responsibility for the Water Shortage in the Occupied Territories', in *Ecotheology* 9 (July 2000), pp. 68–83; B'Tselem, 'Water Shortage in the West Bank: Update Summer 1999', ibid., pp. 107–10.

20. Leonardo Boff, *Letter to the Churches* (Geneva: WCC, 1992), p. 10.

8. Gender

1. Carol Christ, *Rebirth of the Goddess* (New York: Addison-Wesley, 1997); Merlin Stone, *When God was a Woman* (New York: Dial Press, 1976).

2. As Rosemary Ruether wrote, 'Patriarchy', in Russell and Clarkson (eds), *Dictionary of Feminist Theologies* (London: Mowbray, 1996), pp. 205–6.

3. See Augustine, *De Trinitate* 7.7.

4. Dan and Lavinia Cohn-Sherbok, *The American Jew* (London: HarperCollins, 1994), p. 258.

5. Susan Schneider, *Jewish and Female* (New York: Simon and Schuster, 1984), p. 19.

6. See Judith Plaskow, *Standing Again at Sinai* (San Francisco: Harper and Row, 1990).

7. Miriam Peskowitz and Laura Levitt (eds), *Judaism since Gender* (New York: Taylor and Francis, 1997).

8. See Trevor Dennis, *And Sarah Laughed: Women's Voices in the Old Testament* (London: SPCK, 1994); Julia Kristeva, 'Of Women's Time', in *A Kristeva Reader* (Oxford: Blackwell, 1980), tr. Leon Roudiez, pp. 186–213.

9. From this experience has come 'Womanist theology' or the theology of women of colour in the USA.

10. She now teaches at Union Theological Seminary, New York.

11. See Chung Hyun Kyung, *Struggle to be the Sun Again* (Maryknoll: Orbis, 1993).

12. Moses Hess, *Rome and Jerusalem*, in Arthur Hertzberg, *The Zionist Idea: A Historical Analysis and Reader* (New York: Athenaeum, 1969), p. 121.

13. Leon Pinsker, *Autoemancipation*, ibid., p. 188.
14. See Rosemary Ruether, *Sexism and God-Talk* (London: SCM, 1983), Chapter 7, 'The Consciousness of Evil: Journeys of Conversion', pp. 159–92.
15. Beverley Harrison, 'The Power of Anger and the Work of Love', in Carol Robb (ed.), *Making the Connections* (Boston: Beacon, 1986), p. 7.

9. The Family and Community

1. Friedrich Schleiermacher, *Christmas Eve: Dialogue on the Incarnation* (New York: The Edwin Mellen Press, 1990), tr. Terrence Tice.
2. Virginia Woolf, cited in Mary Daly, *Pure Lust* (London: The Women's Press, 1984), p. 298.
3. Lavinia and Dan Cohn-Sherbok, *The American Jew* (New York: HarperCollins, 1994), p. 351.
4. Rabbi Marc Israel, www.routledge.com/textbooks/0415236614
5. Naomi Graetz, 'God is to Israel as Husband is to Wife: the Metaphoric Battering of Hosea's Wife', in Athalya Brenner (ed.), *A Feminist Companion to The Latter Prophets* (Sheffield: Sheffield Academic Press, 1995), pp. 126–45.
6. Carter Heyward, *Our Passion for Justice* (New York: Pilgrim, 1984), p. 191.

10. Racism

1. Mary Grey and Richard Zipfel, *From Barriers to Community: the Challenge of the Gospel for a Divided Society* (London: HarperCollins, 1991).
2. *Guardian*, 23 March 2003, p. 7.
3. Lawrence Durrell, *Bitter Lemons of Cyprus* (London: Faber and Faber, 1957).
4. Michael Ignatieff, *The Warrior's Honour: Ethnic War and the Modern Conscience* (New York: Henry Holt, 1997), pp. 53–4.
5. Will Hutton, 'Heed Not the Fanatics', *Observer*, 11 April 2004, p. 28.
6. Ibid.
7. See the controversial opinion of Samuel Huntingdon in *The Clash of Civilisation and the Remaking of World Order* (New York: Touchstone, 2000).
8. Rashtriya Swayamsevak Sangh, or Association of National Volunteers. In May 2004 the BJP was unexpectedly defeated by the Congress Party in the national elections. Obviously this was not known at the time of writing.
9. Mian Ridge, 'In Fear of the Saffron Mob', *The Tablet*, 17 April 2004, pp. 7–8.
10. Herzl, *The Jewish State*, in Dan Cohn-Sherbok, *Israel: The History of an Idea* (London: SPCK, 1992), pp. 124–6.

EMOTIONS: discussed in the Spiritual Accompaniment literature.

Wendy Robinson (1974; 2000) M:7.8: "There are of course times when one emotion is so dominant that I am drowned in it; an anxiety obsesses me, a depression darkens me to my marrow. It is so that this mood here states. The more I seek myself the more stubborn my become. If he ignored, then it less to the relevant, explored as equal we take just, not left traceun and the confines of my ego. This can be a difficult painful prolonged process of certain moods or states of mind which to do that. There may be something we cannot see of ourselves which is producing this state of ...(8)... mind. Perhaps the mood is making onto we we don't want been to himself to christ (as example, depressia manic aggression, anxious contempt, jealousy). We (accompanist/accompanied) have to be sensible or recognise the times when we need to go to someone for help, or ask for their prayers. And if ears does not seem to be any more we we must ask God to send someone. And he does."

11. Toni Morrison, *The Bluest Eye* (New York: Washington Square Press, 1970).

12. Dan Cohn-Sherbok, *The Vision of Judaism* (St Paul, MN: Paragon House, 2004), pp. 299–300.

13. Stephen Grey, *New Statesman*, 3 May 2004, p. 14.

14. See Victoria Clark, 'Christians of Zion', *The Tablet*, 1 May 2004.

15. According to this, the privileged elite will be 'enraptured', whisked up to heaven, thus avoiding the final destruction that will engulf the rest of the world.

11. *Crime and Punishment*

1. For the Great European Witch Hunt see Mary Daly, *Gyn/Ecology: the Metaethics of Radical Feminism* (London: The Women's Press, 1979), pp. 178–222.

2. See *Catechism of the Catholic Church*, section 2266, p. 488.

3. Translation is from the Jerusalem Bible.

4. See *Catechism of the Catholic Church*.

5. See R. Girard, *Violence and the Sacred* (London: Johns Hopkins Press, 1977).

6. Tim Newell, *Forgiving Justice*, Swarthmore Lecture 2000 (London: Friends House, 2000), p. 92.

7. Ibid., pp. 92–3.

8. For example, by Stanley Hauerwas, 'Punishing Christians', in William Storrar and Andrew Morton (eds), *Public Theology for the 21st Century* (Edinburgh: T. & T. Clark, 2004), pp. 285–302.

9. The encyclicals are *Pacem in Terris* (1963), *Gaudium et Spes* (1965), *Populorum Progressio* (1967), and the cited quotation is 'Message for World Peace Day 1991', reprinted in *Theology in Green* 3, July 1992, p. 19.

10. Newell, *Forgiving Justice*, p. 20.

11. See Leo Driedger and Donald Kraybill, *Mennonite Peacemaking: from Quietism to Activism* (Scottvale, Pennsylvania: Herald Press, 1994).

12. Joseph Montville, 'Looking Ahead: Towards a New Paradigm', in Douglass Johnston and Cynthia Sampson (eds), *Religion: The Missing Dimension of Statecraft* (New York and Oxford: Oxford University Press, 1994), p. 332.

13. Louis Jacobs, *The Jewish Religion* (Oxford: Oxford University Press, 1995) p. 425.

14. Timothy Gorringe, *God's Just Vengeance* (Cambridge: Cambridge University Press, 1996).

15. See Mary Grey, *Redeeming the Dream* (London: SPCK, 1989).

16. Pat Carlen, *Women's Imprisonment: a Study in Social Control* (London: Routledge and Kegan Paul, 1983).

17. Christopher D. Marshall, *Beyond Retribution: A New Testament Vision for Justice, Crime and Punishment* (Grand Rapids: Eerdmans, 2001), p. 25.
18. In Dan Cohn-Sherbok, *Anti-Semitism* (Stroud: Sutton, 2002), p. vii.

12. What Have We Learned?

1. See Ha-Joon Chang (ed.), *Joseph Stiglitz and the World Bank: the Rebel Within* (London: Anthem Press, 2001).
2. Statistics from *The Global Environment Outlook*, commissioned by the UN, and cited in the *Guardian*, 23 May 2002.
3. *Union Prayer Book* (New York: CCAR, 1960), Vol. 1, p. 41.
4. Tissa Balasuriya, *The Eucharist and Human Liberation* (London: SCM Press 1977).
5. Dorothee Soelle, 'Breaking the Ice of the Soul', in Sarah Pinnock (ed.), *The Theology of Dorothee Soelle* (London: Trinity Press International, 2003), pp. 40–1.